DARE TO BE YOU

BREAK FREE FROM THE SHACKLES OF THE PAST TO BECOME YOURSELF, OUTSTANDING AND UNSTOPPABLE!

LYNETTE DIEHM

Dedicated to everyone out there who has gone through adverse times and needed something to give them hope and a way forward.

Recognition And Contributors

Gabriele Engstrom the most amazing naturopath who has helped me through the most recent years of my life. Gabriele Using 30 years of experience when treating people with the SCIO Biofeedback therapies has aided me in breaking down some mental, emotional, physical, and spiritual barriers that stood between me and my success in most areas of my life. After re-evaluating my perspective on life, she helped me to make some lifestyle adjustments to support my overall health and wellbeing. The Coaching Institute for the personal development journey I was on while I was studying with them.
Speakers Institute for the personal and professional development journey I am currently on with them.
The Salsa foundation for the wonderful instructor led lessons and for always making me feel like I was a part of their family.

Disclaimer: All the names and timelines have been changed to protect people in this book. A couple of themes such as rape and depression have been written about in this book and may trigger emotions from past events in the readers lives that they may have not properly dealt with

"Be the change you wish to see in the world."
- Gandhi

Prologue

Life is a journey that is full of twists and turns. We fight every lion, tiger, and bear in a quest to reach our own personal nirvana, a place of success, peace, and happiness.

So many variables impact living a successful life, including unresolved childhood issues, identity issues, relationships, professional woes, as well as financial burdens. Being an adult with heavy responsibilities who is true to themselves is not a simple thing to do, as we try to please everyone but ourselves. We fight to make our kids, spouses, employers, and churches happy. We compromise to get a meaning for our lives to the extent that we no longer know who we are or what we really desire in life.

This book is a direct call to be yourself and let the chips fall where they may. You can never be happy if you don't know who you are.

In our quest to find true happiness, there are a multitude of pitfalls along the way, such as failure, despair, and heartbreak. Like hamsters on a wheel, we lose who we are to an endless repetitive groundhog day cycle. Who we are, our dreams and desires become blurred as we navigate the matrix of life.

We submit to the schedule of life without question, only then left to wonder where the time went. Just yesterday you were in bed with your childhood sweetheart and so happy. Now today, three lovers later, your body has morphed, and you have a bulging waistline and breasts that have been affected by the gravitational pull.

It was just yesterday that you took an entry-level job, and it feels like nothing has changed since. Because of this, you have lost all enthusiasm and zest for life; you are divorced, supporting a partner who spends all their time at the mall, and your ex is messing with some douche with a six-pack, compared to your rather round pot belly. You have lost yourself and who you are. In the here and now, you no longer recognize yourself.

We have taken a detour from what makes us happy regarding our dreams and destiny. We are hanging on to life by a mere thread, but it is not too late. Despite everything, it is still possible to turn our life around and fulfil our heart's desires.

We live behind a mask to conceal our pain and identity in order to not only conform to other people's expectations, but to silence the trauma that has already occurred in our lives.

I am Lynette Diehm, and I am going to share with you my own experiences in life which gave me the tools I needed to find true happiness, wealth, love, and success in my personal and professional life.

It is time to breathe, step out from behind that mask and shine brighter than we have ever shone before as we dare to be our truest self and live the life we were truly destined to live...

The beginning of my fears and limiting beliefs as a child

"How parents behave, speak to, and treat their children will either build up the child or tear them down and create fears and limiting beliefs. Parents should be respectful, loving, considerate, supportive, encouraging and build their children up positively if they want theirchildren to thrive in their adult years."

When I was five years old, my parents used to put my older sister and her needs first and it felt like my needs never really mattered to them. When I had problems and I needed their help, they would tell me to go away and to sort it out on my own. But it was a completely different story for my older sister, as she would go to them all the time and they were so loving and understanding of her. They gave her many things that they never gave me, including all of their attention.

Almost every night they would take her into the study with them and shut the door on me, leaving me outside in the hall. I often wondered what went on in that room with the three of them. One evening, I plucked up enough courage to open the door.

They immediately yelled at me and told me to get out and close the door. I did so, with my eyes full of tears, and feeling hurt and angry that they did not want me in the room with them. I had seen them all playing a board game at the table in the study. They were smiling and laughing loudly at each other. It looked like they were really having fun. This was one of the most significant times in my childhood that really affected me as I developed fears of not being good enough, not belonging, and not being loved.

When I was six years of age, I had a brilliant memory. Some said it was a picture- perfect memory. I could remember the lines of a song I had only just heard that day and sing it without having to listen to the song again or see the words written.

I also had a wonderful imagination. I used to sit and daydream about being an entertainer for a living, making people happy through publicly singing, dancing, acting, and modelling. I thought I would be amazing at being an entertainer. I thought I had a magnificent voice, that I was a wonderful dancer and actor, and that I could become anything I wanted to be. I thought if I wanted to, I could rule the world as I had so much confidence and self-belief in my abilities despite being made to feel by my family that I was not loved, not enough for them, and did not belong. This was before my parents kept me down a grade at school.

At that point in my life, I thought I was good enough and that I truly could become whatever I wanted to become. I told my mother I wanted to become an entertainer, to which she completely shattered my dreams and goals by saying I was being stupid, that I wasn't good enough, smart enough, I did not have a good enough voice, that I had two left feet, and was not pretty enough to be an entertainer, to sing, dance, act, and model. She said I should just aim for a job which would be far less work and far more achievable like a housewife and mother. I was heart-broken and devastated. I wanted to be more than just an ordinary housewife and mother. I had ambitions to do more, to shine.

Because of my mother, I formed some really heavy self-defeating and limiting beliefs, especially when I was told by the principal of my school that my parents insisted I repeat the grade. Everything just seemed to go downhill with my self-esteem and confidence from there.

I became shy and withdrawn as I had no confidence in myself, and I self-sabotaged when I thought things were going too well for me. It was like I was constantly waiting for the penny to drop.

At church, the other children alienated me as I was the only child born in 1977 and all the other children were older or younger and they wanted to stick to being friends with children their own age. I felt like an outcast.

At school I was teased, tormented, and bullied because mainly I was older than the others in my class by a year and therefore, they all thought I was dumb and stupid and that they had a right to bully and be mean to me.

My Special Place Where I Could
Just Be Me Without Fear

*"Imagine having that special place where you can
just be you no matter what."*
"This place does exist you just have to find it."

I went down to the beach one day during my lunch break and it was nice. It was silent, with no other people around, and as I walked across the joining of Albert Road to Victoria Avenue, I noticed the path was so beautiful. It was spring and all the flowers were coming out to blossom and bloom, dogs were roaming around, and children were out playing in playgrounds while the birds chirped.

It made me feel so very blessed to walk down there and experience it and have the time to myself. I love spring, with the different colored leaves and flowers, the different scents blending into each other, giving off a fresh and vibrant fragrance. That smell took me back to my childhood's secret place when I was eight years old.

The secret place was in the rainforest, out the back of my parents' home. I used to go there and hide when things got bad for me. It was my special place where no one could find me. I used to go there a lot to get my thoughts together and to let the sounds of the birds chirping and the water trickling slowly in the stream calm and soothe me.

I was so blessed to find that place as I could be anyone I wanted to be there. They loved me and I could pretend that was the case. I felt like I belonged there, as the animals in the rainforest did not judge me or hurt me by saying mean things to me. I wished I could live and be in that special place forever, but this was not possible, as I had to grow up and move on.

Often, when I meditate now, I take myself back to that rainforest behind my parent's place. Nature has a way of opening itself up when we are little.

As we grow up, sometimes it is not possible to have a special place like that where we can really let our hair down, have an imagination and be free. As we grow older, we focus on getting good grades, a good job, and earning an income to survive - and this is how we forget that we still have to nourish and nurture ourselves.

I often wonder when life became so rushed, full of prying, judging eyes and complications, so much that we hide our true authentic selves. We want to feel loved; we want to belong, and we want to feel as though we are enough. There is not a single soul on this planet who is truly and completely themselves. As we grow up, we get increasingly shaped by society, the rules of society and every other person we come into contact with. We lose more of our innocence, courage, and tenacity to be ourselves as we try to fit into the societal stereotypes forced upon us through family, school, cultural heritage formed eons ago by less civilized and less evolved societies and governments.

Let's face it, we all become someone very different from the person we were as a child. We become more serious, more sensitive, needier, constantly looking to belong and to be loved and enough. We forget that for us to be truly happy; we have to look inwards and work on our relationships with ourselves. We forget that to be loved and to love fully and unconditionally; we have to love ourselves and to fall in love with our lives again instead of looking for love on the outside.

Relationships and marriages break up, families judge before truly seeking to understand each other, friends eventually move away and fall out of contact, and then all we are left with is an empty shell. We know nothing because, for most of our lives, we were someone else for everyone else.

What if, instead of searching for love, belonging, and being seen as enough by external forces, we looked deep within ourselves? What if we got to know that person deep down inside of us for who they really are? What if we developed the person hidden within and then learnt to love ourselves unconditionally? Maybe then we can love others unconditionally.

A Childhood Experience That
Impacted My Life For Many Years

*"No, there are no books that teach you how to
be a great parent, but there is a thing called common
sense that can guide you to raising them properly."*

Being forced to repeat first grade had a deeper impact on me than my parents had probably imagined. It seemed like a very cruel thing for my parents to do, considering I had teachers and extended family members compliment me on my ability to memorize things quickly. I could, after only just hearing a nursery rhyme, recite it back the day after with no problems. I was even told many years later by my mother that I had a photographic memory at that age. This made me feel like the reason behind being kept down in grade one was that my parents did not want people to see I was smarter than my sister who was eighteen months older than me. Later in life, I was told by a family counsellor that this was probably the most credible and reasonable explanation for being held back in grade one, given that I had a picture-perfect memory at that age.

The family counsellor told me they may have thought that by doing this we would be a few years apart at school so no one would notice that their favorite child was not the brightest child in the family and therefore the other children would be more inclined to leave her alone at school.

When they did this, they did not consider the impact this action would have on my life for many years to come. They made me feel like an outcast by those my age who were in a higher grade than me, and those children in the same year at school as they were younger than me. The children my age thought I was dumb, so they never wanted to be friends with me. Often, I was bullied by my classmates for being kept back in year one, as they thought I was not as smart as they were.

This bullying happened all the way through my primary school and high school years. Because of this, I dreaded going to school. I struggled with the biggest and strongest fears a child could have, which were not being loved, not being wanted, and not being enough.

My parent's actions and the actions of the other school kids affirmed these fears each -and -every day of my childhood. So, I felt:

- Angry.
- Alone and frightened.
- As though no one cared.
- As though I was unwanted.
- As though it was me against the world.
- As though I was dumb and stupid.
- As though I did not deserve and was not worthy of having a good life.

This treatment from the other children made me feel as though there were very few people who liked me and really got me at that age. I even believed for a long time that I was dumb and stupid and that there must have been something wrong with me to have been held back by a grade. This made me feel depressed and have very low self-esteem. I developed terrible soul-destroying limiting beliefs and had fears that regularly would overcome me.

It was not until I moved out of home when I was fifteen that I saw things differently. I used these challenges to fuel and empower me to prove to everyone, including myself, that I was, in fact, a very smart person. I became more focused, driven, and motivated to get what I wanted out of life.

The Effects Of Bullying On Our Lives

"Children become bullies by following their parent's example, so watch your temper and treat everyone equally and with respect around them."

The other children used to bully, tease, and harass me in their clicky little groups as they felt very insecure and threatened by me, as I was different from them.

They had new clothes, books, bags and were not very intelligent themselves, but I always saw them as more fortunate than I was.

I, on the other hand, was given all my older sister's hand-me-down clothes, and I had to wear them to school every day. I had all my sister's old books and the other kids saw me as poor and not very bright because I had hand-me-down bags, books and clothes and they would tease me about them regularly.

One particular popular girl, Kimmy, was the worst of them, as she would never leave me alone. She told lies to the other school kids about me to make herself look good and bullied me day in and day out at school. She would throw bits of rubber and pencils at me, and she constantly called me dumb, stupid, fat, and ugly.

One day she made me so angry I could not take it anymore. I stood up in the classroom before the teacher arrived and tipped the desk over at her. My books, pens, and pencils, which were on the desk, ended up flying everywhere.

The teacher came in and asked what happened and Kimmy said I had thrown the desk at her. When I tried to explain to the teacher why, she would not listen, gave me detention after class, and sent me out of the classroom to sit outside the door until class was over.

When the school told my parents about it, they were extremely angry, yelled at me, and sent me to my bedroom with no dinner that night.

Because of the bullying throughout my childhood years, I became a people pleaser because I wanted to be liked, to belong, and I wanted to be popular, so I let people push me around. I did things people wanted me to do so that I could be in the "In" crowd and fit in. I did their homework, gave them my lunch, carried their books for them. Still, nothing I ever did seemed to please these people, particularly the girls.

I became very withdrawn and shy and fearful of others to the point where I would not express myself, what I felt, or what I wanted at school. At home, when I needed support and attention, I was told to toughen up and to go away and deal with it on my own.

As I got older, I realized five very important things that really helped me deal with the bullying and move forward with my life. These five things were:

If you do not stand up for yourself, then people will push you around all the time.

To be popular does not really matter and does nothing for a person, because what really matters is what you think of yourself and how you feel about yourself.

Life is not easy and was never meant to be easy. Life has and always will be full of difficulties, good times, and bad times. And if you only have the good times, you will never grow, learn, and develop into the amazing person you know you can be.

Not everyone will like you, no matter who you are or what you do, so it is always best to be yourself. Let your inner light shine. Love and respect who you are and put healthy boundaries in place, so you only attract like-minded people who will love and respect you and your boundaries.

There are always going to be people out there who will not like you and who will feel insecure/threatened by you and will do anything to hurt you and bring you down to their level. You do not have to take on board what they say or do. It is their insecurities that they are projecting onto you and really have nothing to do with you personally. So, continue in daring to be you, outstanding and unstoppable in everything you do.

A Traumatic Experience From The Past

*"You are doing damage by not treating
all of your children equally."*

To everyone on the outside, my family was just a normal family. But behind closed doors, it was a different story.

I grew up in a strict religious household. My parents were very controlling with what we should and should not do. They treated my sister like she was the perfect child. She could do nothing wrong. I was always treated as the wicked child, the one they never wanted, the mistake.

I tried to tell my parents that my sister was holding knives against my throat, and they automatically assumed that I had provoked it. They told me it was my fault and told me to go away.

One time when I was ten years old, screaming when my sister held a knife against my throat in the kitchen, my father came in and yelled at me for provoking my sister.

I ran out of the kitchen and into my bedroom and hid under the bed. I was then dragged out from under the bed, bruised and scratched along the way. My father was so angry he wanted to belt me.

He kept yelling at me, "You'll drive your mother into an early grave!" "You're a naughty child!" "You are good for nothing!" "Why can't you be like your sister?" He then put me over his knee and hit me with the buckle of his strap.

I felt the pain of the buckle smashing down on my bottom while my father was hitting me, the only thoughts going through my mind besides the agonizing pain was that I could never do anything right; I was not loved; I was not wanted; I was not enough. I could never do anything right, even though I had done nothing wrong.

From that moment, the trauma of being beaten with the belt buckle caused me to think and feel badly about myself. Before then, I never would have thought that a parent could do such things to a child.

My bottom was bruised and scraped from the buckle, and I felt as though I could do nothing right, as though I could never, please them, and this made me angry at myself for making my parents aware of what my sister was doing to me in the kitchen. I thought maybe if I had kept my mouth shut and just put up with my sister and what she was doing to me, then I would not have been beaten with the belt buckle. This made me feel insecure, scared and alone and I vowed never to make my parents aware of what my sister was doing to me again, as it would mean more punishment for me while she got off with her unacceptable behavior.

These thoughts throughout the years then became negative beliefs and fears of not being loved, not being wanted, not belonging and not being enough that I could do nothing right. And throughout the years I gained more evidence of this, and I believed them even though I did nothing to provoke my sisters' actions.

I am constantly making progress towards no longer seeing myself as a victim because that was the past and I am a completely different person now. I have learnt a lot of lessons in my life that have strengthened me:

- There wasn't anything I could have done differently to prevent it from happening.
- I can't control other people's actions.
- If anything like that ever happens again, I need to stand up for myself.
- My past does not dictate who I am now and what my life will be like moving forward.

A Best Friend's Betrayals And
What I Learned From Them

*"Be careful who you trust as your friends
may not turn out to be true friends."*

I met Ange when I repeated grade one. She had joined the class mid-way through the year. She got teased by the popular children in the class just as much as I did, so I decided one day to sit next to her in class. The next thing I remember, we had become the best of friends.

I was in year nine when Ange first betrayed me. I slaved for weeks and weeks over a history assignment. During those few weeks, Ange was playing hooky from school and when she came to school the next day, she bragged about it to me. When Ange finally came back to school, the assignment was due and the teacher we had for that subject knew we were close friends, so she told Ange to borrow my notes, knowing that I paid a lot of attention in class. Ange borrowed my notes, but the next day came to me for help as she was struggling to put her assignment together. I agreed to help her, not knowing that she really wanted me to write her assignment for her.

That night I went over to Ange's place, and she just sat there cried, and said, "I cannot do it." She made a big fuss about it, and I felt sorry for her, so I showed her how to rearrange the sentences in such a way that it did not look the same as my assignment and notes.

I was young and wanted to be liked at the time since my family life was not the best, so I wanted to help Ange. I restructured all the sentences for her and then told her not to submit it as it was. She would need to have a go at changing it to suit her understanding and her wording. The very next morning, she submitted the assignment. I asked her how she went about changing it and she said really well.

A week later the results had come out, and I had gotten a "B+" and she got an "A" which was impossible for her to get as she had missed so many of the classes for that subject and only had my notes from which to get an understanding.

Me being curious; I went and queried the teacher about her assignment, and the teacher showed me what Ange had submitted. It was all the work I had done when I was at Ange's place the night before. She did not change a thing about it, not even a full stop or a comma. It was, word for word, exactly what I had written the previous night.

That made me so angry as I had trusted Ange to restructure and put the assignment into her own words. Instead, she had handed my work to the teacher and taken the credit for an assignment that was not her work and had gotten higher grades than me for it.

When I queried Ange about the assignment and not letting on that I had spoken to the teacher and seen what she had handed in, she said she had studied what I had written and changed it into her own words.

It was the lies which hurt the most. I had never felt so betrayed by someone so close to me in my teenage life as I did at that moment.

It was at that moment that everything had changed for me. I became less trusting of others and more skeptical. I started questioning myself, who I was, and all the surrounding people. I eventually forgave her and became friends with her again.

A couple of years later, she went and told some of my deepest secrets I had told her in confidence to a couple of girls who used to bully me, hoping she could become their friends. She also told them I was talking about them to other people as she had overheard me. Which I never did.

They threatened to beat me up. When I stood up for myself, they went and beat Ange and another girl up that we were friends with instead of me. They beat them up really badly. I felt as though this was my fault for a few months.

Then one day it clicked to me that if I had not of stood up for myself and told the truth, then they would have beaten me to a pulp and that what had happened was not my fault but her doing as she had lied to those girls about me and they realized it when I built up enough courage to stand up for myself.

Ange and I reconnected and became friends again several years after that. Here I was thinking she had changed, but she had not. I got engaged to her husband's best friend. That friendship ended after she had a threesome with my fiancé and her husband, and I found out about it. My engagement also ended that night.

She tracked me down many years later on Facebook, and she told me about how she has a new husband with lots of money and that she did not need to work and that she was only with him for the money. That was when I finally, for the last time, cut ties with her, as she was definitely not the type of person I wanted to be around.

She never apologized for any of the times she had lied to me and hurt me in the past. I honestly thought that this last time around would be different, that she would be different, and you know we should learn and grow from our mistakes, but she never did, and she was not any different from all those times she had hurt me. She was still the same lying, selfish and nasty person she was back then.

I did a lot of soul searching after that and could not trust or let people get close to me without putting a wall up to protect myself for a few years after that. I did, however, heal from this experience and move on with my life.

What I learnt from this is that:

- In life, you must be very careful who you care for and let into your life.
- Never give people too many chances.
- It is not my fault that people are the way they are, and I am not to blame myself for standing up for myself and telling the truth.
- No matter what, the truth will always set you free.
- Be careful with your heart.
- Do not have people in your life that do not have the same principals, morals, and values as you do.
- Always ask questions and seek answers first before getting in too deep with people.
- Sometimes the best thing you can do is walk away, especially if the friendship is toxic.
- If I do not set expectations and put boundaries in place for who and what I will accept into my life, these types of things will happen and although we are creatures of habit and like to go back to what is familiar, sometimes it is for the best that we do not accept the familiar back into our lives as it can do more harm than good.
- I also learnt many years later that Ange had conceived that night after they had the threesome and that it was possible the baby was my ex-fiancé's kid and not her husbands.

What Is Really Holding You Back?

"To change your life, you have to dig deep and find that defining moment that has caused you fear or limiting beliefs and change your emotional attachment to it, because if you don't you are doomed to live in the past."

Procrastination and not being perfect enough are not the actual fears that hold you back. So, let me share with you my story regarding procrastination and perfectionism.

From a very young age, they taught me that if you are going to do something, you must do it properly and perfectly. I remember being in junior high school doing home economics, where we were taught to cook and sew.

Here is a little background on my family before we delve deeper into the memory so you can understand the story a little clearer. My mother was an amazing Sower, and she used to sew the most wonderfully perfect dresses for my sister as a hobby. Once my sister had grown out of them, she would sew them in for me if I wanted them. Anyway, she used to sew, and she used to do it so perfectly and it used to take her a very long time to sew clothes, as it all had to look perfect all the time.

I remember in home economics when I was twelve, sewing a pair of board shorts in class. Once I had completed sewing them, I was so proud of them. So, I took them home to show my mother I could sew just like her. When I showed her, she was not all that impressed, and she looked disappointed in me and told me I had sewn them all wrong. Apparently, it was because I had made a few mistakes in the stitching, as it was not straight enough at the seams, and I did not tie off the ends of the stitching so the threads could be cut short.

I remember the look on her face as I showed her. It was not the look of a mother that was proud of her daughter, but a look of annoyance that I had brought something less than perfect that I had made home to her.

She took them from me and unpicked all the stitching and sewed them up again with perfectly lined up straight stitching at the seams and tied off the threads and cut them off short and gave them to me all perfectly stitched up, and then she growled at me for not having them stitched up properly in the first place.

I was so upset with myself as I thought I could never make her proud of me, and so I vowed from that point forward to always try to get everything I did as close to perfect as I could. For many years, I did everything I could to my perception of what perfect was and sometimes I used the excuse that because I did something and it was not yet perfect, that I could show no one those things. That only spurred on and gave me an excuse for procrastinating when it came to doing things, as I did not want to show people what I had done in case they criticized and judged me for it not being perfect.

I remember feeling hurt, angry, stupid, and as though I was not good enough and not perfect enough for her.

I guess that is also what made my fear of speaking in front of an audience and in front of a camera even worse, the fear of not being perfect enough and of being judged. It was not until I started working for a recent employer and started doing the coaching courses I realized those fears were linked to the bigger fear of not being enough.

Because of this, I did a lot of soul searching and dove deeper into why I was that way. Through this soul searching, I traced it back to the sewing incident and when my mother told me I was aiming too high with what I wanted to be when I grew up. I then changed what those moments meant to me in order to move forward more positively. Now instead of working alone, I work collaboratively with people at my work and let them know when there are problems and when I need help, and I know I do not have to be perfect to do the job I do. I also completed a challenge another coaching student gave me to do, which was a thirty-day video challenge on Facebook which is how I got to where I am now with Facebook live videos and looking for the next challenge to smash what remains of that fear out of the water.

I did the thirty-day challenge, and it turned out to be a ninety-day challenge and I got some amazing people encouraging me and cheering my video posts on, which made me feel more confident in myself and who I am when it comes to being in front of a video camera and speaking. My videos are not perfect, but they are genuine and authentic and that is what people like about them.

The thirty-day video challenge made me face my fear of being judged, not being enough, and of not being perfect. Now I do not procrastinate or put things off and I get things out there as I know that there is no such thing as perfect.

Sometimes we judge ourselves a lot more harshly than other people judge us, and I have had to let that go, ease up on myself over the past year. I am much happier and better for it, but it was difficult, and the feedback I gained from those Facebook live videos have had a massive impact on me with such amazing words of support and encouragement posted in the comments below my posts.

Here is a YouTube link to a video I did that may help others out there with what is holding them back: https://youtu.be/E2j5ZXhhxzE

Personal growth and breaking out of the people pleasing cycle

"Learning, growing, and changing is what life is about. If you aren't learning from your mistakes, changing and growing from them, you are doomed to repeat the same negative patterns repeatedly until that lesson is learnt."

I used to be in a horrible place in my twenties because of circumstances beyond my control. I was depressed, angry, and withdrawn from the world. For me, this was the worst possible place to be, as I felt lost, alone and without direction. I struggled to be in this situation because I was a deep thinker and could not recognize there were other options and possibilities out there for me. This would lead to a standstill in my life and me constantly repeating the same choices, which lead to the same patterns in my life happening repeatedly.

I was like this because of my childhood and having been raped and abducted by a stranger at twenty-two years of age, in Queensland. I did not know what personal development was about, or even that it existed. I was born into a strictly religious family of which I was an outcast, bullied and treated as though there was something wrong with me at school and at religious youth group functions. Religion and school always taught that to be successful in life, you had to be married with children and possibly have a job by the age of twenty-five.

After my ten year de facto relationship split up when I was twenty-nine, I moved into a place on my own and that was very scary for me having been through what I had already been through in my life. Having sent a rapist to prison for what he did to me, as well as the fact I needed to reinvent myself, as the old me was not working anymore as I had to leave my partner, Martin, and my best friend, Melissa, behind me and start a new life because they had cheated on me with each other. I was a people pleaser and could not understand how this had happened to me.

The only reason I knew about them cheating was because Melissa had emailed my work email address, bragging about it a day or so later. This broke my heart, as it was not just Martin's betrayal. I was hurting from Melissa's as well. Two days later I moved out of the house I loved so much. I did not want to have anything more to do with Martin. He served me with legal papers for the house.

I was vulnerable and angry and could not stand the sight of him, and so I signed away the house I loved so very much to him to get Martin out of my life. I was the only one paying the mortgage for this house on my own, as he did not have the money to help.

The day after Martin had served me with the papers for my house I woke, and I remember it being a cold overcast, wet morning and I was feeling extremely down and depressed and could not bear to be in the world anymore. I got up out of bed, dragged myself over to the mirror in my room, and looked into it. What I saw staring back at me was a sad, angry, bitter, broken shell of a woman, a stranger in her pajamas staring back at me with a very blank, distant, depressed, and hollow look on her face.

In that moment, I realized I knew nothing about that stranger staring back at me because in my prior relationship; I was constantly suppressing my true authentic self so that I could feel loved and have a sense of belonging. Because of this, my needs were never met by myself and the people in my life, and I was constantly changing to meet the needs of others, so I felt completely lost and as though I did not matter to anyone.

This was when I knew things had to change. I could no longer go on living my life the way I had been because I was a people pleaser. I hated the person I had turned into.

I then questioned myself as to why I let others treat me so badly and turn me into someone I was not. The answer was simple: I wanted to feel loved and to belong, and I realized I had gone about things the wrong way my entire life until this point. I thought there had to be a better way to belong without suppressing my true authentic self to meet the needs of others all the time.

So, I picked myself up, did some research, and started a journey of self-exploration.

On that journey, I developed a holistic health support system to help me get to know, love, and respect my true authentic self and to attract the right people into my life.

Now, because of the holistic health support system I developed, I love and respect myself, have boundaries I enforce with others, and they love and respect me for it. I now feel as though I belong, and I am enough. I no longer suppress my feelings or let other people treat me like a doormat. I now speak up about what I want and how I feel and now my needs are being met by myself and others and it feels amazing.

This system is a holistic health support system I put together throughout my life, which dragged me out of the depths of depression, saved and improved the quality of my life. I will tell you more about it in later chapters, but for now I will continue telling you about the events that happened in my life that got me to compile and complete the system and want to share it with others today, and also to inspire you more so that you see that no matter what happens in your life you can and will get through it with this system.

I remember many years ago, being that person who let her

fears overrun her life. These were fears of not being enough, not being loved, and not belonging. Although I practically raised myself from the age of fifteen and was very independent, I still wanted to belong, feel loved, and have enough for others. Because of this, I was quite the people pleaser, always doing everything others wanted me to do, always bending over backwards for the surrounding people, always being who and what they wanted me to be.

It was not until after my long-term relationship ended that I realized I no longer knew myself.

When I looked in the mirror, I did not know who I was anymore and had no self-respect and very low self-esteem. I could not voice my expectations to others as I felt depleted and had no voice. I was depressed, and I was in a lot of pain, having been betrayed by family and the two people I held dearest and nearest to my heart.

When I looked at myself in the mirror, there was this depressed, empty, broken- hearted shell of a woman looking back at me who I did not know. While looking at her in the mirror, I cried with her and for her. She was not at all the woman I grew up fantasizing she would be.

She had needs that were shoved so far deep inside of her it hurt, and those she loved did not meet these needs. She had cried herself to sleep many nights, wondering if this was all she was meant to be and asking why these things had happened to her. Whilst looking in the mirror, it finally clicked for me that if I wanted my life to change, it was time to stop feeling sorry for myself and reinvent myself and my life to the way I wanted them to be.

This was not the first time, but this time I was stronger. I had picked myself up and reinvented my life once before. I knew I could do it again. This time was different. I could see the patterns now and I was so determined not to repeat the same patterns and to learn, grow and change from the experience.

I promised myself this time, my life would be different. I would be different. I embarked on a self-discovery and self-empowerment journey; I researched what was working for others to make them feel good and satisfied with life and experimented with those things and built up a holistic health support system that empowered me to be myself, helped me heal and feel good about myself and supported me through some of the toughest times of my life which were yet to come.

To this day, I still use this system, and I love using it. I am no longer a people pleaser as I have given myself standards, values and expectations and an amazing lifestyle which I love, which has given me self-love, self-respect, and some healthy boundaries in my life. My life is no longer built around other people and what they want but built around me, my wants, my needs, my likes and dislikes, my health, my relationship with myself and others, and my career. I no longer feel weak but strong and loved, as true love comes from within oneself and not from external sources. My life is powerful!

Sure, I still have fears and some limiting beliefs to replace and overcome, but I see them as challenges that I can and will overcome. Life, to me now, is a journey full of healthy living, self-discovery, change, and personal development.

Here is a newsflash for you "being single does not necessarily mean you are lonely and constantly seeking a relationship." Relationships happen when the universe sees you are ready for one and there is no point looking for one or forcing one to happen. It is incredibly powerful to be yourself and live life on your terms, doing it your way.

If I were the same person as I was back then I might still be in one of those toxic relationships now, but lonely and powerless and constantly letting other people walk all over me to get what they want. I would never have had the career I have now or the strong positive, loving mental attitude/outlook on life. I would never have known that I could change lives through my writing and coaching. I never would have known I could write, as I thought I had no imagination and needed an imagination to be able to write. I realized that the most powerful writing is not about having an imagination; it is about writing from the heart, from experience and from passion. These are the things that impact people's lives and inspire people the most.

I reinvented myself on my own, but you don't have to do it alone. I dare you to be yourself, outstanding and unstoppable in your life by reinventing yourself and your life to be the way you want them to be. You can do this because I have done it. It is difficult, but it is possible and very worth it if you are willing to invest in yourself.

Limiting Belief And Fear Of Reading Out Loud

"What the mind can conceive and grasp as possible in regard to your hopes, goals and dreams you can achieve if you are persistent in implementing your plan to achieve them. Only through persistence in the implementation will you achieve your desired outcome."

When I was in my twenties until the age of twenty-nine, I hated reading because it had led me to believe as a child that I was a slow reader, that I was dumb and stupid, and so I simply hated it. The reason for this was my parents neglected me at home. They did not spend the time with me to help me get my reading and writing skills up to the level they should be. I used to compare the speed at which I thought I could read with the reading speed of the other children in my class when they got up and read out aloud. I would sit there and try to follow along as they read to the class, but for some reason, I could not. It felt as though I was a couple of words behind them all the time and I hated that, so I developed the limiting belief that I was a slow reader.

I can recall being in grade six at school and the teacher telling me to get up and read in front of the class. I was so frightened, nervous, and afraid of being judged by the other children, as it would give them yet another reason to bully and tease me.

I got up and I read and sure enough, because of fear I did not read properly and to my full capacity as the nerves made me lose track of where I was on the page. Because of this overwhelming fear, I felt like I was going to die of embarrassment without delay. I got halfway through the paragraph, then one of the other children in the class yelled something out at me. I cannot recall what it was, but I ended up running out of the classroom in tears because of it.

After class had finished, the other children found me and teased and taunted me about my reading, which only made me feel worse about myself. This gave me the evidence I needed to believe the limiting belief I had, and to feel even more afraid of reading.

For the self-exploration journey at the age of twenty-nine, I had to really push myself out of my comfort zone and do the reading, so that I could personally and professionally develop, and I had no one to help me do this, but I was so determined to do it. My life needed to be improved. I wanted to feel joy, happiness, excitement, and love, and I knew being able to feel those emotions, I also had to feel the negative emotions of anger, sadness, guilt, and anxiety. I was not a fan of feeling the negative low emotions, but the alternative of not feeling anything at all was not working for me.

So, every day after work, I would push myself to read at least a chapter of a book.

Eventually, I got rid of that limiting belief and past that fear to a point where I enjoyed reading. These days, reading is one of my favorite pastimes, both in learning and leisure.

I am so glad I moved out of my comfort zone with reading, as it helped me with many things in my life, both personally and professionally. I now have people telling me they see me as the type of person who loves to learn, and they do not know how I do it as I am always doing some sort of personal or professional course after work every day. For the record, now I love to learn new things as they help me improve on myself. I am still not as fast as some people with my reading, but I realize it takes time and practice to get better at it and I know now that I read at the same pace to many people in the world, and I am good with that.

The New Girl In The Group

"There are some true friends that stay forever and stand by you through thick and thin, there are friends that stay for a season and then move on like a seasonal carnival, there are some friends that come into yourlife for a short time and are light and flighty who teach you lessons and then leave your life as fastas they came into it."

I remember in junior high school, when I was fighting with my friends and spent quite a few lunch breaks on my own. Wandering into another area of the school from my original bunch of misfits, I saw a girl. She was a little large, and a little smelly, sitting on her own crying near the girls' toilets. I had seen this girl, Amanda, around the school in a few of my classes. She would get bullied by the other children a lot more than I did. They used to bully her about her dyslexia and the funny glasses with pink lenses in them she wore to help with her dyslexia, her weight, and how she smelled, as she had a bladder problem.

I felt sorry for her, so I started to talk to her one day as she sat crying. Yes, she smelled quite bad and was overweight, but to me that did not matter, as I could see she needed a friend. I got to know her.

I even went over to her place to study with her after school one time for an exam. I was shocked and heartbroken by what I saw when I got to her place. Her place was a two-story housing commission house on stumps. She had four sisters, one I think was not even a year old and the other three were a year apart from each other and she was three years older than they were.

Coming back to her place on the outside in the yard, the grass was overgrown and there was rubbish all over the yard. As I walked inside her place, I could not even see the floor, as it looked like no one had ever cleaned the place. There were dirty disposable diapers, food scraps, dirty dishes, piles of dirty clothes all over the floor and on her family's old broken second-hand furniture. Amanda's youngest sister was crying and crawling around on this filthy, smelly floor, and no one bothered to pick her up. They also had three unwashed dogs running around inside the house. Amanda's mother was too hyped up on drugs to care about her and her sisters, and her father was a loud, violent, scrawny old fellow.

I studied there with her for half an hour before the smell started to really get to me and I had to make my excuses and leave. I remember thinking that even though my childhood was not the best; it was better than hers and I was grateful for that.

Amanda was expected to look after her younger sisters as her mother did not, and if she disagreed with her father or if he had had a bad day, he would yell at and beat her and her sisters. He had a foul mouth and used to curse and swear at them all the time. He also used to punch them, knocking them to the ground. Often, Amanda would come to school with bruises all over her face and body and when she was asked about it, she would say she fell or walked into something covering up for her father's violence. She was too afraid to say anything in case family welfare got involved and split her and her sisters up.

I felt so bad for her and thought she could do with a friend, so I became that friend to whom she could talk. When things had settled down with my old group of friends, I introduced her to them, and we all sat together and played handball and elastics in our lunch break. I made sure that they all made her feel welcome.

As I got older, and my best friend Ange had hurt me several times throughout the years with her lies and actions, we grew apart. Amanda was also there in the background, putting a wedge between Ange and me because she wanted Ange for herself.

At eighteen, me and my fiancé moved an hour's drive away from the old suburb, so I lost touch with the girls. That was until my fiancé, who had been friends with Ange's fiancé, started speaking to him again. This, in turn, rekindled my friendship with Ange, and she would tell me all the negative things about Amanda, as they were still in contact.

Despite being somewhat guarded towards Ange, I gave her the benefit of the doubt from our previous friendship and we became friends again.

One day Ange told me she had gotten married, that she and her fiancé had had a small wedding and she could not invite me to it because of the size of the ceremony despite the fact Amanda was her matron of honor. That broke my heart. I had thought we had grown really close again, but obviously not, as she kept her wedding a secret from me for months. Ange and her husband invited me and my fiancé over to their place for dinner one night and that was when the three of them had the threesome and ripped my world apart.

I realized something from this, and that is Ange had not changed from years ago at all. She was still the same selfish person who had to have what I had no matter what the cost was to me and so I never spoke to her again.

From my friendship with Ange, I learnt I was too trusting with people and I needed to stop being that way. If you give someone too, many chances and they do nothing to change, then they will never change and they will continue to hurt you with their deception and lies.

I also realized that Ange and Amanda were cut from the same cloth and neither of them deserved my friendship. They were not honest, loyal, genuine friends. No matter how much you want or think these types of people will change and learn from their mistakes, they never do and they like being selfish and dishonest.

It took a lot for me to get over Ange and Amanda treating me this way but eventually I healed; the pain eased off, and I moved on with my life. Now I only surround myself with people who are honest and who support me and who are of a much higher standard, morals and values, and I am happier for it.

Sometimes, no matter how much history you have with people, cutting ties with them and their behavior is the best thing you can do for yourself. You need people around you who will love, respect, and support you in your life.

My First Rejection

"The ugly duckling transforms into the beautiful swan when she lets her inner beauty shine through the outer layers."

I remember when I was thirteen years old; I had a massive crush on one guy at school. Everyone liked him because he was hot and cool. He was great at sports and also clever. He was a year older than me, and he was new to the school.

I remember when the year first began, and I would see him around as I was also into playing sports. Our eyes would meet as we passed each other, and he would say hi to me.

It was such a good feeling having someone notice me in the same way I noticed him.

I was so into him. He seemed like a very nice guy. My older sister also liked him, and she made it known to everyone.

There was a school dance happening in a couple of weeks' time and I had built up enough courage to ask him to go with me, as he seemed shy when it came to girls. Mid- conversation in the library, I asked him about the dance, and he instantly said he was not going as there were not any girls at school that he wanted to take. The next day he had told almost the entire school I asked him to the dance, and he joked around about it to the other children.

Word of this got back to me and I felt incredibly humiliated, rejected, and embarrassed by it. I just wanted to skip the afternoon classes and find a quiet place to cry. Instead, I thought I would confront him. Upon approaching him, I heard him telling my sister that he thought I was a joke, and I was not his type. This made me feel even worse.

I was so angry at myself for liking someone without getting to know them first, and realizing they were like this.

When I got home, I went straight to my special place in the rainforest behind the house so my parents would not know I had skipped class, and I cried and let all the negative emotions out for a couple of hours. Then I fell asleep underneath a big old tree near the creek. I woke up a few hours later and ran home and straight to my room, which I was sharing with my sister.

When she arrived home from school, she came to our room and teased me, which made me feel even worse. I screamed at her to get out of the room and slammed the door on her. I wish I had not left my special place, as that was the only place, I felt safe to be myself.

In my head, I was telling myself so many terribly negative things about myself. I got furious and screamed into a pillow and then fell asleep.

The next day I did not want to go to school, but I knew I had to, so all day I pretended as though I did not hear what this guy and all the other school kids were saying about me. It hurt like hell, but eventually the other kids stopped tormenting and teasing me about him.

As time and the years went on, I got over the pain of the first rejection, as I had many other crushes and rejections throughout my high school years. Each rejection made it easier and easier to bounce back, as I became more resilient and did not care so much about it afterwards.

I moved away from my family home at the age of fifteen and never saw him again until our paths crossed at a supermarket in the new area I was living in. I must have been in my early thirties, and I had grown up and changed quite a lot. I was not that same awkward little teenage girl anymore. Everyone at school used to make fun of me, but I was no longer the ugly duckling.

I was this confident, powerful, fit looking, stylish blond-haired woman who demanded respect from those around her. As he passed me, he said hello, and I simply walked on by as though I did not recognize him at all and continued on my way. As I walked past him and got further and further away, he could not take his eyes off me. I felt his eyes piercing the back of me as I walked.

On the inside, I was chuckling to myself. I could tell he then knew what he missed out on throughout the years with me, and it felt great. To this day, I still remember that moment so clearly, as I felt so powerful and strong. Those feelings will stay with me for the rest of my life.

I learnt the following things from that rejection and followed on in my life after it.

When it comes to liking someone, if they like me, they like me, if they don't it is not really my problem as there are plenty more fish in the sea

I deserve someone who will love and respect me for the person I am, not just for my outer appearance.

Sometimes the most good-looking people on the outside can be the ugliest people on the inside, and vice versa.

Sometimes rejection is not always a bad thing as it prepares and makes you more resilient for what is yet to come in your life.

Facing Your Fears Head On With No Regrets!

"Can you ever truly say that you have fully experienced
life from within the boundaries of your comfort zone?
If you never try to accomplish the impossible, then you will
never know what is possible in your life, so get out there,
be bold and be daring."

I had the biggest fear of heights throughout my childhood, teenage and early adult years. This fear was so frightening for me that when walking up too many stairs I would get vertigo, and when up higher than one or two floors out in the open air, I would get panic attacks. I remember one time on holiday in Sydney when I was eleven years old, being teased by my cousins and my sister as they asked me to go with them up the Sydney harbor bridge and I completely freaked out and cried. The mere thought of even going that high and looking down from that high up scared me. The fear was that bad.

Have you ever had a fear that bad that you just could not shake it off?

Well, this fear was that fear for me, and it prevented me for a long time going up high.

The thought of it paralyzed me, so I did something about that.

I was having to spend my birthday on my own, as all my friends were going away because it was the school holidays. I decided I would do something very daring, something so completely out of my comfort zone and out of character for me. I went and bought myself the most amazing experience of my life, a skydiving experience. For me, this was not just a small leap of faith but a massive one, as it had the potential to go horribly wrong and send me plummeting to my death.

When I got to Willowbank in Queensland where the skydiving was to take place, I had many thoughts running through my mind before getting out of my car. Thoughts like: You are being stupid doing this, you will die or end up as a cripple after it. What if the parachute does not open? What if I run into a bird and go plummeting to my death?

I nearly vomited when I opened the door to get out of the car. I pushed myself so hard to walk to the area where they were instructing people how to do the skydive and strapping us into the parachutes. We jumped off boxes and chairs as a practice run and I was ok with it then. We then went over and boarded this tiny little plane.

As the plane went up and up into the sky, I was in denial, thinking it was just a dream and I would wake up soon from it, but it was not just a dream. This was real. The next thing I knew, we were at some ridiculous height, and I remember sitting there thinking I needed to be let out. I was so frightened.

It was a fairly windy day, so there was a little turbulence which did nothing to calm my nerves. The door of the plane opened, and I began to shake. There were two other people to go before me, and neither of them would jump.

And then it was my turn. I built up enough courage, clenched my jaw, sitting there with my legs dangling out of the plane, nothing but me and open air, and I then pushed myself out into the void, taking the plunge and letting gravity do its work.

For the first three seconds when free falling, I was so terrified, but as the parachute was released, it felt amazing. It was a life-changing experience for me and one that helped me reassess my entire map of the world and who I thought I was.

I remember the emotions I had that day so clearly and the overwhelming crippling fear I felt I had pushed myself through. I also remember the amazing experience of seeing the world from so high up, slowly gliding down back to earth. In those moments, I realized I was not so much afraid of heights, but more of falling without anything to stop me from plummeting to my death.

Being up there and gliding down made me feel powerful, invincible, and strong. All the problems and dramas I had in my life seem so small and insignificant from up there, with the adrenaline pumping through my body. It felt absolutely amazing, and the best part was I had done it all on my own accord, with no one close to me there to cheer me on and support me during the process. It was a once in a lifetime experience, I would do all over again if I had the chance to.

I am smiling while I am writing this. I guess what I am getting at is if you let fear rule your life, you will miss out on some truly amazing moments, and some will be life changing. So why not just push through the fear and get out there and do things even if you are afraid? The fear is all in our heads and if you do not push through it, you will never truly know what you are really capable of.

Because of this experience, in 2017, for my birthday I went in a hot-air balloon up over Melbourne City Centre and saw some amazing sights. I also did this on a fairly windy day. This was my attempt to conquer my fear of falling as when we came down to the ground in that basket, gravity literally pulled us down as the wind pushed us along. It was a very bumpy ride at the end, skidding along the ground in those final moments in the basket before we were secure once again.

From those two experiences, I learnt so much about myself and really grew from them to the point where I changed a lot of my life afterwards for the better.

The Yearning For Meaning And Purpose!

"What is life without meaning and purpose? Every day without meaning and purpose is like being in a black hole of nothingness with no direction and worth, so one must always seek meaning in purpose in life to gain fulfillment."

In my teenage years up to my twenties, I used to sit and often wonder what if I could do this, what if I could do that, and what if this happened and what if that happened? It used to make me sad as fear, and the limiting beliefs programmed into me as a child would impede me from doing what it took to get out there and live and speak my truth. I was trapped, because my mind was not open to the possibilities that I could actually be who I wanted to be, and do what I wanted to do, or even have the things I wanted to have.

I used to be a deep thinker, and I wanted and yearned for more out of life. I knew I could be more, and this frustrated me as my fear, limiting beliefs and comfort zone would keep me stuck. I had friends who told me I was strange and weird because I did not want to just live life for the moment. I was searching for more. A purpose and meaning for my life, but fear stopped me from being open enough to find the answers I was seeking.

Many times, I sought professional help for this because I thought there was something wrong with me, but counsellors wanted to talk about the past. I did not need to talk about the past, psychiatrists would try to push medication on me for depression and this would stop me from feeling any form of emotions, even though I so desperately needed and wanted to feel something, anything other than despair and that trapped fearful feeling. Phycologists would try to psychoanalyze me with no ability to help me move out of my comfort zone past my fear and limiting beliefs.

I embarked on this journey of self-development and self-exploration thirteen years ago after I had had a nervous breakdown from multiple things which had happened in my life and had built up. I had held in so much anger, pain, resentment, and frustration inside that it almost broke me. I became withdrawn, quiet, and closed off from the world around me.

What if I told you there is a way to regain who you are and to be able to speak your truth, being the truest version of yourself that you can be? Would you believe me?

Well, there is, and I am living proof of it, but it comes with a lot of hard work and determination on your part. It all starts from within and you really wanting to help yourself with most of the effort, as no one else can do it for you. Be strong, be brave and explore the deepest, darkest parts of your soul and you will be amazed at what you will find out and how you will change after you help yourself. The power is within you.

When I started on my journey of self-exploration, I didn't have anyone else there to love, support, understand me, and to help me along this journey. The only person I had to rely on was myself. It was extremely hard to figure out who I was, why things had happened to me the way they had, and what I really needed to do to stop feeling the nothingness and longing I felt inside. I was stuck in an endless, repetitive, negative cycle of depression.

Then through exploring every inch of the deepest parts of my soul and experimentation with modalities, therapies, remedies, things other people said worked for them and the things that made me happy years before. Over the past thirteen years, I ended up creating a complete life changer of a holistic health support system that actually worked for me.

Supporting a balanced mood is a key role that it performs. I will not lie to you and tell you it was an instant overnight thing, or that it was a simple thing to turn my life around and give it purpose and meaning and break out of the fear and depression that had consumed me for years. I had to really want to change for the better. I completely changed my lifestyle, and it has worked for me for the past eight years.

There is no one size fits all in this, though. You have got to experiment, mix, and change things around to suit you, as we are all different and individuals in how we feel, see, think, act, and experience the world around us. What I can tell you is that this system saved my life and completely changed me forever. I am now eight years out of the depression and have not relapsed since and I now have a sense of purpose and meaning in my life.

Being Human And Having Emotions

"To be a true leader and manager, you need to have empathy and you need to be understanding of your team's personal situation and be approachable about it."
"You build people up. You do not tear and knock them down."

It is human to have and to show emotions to others.

Have you ever felt like you could not be yourself because you could not show your emotions in specific situations around others?

It sucks, doesn't it?

I worked for a large fortune one hundred company years ago where they had their favorites who they would let get away with things, like dressing unprofessionally and making loud outbursts in the office for no apparent reason, then there was the rest of us who they would not let anything slide with. While I worked for them, my cat died.

Silky was his name. He was a wonderful little red point Persian. When I first saw him in the window at the pet store, he was all alone and looked really sad. The way he looked at me when I tapped on the glass to say hello to him made me realize he was destined to come home with me. You could tell he was afraid and alone and just wanted a loving home.

He was six months old. When we got him home the first night, when we went to bed and shut the door to the bedroom to go to sleep, Silky meowed for hours, wanting to be let in as he was afraid.

I ended up lying beside him on the couch until he fell asleep that night. From that night onwards, we had such a strong bond. He was like a child to me. I remember whenever my partner came near me when Silky was around, the cat would hiss at him, as he could sense that my partner was not doing the right thing by me, and he wanted to protect me. We had Silky for about four years and the bond I had was very strong with him.

Silky almost died that day. I was at work that morning when my partner rang me and told me that my cat, whom I loved dearly had at tick and looked like he was dying, and he wanted to know if I wanted to come home and go with him to take Silky to the vet.

I asked my manager if I could take the rest of the day off so I could go. I was in tears and very upset about it. He told me I really should not be showing emotions at work as they make me look weak and that they really needed me at work for the rest of the day. He then told me that my cat was just a silly animal and that a cat should not mean that much to me. He told me to toughen up, wipe away my tears from my eyes, and get out of his office to continue working.

This sort of behavior from someone in management horrified me. I was angry that a manager could be so cruel and nasty, and I felt so very alone.

I rang my partner and told him I could not go as they needed me at work and that was that.

That night, I got home and asked my partner about Silky. He told me in the car on the way to the vets, Silky had gotten worse. My wonderful little friend was now being kept overnight at the vets to make sure he was ok.

I broke down in tears hearing this and I thought to myself it is human to want to cry, scream, shout, be angry, upset, disappointed, annoyed, be vulnerable at a time like this. And then I thought if I had been one of the other employees that the company was letting get away with things, then I probably would have been allowed to leave work when I needed to and that made me even more angry. I was so angry that I got on my running machine and ran 2kms nonstop at a quick speed setting. I had never run with that speed setting before. After that I went to bed with my negativity purged from my body from all the running.

The next two days dragged out very slowly as Silky's health was degrading rapidly.

At work I was expected to carry on doing the work like Silky was not dying. The vet had Silky on an IV drip and pumped liquid into him and gave him the anti-venom, but he had arrived at the vets too late as the venom from the tick was already circulating through his tiny little system. The vet told us that because Persians are inbred cats, that their systems are weaker, and they are more prone to kidney and liver disease.

I remember hearing in Silky's final hours the vet saying that his kidneys are not functioning properly and that they would give way soon. The vet said he could not stand to see Silky in so much pain and asked that we have him put down so that they could put him out of his misery. Although I did not want to lose Silky, I said yes, as I could not bear to see such a lovely soul in so much agonizing pain.

To this day, I really miss Silky as he was like a child to me.

I recall another experience when another manager I had at another company treated me much worse and that was when I was contracted into a big four company in a different city doing a managerial position by an offshore resourcing company.

This manager was new to the role and had started a few months after I did. We worked on a client site doing a technology migration project.

I was an early riser and used to start work at 7am in the morning and finish at 4pm with an hour's lunch break. The company had multiple vendors pitched against each other in competition to get the applications and data migrated on to a cloud solution from an on- premises infrastructure environment.

Prior to the manager coming on board, I was directly reporting to his manager, and we got along really well. I was originally hired to fix a project that had gone south because of poor planning and management by the previous person in the role.

The team I had was on an onshore\offshore rotation every 4 weeks. I organised and facilitated the team meetings mainly from 2pm to 4pm and was also available for the team to contact me after hours on WhatsApp if any issues arose. I also worked some late nights and weekends when needed.

A week before my new manager came on board, they made me work on a weekend to help with the management of an urgent issue that had come up on a delivery piece. The issue was resolved that weekend and they compensated me for the use of my personal time to work, as I was a contractor. Another time I had to work late was after the new manager came on board. It was arranged by my old manager for me to stay back and that I would get paid for working. My old manager asked me to stay back and work, and I did the extra hours.

The main reason for this was so that I could have meetings with the offshore team and coordinate with them who did what and then reviewing and changing the artefacts to make them fit for purpose after the team had created them and sent them through to me. We delivered the artefacts to the client, and the client was happy.

Some information you need to know about my new manager was that he had anger management issues and would yell at the offshore and onshore team members regularly. Often, he was not happy with anyone. He had yelled at me a couple of times in the office when no one was around prior to the two days I had to work back at night to get the project artefacts completed and delivered to the client.

Even though he was there in the office and finished at the same time I did those two nights, he disputed my timesheet and would not let the offshore resourcing company compensate me for the extra hours I worked. The offshore resourcing company decided that even though I had pre-approval from my old manager two levels higher than me to work back those two nights, that they would not pay me the money for the extra hours as according to them the pre-approval needed to come from my new manager who was disputing the payment of the extra hours I worked.

The day after I submitted my timesheet, and he disputed it, he came into the client's office early and yelled at me for putting the extra hours I had worked on my timesheet. His yelling at me while no one in the office was around terrified me, so I did not yell back. I just stood there and took the abuse, as I could tell he was close to cracking and might hit me.

I could see how angry he was in his eyes and in his body language and the tonality and level of his voice.

A week later, I got a phone call saying my aunt on my mother's side of the family had died. The call came in while I was at work. I told my old manager about the call, and he told me if I needed to leave early that it was ok to do so. I told him no and that I would do my eight hours and leave at 4pm as per usual. He then told my manager about my aunt dying and he sent his condolences to me via email.

3:55pm came around, and our team meeting with the offshore team members had just completed. I was getting ready to leave the meeting room on ground floor to get my belongings and go for the day when my manager told me I could not leave as he had arranged another meeting with some of the offshore people directly after the meeting we had just finished.

I told him I had to leave as I had to get to an appointment to deal with my aunts passing away, and he stood part way across the door and yelled at me in front of the other onshore team members because he did not want me to leave. The thing is that he never sent me a meeting invite prior to the meeting we had just had, and he never verbally told me about it until he was there yelling at me for needing to leave since I had completed my 8 hours that day. I got past him and to the elevator to go upstairs to get my belongings. He followed me into the elevator and continued to yell at me and he raised a fist at me when the doors had closed. I really thought he was going to hit me; I was so scared.

Lucky it was only one floor. I had to be in the elevator with him and as the doors opened; I bolted. Others on the floor could see I had been crying and asked me what was wrong, but I did not tell them, I just went over to my old manager's desk to see if he was there to get him to sort out my new manager, but he was not there. Instead, I got a friendly co- worker to escort me out of the building to make sure he did not follow and harass me anymore.

The next day I worked from home as I was so afraid for my safety if I had gone into work given what had happened the day before. I put a complaint in to the offshore resourcing company who had me contracted to their client, and let the client know that while on their premises during work hours this had happened, and they investigated it. Other team members came forward with their statements about what had happened, backing me up.

Instead of giving him notice for unprofessional bullying and harassing behavior, they gave me two weeks' notice to finish up. During those two weeks, the client let me work from home as they also feared for my safety.

If you ever get a manager and you can see early warning signs that they have anger management issues, raise it to management above them as soon as possible, and I would suggest looking for another job as it is not worth your health and safety staying in a working environment like that.

What I learnt from the two above experiences is that it is ok to be emotional and to be vulnerable, as it is not every day you face the death of a family member or a pet, and anyone who tells you otherwise is wrong. We are not robots and we do feel emotions such as:

- Love
- Hate
- Happiness
- Excitement
- Anxiousness
- Betrayal
- Weak
- Strong and powerful
- Stressed
- Exhaustion
- Frustration
- Anger
- Sadness
- Pain
- Frightened
- Fearful

These are all human emotions and feeling them is a part of life.

Please do not let anyone sit there and judge you for having emotions, showing them, and letting them out when you need to.

Do not hold your emotions inside you for too long just because there are people out there who have difficulties processing and showing emotions themselves.

You are doing more harm than good when you hold your emotions inside for too long.

Process them as and when you need to in the way that best suits you. When you hold them inside to the point where you explode, you run a higher risk of emotional, mental, and physical illnesses and emotional instability. If you cannot process your emotions around loved ones or on your own, then talk to a coach or counsellor or any other qualified health care professional that you think will help you process them and get them out safely.

It is not mentally unstable to have, show and let emotions out, no matter how many people may be there watching you. Those who judge you are those people who cannot process and deal with their own emotions.

The Role Of Exercise In People's Lives

*"Change your lifestyle before it changes you by adding
exercise as a daily ritual to enhance and improve your life."*

Exercise has been an intricate part of everyone's lives for so long now, whether or not you like it. If you are not running, you are walking, if you are not walking, you are skipping, and if you're not skipping, you are cycling, rowing, or jumping. Many of us love to dance and do athletics, and many of us like to play sports, which involves some form of cardiovascular exercise. There are also those of us who enjoy a decent workout with either core or weights at the gym.

Exercise decreases the effects of anxiety and depression, making these conditions easier to manage daily, and it is clinically proven to support a balanced mood as this is one of its key roles. Exercise increases our productivity by 10% as it makes us happier and more focused, less stressed with a better ability to concentrate due to all those endorphins and healthy doses of serotonin pumping through our bodies.

If you do not know what serotonin is, then let me tell you. Serotonin is a chemical that has a wide variety of functions in the human body. It is sometimes called the happy chemical because it contributes to wellbeing and happiness. The scientific name for serotonin is 5- hydroxytryptamine or 5-HT. It is mainly found in the brain, bowels, and blood platelets.

Serotonin delivers messages between the nerve cells, playing a massive part in our wellbeing and happiness.

It is a predecessor for the chemical called melatonin, which is used to help regulate the body's sleep-wake rotations and the body's internal biological clock. It helps to regulate our appetite, keeps our emotions in check, and motors the autonomic and cognitive functions of our bodies. It performs a key role in supporting a balanced mood. Low serotonin levels have been known to have links to depression and anxiety.

I personally cannot remember what it was like to not exercise, as I have exercised in one way or another my entire life. It was not, however, until the year 2008 that exercise helped me to turn my life around. Because of circumstances externally to what I could control eight years prior to 2008, I had become depressed and had a nervous breakdown.

A huge part of what had gotten me out of depression when turning my life around with my holistic health support system and daily rituals was exercise. I am truly grateful that I had included exercise into my holistic health support system and daily rituals, as it helped to make me happier by making me more active, more social, and more productive in every area of my life.

These circumstances behind the depression and the nervous breakdown I had were several distinct factors. In 2008, I had hit rock bottom and had no support from anyone, so I had to pick myself back up and move myself forward in the best possible way I knew how to at the time. Lucky for me, I was a very mentally strong person because of what I had already gone through in my life, and I had already reinvented myself and changed my lifestyle previously a couple of times.

Exercise stabilizes and rebalances hormones and chemical imbalances in the brain.

The downside to it is that unless you exercise every day, your hormones will become unbalanced again and the chemicals in your brain will end up becoming unstable again because of the lack of serotonin being pumped through the body.

If you look at some of the most successful people of our time, you find that they have daily exercise routines, and they eat reasonably healthy. I for one, am truly grateful to be able to exercise and reek the benefits that exercise has brought to my life, and I would not be the same without it today.

There is only one downside to exercise, and that is that you can become addicted to it and the feeling you get from exercising if you do it too often. Therefore, personal trainers and exercise therapists advise you to only workout four to five days a week and only for a maximum of 45 minutes each time and to rest for two to three days in between times so that your body muscles have enough time to rest, rebuild and recover from the intensity of the workout you did. Forty-five minutes of exercise puts you in a peak state physically, mentally, and emotionally for the rest of the day.

I was physically active before I got my driver's license and car at the age of twenty-one because I used to have to walk everywhere to get to the places I needed to go, as I was not a fan of taxis or public transport.

After I got my car and driver's license, I became lazy and accustomed to driving everywhere I needed to go, as it was quicker. I bought a treadmill, thinking I would use it at home, but other things became more of a priority for me, and I hardly touched it. In the year 2000, I was raped and abducted from a shopping Centre carpark in Brisbane. I will tell you about this later in this book, as this is not the right time to be getting into it. The Rape and abduction put me into depression where I was on antidepressants for several years.

To get myself out of depression, I got myself a gym membership and got myself a personal trainer to help build up my physical and mental strength. This was a big part of what snapped me out of the depression after taking myself off the antidepressants. The PT sessions and my gym membership were the beginning of me turning my life around and getting me to see that my entire life-style needed to change if I wanted too ever be happy again.

To this day, I am glad that exercise started me off on the journey I have been on for many years. It got me to develop my holistic health support system that saved and dramatically improved my life.

Losing The Truest Love Of My Life

*"To love so deeply and to lose that love is better than
to never have felt that love at all."*

*"When you have a love that is so strong, deep, and true that
could have stood the test of time but due to natural causes it perishes,
you must grieve and move on no matter how much it hurts to do so."*

This is a memory I had locked away in a little box in a corner of my mind because the ending for me was quite tragic and deeply hurtful.

Many years ago, I had my life sorted out. I had a wonderful job with a global organization, amazing friends, and a wonderful, spacious place to live. I practically had it all. The one thing I did not have was a loving partner to share the trials of life with and eventually marry.

This was after the two times two different long-term partners with my so-called best friends had cheated on me. I had literally picked myself up, reinvented myself, and gotten myself to a point in my life where I was ready to let someone special in again. I had sorted out all my emotional baggage from past relationships, gotten quite comfortable within my own skin and my self-love and self-respect were at an all-time high. I loved my life and had decided it was time to date and get myself out there again to find love.

I did not know how to meet men at the time, so I got myself a profile on the Facebook dating app. For a couple of weeks, I was chatting with a really nice guy. I was away in Central and North Queensland for work and during that time; he kept me company over the dating app. He seemed quite nice, not like the other guys I had chatted to on the app before. He was respectful, honest, funny and a brilliant conversationalist.

The guys I had chatted to previously were twisted, perverted, and kept asking me what I was wearing as under garments to move the conversation to more of a perverted sex chat, which I found very disrespectful, especially since I had not met them face to face and therefore did not know them from a bar of soap.

He was very different in his conversation topics and very respectful in what he said to me. Our conversations were deep and meaningful, and they showed me the type of person he was as we would talk for hours and hours either on the phone or messaging about everything.

He let me in, and I let him in, and we just got each other. He was a true gentleman.

The night before I was to fly back to Brisbane, he asked me if I would like to go over to his place for dinner as he would cook something special. Naturally, I said yes, as my intuition and instincts told me I would be safe. We had arranged for this dinner to happen the following week after I got back from working away.

We spoke on the phone a few times before the night we were to have dinner. That week I felt a little giddy and nervous and I really had to talk myself into going over to his place for dinner, as meeting someone for the first time in person at their place was not something I would normally do. It was not the safest of situations to put myself in and I was very safety conscious, but I took a chance on him.

The day of our date arrived, and I put on something special, sophisticated, yet very elegant and drove to his place. I parked my car on the side of the street and went up the stairs to his apartment

DARE TO BE YOU

block and knocked on his door, not knowing what to expect when he opened the door.

He answered the door with a massive smile on his face, invited me in and offered to take my coat. I went inside and took off my jacket and gave it to him. I was instantly surprised by what I saw when I walked through the front door. He had a really nice posh upper market type of place with stylish newish furniture, and it was immaculately clean and tidy. The reason I was so surprised by seeing his place was because I have been over to male friends' places before to watch movies, and their places were not as neat and stylish, and I thought that all Batchelor pads were similar.

I could smell the delicious aromas of his food as he was cooking. He had candles lit to give it a really romantic atmosphere, and he was wearing really nice casual slacks and a shirt. He was clearly a man who knew how to live and impress.

We had a glass of expensive red wine before he served up dinner. The food tasted amazing. After dinner, we sat and talked for hours. What I really liked about him was he tried nothing on me that night. It was just a superb evening getting to know each other on an intellectual and emotional level. When it was time for me to leave that night, he hugged me goodbye, and the night ended. He was the perfect gentleman.

The following week, he took me out for dinner at a fancy restaurant on the river. I believe the restaurant was called Oxley's on the river. He picked me up from my place and drove me to the restaurant, and for the walk to the restaurant, he offered me his coat as it was a fairly chilly night. When we were being shown to our table, I had a good look around and the place was very romantic. It had moonlit views of the water and of Southbank, and the table was lit up with candles. Part way through dinner, we had a band serenading us and it made me feel so special and like we were in a fairy tale. During the serenade, he held my hand and gazed into my eyes.

Before we left the restaurant, he kissed me, and it was like no other kiss I had ever had before. I had butterflies in my stomach, and I was feeling lightheaded from the entire night. He was yet again the perfect gentleman who had the view that if he wanted a relationship with me, he would take the time to woo and sweep me off my feet, and that we had all the time in the world for things to get physical. He was good to wait until I was ready, and he would not pressure me into anything.

We were together for about six months, and madly in love with each other. He worked as a trainer for a mining machinery reseller, which meant that often he would have to fly out to mine sites around the world for his job. Over the next year, we spent half of that year apart.

Towards the end of that year, he told me he loved me and that he wanted to have a family and settle down with me. So, we made serious plans together.

Two weeks after that, he went to get an x-ray done and then found a little black spot on his right lung. On closed examination and further x-rays, they confirmed it was lung cancer he had from all the dust and dirt on the mine sites, and his smoking.

When he told me it broke my heart and he also told me he had to leave for the USA as they had better specialists and healthcare insurance over there. Another reason he was leaving, he said, was that he had seen what having lung cancer does to people and their loved ones who end up caring for them and he did not want to be a burden to me or any of his loved ones.

He left on a plane to the USA the next day while I was at work, even though I told him I did not want him to go and that I wanted to take care of him. I tried to contact him after he got to the USA but got no responses to my texts, emails, and messenger messages, so I never heard from him again. Not hearing from him after that shattered my heart into very tiny little pieces and it took me a while to recover. I eventually recovered from it, but it took a few years because that was a love so intense, so strong, and so very deeply passionate that I had never experienced before. The way I recovered from it at the time was by packing all the good and bad memories of him and us together and putting them in a box and locking them away. For years, because those memories were in a box locked away in my mind, my mind would not let me remember anything about that relationship until years later, when I was strong enough to deal with the emotions properly from having my heart shattered.

I have moved on a couple of times and dated but have not really found anything that even comes close to or even measures up to what I had with him, and I could not see those men as long-term relationship material. I am not looking for a relationship now, as my life is pretty full. Not that I am not ready for or that I do not want another long-term relationship because I am totally open to it, but just not with any old riff raff. I now also believe that if a man is interested, he will do the chasing and ask me out on a date.

The Violent Womanising Cheater

"Never judge a book by its cover as the cover may have been mended or replaced to only show you what you want to see and not the truth which is hiding behind the front cover or what has been torn out of the book."

I remember being a little lost and wanting to be loved in the year 2010, so I had profiles on multiple dating apps and sites. At that point in my life, I did not really know how to meet good people, especially men. So, I joined hoping that I could meet a good man as I was not getting anywhere with meeting people at work, bars, and clubs. I had heard of success stories from people I knew who used dating apps and dating sites. I was not lonely. Someone special to complement my life was what I wanted.

I was on those dating sites and apps for about a month, and I was tired of getting rude, disrespectful men wanting to do sexting and asking me for sex and about sexual orientations. I never used to respond to them, I just used to block them. I probably got about thirty to forty of those characters in a week hitting on me and it really annoyed me.

Their messages would start off with hey baby, hey babe, hey sexy, hey hottie and then they would ask me out, to go to their place to meet them, or they would just jump right into asking me to meet them for sex, tantra, bondage, fetish stuff and go right on into what my favorite positions were, and so on and so forth in their rather lengthy messages of what they wanted to do to me. I would get to about halfway through the first sentence of the message and skim through the rest of the message and then delete them and block them, as their messages were so disrespectful to women.

Do not get me wrong, there were a few decent ones on the apps and dating sites and I chatted to them for a while, but they just did not seem to want to meet in person and only really wanted a pen pal. Anyway, a message came up for a man ten years older than me. I did not know how old he was at the time as his age was not in his profile and we chatted for a while. Then he asked me to meet him at the RSVP singles night in the city. He said that he was also meeting another single female friend there as well. I said yes as it was in public and others were going to be there so it would be safe and he not once spoke about sex, undergarments, or anything sexual, which to me was a plus as it meant he may have been half decent. He also mentioned he had an eleven-year-old daughter, which to me meant he was a responsible type of person.

On the singles' night we met, he seemed nice and so did his friend. She was Scottish and seven years older than me and he was English and ten years older than me. We all got along extremely well and became friends.

As time went by, we all became the best of friends and used to go out to dinner, drinks, and dancing at least once a week. During that time, I learnt that he was a womanizer and had a couple of different partners, which did not bother me because we were only friends.

A year later, he went on vacation with his daughter to the UK to visit his parents and he sent me a message telling me he really missed me and wanted to be more than friends. He told me he would break everything off with his sex buddies if we could become a couple. I thought about it for a while and then I said let's take it slow, dating for six months first and see where that goes. At that point in time, I did not know he abused women or was a narcissist.

Four months went by, and he lost his job and could no longer continue to rent the place he was renting, so he invited himself to move into my place and stay with me. Things were good for a month and then his other side came out. The side of him that was verbally abusive, narcissistic, and sexist. At that time, I was working full time, studying part time, and battling cervical cancer.

He used to make remarks like have you made me and my daughter dinner yet, the only good woman is one that is barefoot, pregnant and in the kitchen cooking dinner and getting me beers from the fridge. He not once offered to cook or clean even though he and his daughter were staying with me, and he was not working anymore as his employer had found out he was stealing all their clients for his own business. He was a tradesman, and his trade was installing and fixing garage doors.

When things were good between us, he used to tell me about his previous relationships which he so obviously never got over the fact that these women broke it off with him because of his tendency to verbally abuse them and narcissistically twist and turn things around on them so that they would feel bad and give him what he wanted. From what I heard, he would get them to rely and depend on him and make it, so they became really attached to him and then turned on them when they did not want to give him what he wanted. I know this because toward the end his daughter told me, hoping it would scare me.

He also told me of a couple of times where his ex's got him that mad. He could not help himself and he would lift them up by their necks against the wall and yell at them. Yet he could not understand why after they broke up, they put restraining orders out on him.

The narcissistic verbal abuse he was doing to me, and these stories he and his daughter told me about regarding his past relationships, really concerned me and rang warning bells in my mind.

I needed him and his support as I was going into day surgery and was told by the doctor, I would need complete bed rest for a month or two, and not to lift a finger for at least two to three months after the operation.

I gave him the benefit of the doubt because of this and thought if he were supportive and looked after me during my recovery period and picked me up from the hospital that maybe we could work.

The day of the operation came around really quickly, and he drove me to day surgery but when it came to picking me up and driving me home as that was when I needed him to be there for me the most, I waited two hours at the hospital, and he did not come so I ended up calling a taxi and getting the taxi to take me home. I was so disappointed and upset with him for not showing up to pick me up from the hospital in my time of need.

Three hours after I had gotten home, he arrived home without his daughter, who was supposed to be staying with us for the weekend. He was in a really messy state as his ex-wife, the mother of his child, had called the police on him as they had a massive fight, he was very abusive to her and apparently the police dragged him off her property. He was so fixated on himself and what went down with his ex-wife that he didn't even ask me how I was feeling after surgery and told me I should cook him dinner even though he knew I had just gotten out of day surgery that day and was not supposed to lift a finger.

That was the moment I knew I had to get him out of my life as I needed support and rest, not drama and someone so self-consumed telling me I needed to wait on him by cooking him dinner.

That night I could not sleep and so I laid in bed trying to figure out how to get him out of my home and out of my life because, as far as I was concerned, we were over.

The next day, his daughter told me in a text message why she was so set against me and why she was always fighting with him.

The reason was that he was still sleeping with her mother even though he was with me, and she did not like it as she wanted them to get back together.

He left for work that day and as soon as he left; I started shifting all of his furniture out of the house.

To give you a bit of history into the type of relationship we had. We had had several fights previously, and I had also asked him to leave/move out a couple of times in the past, but he never did as he said I would have to force him to leave, and I just did not have the time or energy to do so. He was supposed to be paying me some rent for staying with me, but he never paid me a cent for rent, utilities, or food. He just bludged off me. He was the type of man who expected a woman to work, pay all the bills and wait on him hand and foot, as that was what he thought a relationship was all about.

I spoke to my neighbors upstairs in the body corporate, and they said they would make sure that when he arrived back at my place from work, he gets all of his stuff and leaves peacefully. He did not have the key to the deadlock, so after I moved his stuff to the area closest to the front door in the lounge, a friend came and picked me up.

Before I left my place, I locked the dead lock so he could not get into the place while I was out. He was not very smart because when he moved himself into my place; he did not ask for a copy of the dead lock key.

While I was out, I got a couple of text messages from my neighbors upstairs telling me that when he got there and could not get in he tried to break in the front door and when he could not do that he went around to the front of the unit block and put a ladder up against the front wall to climb up to the balcony to break into the place through the sliding door. He scared the crap out of the neighbors who lived downstairs because of the noise he was making, and they told me if he got inside then they would call the police as he legally was not supposed to be there. I would then come back and allow him to get his stuff with the police present.

When I got home, I entered the unit block through the back entrance as he was out the front sitting in his car, waiting. I unlocked the unit and got inside and locked myself in and then called my neighbor who then came down and collected him from his car and helped him get his stuff out of the unit as everything was in the living room near the front door packed up and waiting for him to take away.

Because of the type of person, he was, I was frightened he would get violent with me and so I stayed in my bedroom while my neighbor dealt with him and his stuff. While in my room waiting for the "all clear" from my neighbor, my heart was pounding one hundred miles an hour, and I felt dizzy and exhausted. I was also very sore in the area I had the operation, which concerned me greatly. I know I probably should not have moved his big heavy wooden furniture around the unit on my own, but I just wanted him out of my place and gone so badly as I knew that if he had stayed, I would not have been able to recover from the operation as quickly as I needed to.

My neighbor gave me the "all clear" to come out and told me he put all his stuff in my garage because he had nowhere else to put it, and he had changed the frequency for the electric garage door opener to work with the remote he had for it so I could not get in there afterwards to park my car. He hung around the front of the unit block for three hours, making quite a ruckus, loudly yelling at me, so I made sure the deadlock was locked while I was in the unit, as I was so afraid of him. There was only ever one time I felt more fearful for my life and safety than that time, and that was when I was raped and abducted many years earlier. I was so glad when he finally drove off that night.

The next day I rang the doctors and told them I had pains where I had been operated on and was bleeding and they got me to go to the hospital so that they could check it out.

Apparently, all the sliding and lifting of heavy furniture on my own had busted the stitches, and it had got infected. This explained the bleeding and the stomach aches I was getting.

I think it took him approximately three weeks to get all of his stuff from my garage and give me back all my keys and garage door opener. During the following eight months, he texted me abusively nonstop every day threatening me and also trying to make me jealous by sending me pictures of other women and saying he was in a wonderful relationship with them and that they were better than me in every way. I tried to get my ISP to block his number so he could not do that, but they could not do that without a court order and that far back technology was not advanced enough for me to block his number on my phone myself. I told the police about my situation and his messages, and they said that unless he had physically harmed me, and I had proof of it, that they would not help me get a restraining order on him.

When it got too much, I threatened him with going to the police and taking him to court, and he then stopped harassing me.

This taught me to be extremely careful who I choose to let into my life and that people are not always the way they first make themselves out to be. They may be a wolf in sheep's clothing. It also taught me to be stronger and to stand up for myself around men. To make sure they hear me the first time when I ask them to leave and not to let them shrug things off. I also learnt that I deserved to be with someone who will love and respect me for who I am and not for what they want me to be or what they think they can turn me into. If you are fighting a lot, then it is not worth your mental and emotional wellbeing to continue being with that person, as things will never change. I also got to know some significant warning signs to look out for with men when dating.

The Internet Dating Scam

"Dating is risky even for the weariest of souls as there are many types of people out there. You may date someone who you think may be a frog but he ends up being a toad and so you release the toad into the wild and the vicious cycle repeats until one day you find a frog and kiss him, and he turns into a prince."

I have been single for sixteen years but dated on and off during that time. I remember the vicious cycle that used to repeat so that I could feel loved, enough and to have a sense of belonging.

After the love of my life left to die in the USA, every now and again I used to get frustrated with life, not because I was lonely because I was not as I had my friends, hobbies and so forth to keep me busy, but because I felt like it was time to share my life with someone special. I also had friends and family pressuring me to find a man and settle down and have a family. I was constantly asked by loved ones:

- Have you found someone yet?
- There are plenty of decent men out there, so why don't you find one and settle down and have a family?
- When are you going to have a family?
- When are you going to give us grandkids?

My answer was always the same when I felt I was ready to do

so. It did not mean that their questions did not annoy me or did not get to me. What used to get to me more was seeing how easily others could find themselves good stable relationships where their partners were supportive caring and thoughtful, and there were only a couple of experiences I'd had in my lifetime where I had met princes, but those princes were not the right princes for me no matter how hard I tried to make things work in those relationships. The universe, it seems, has other plans for me.

Due to peer pressure, I would every now and again buckle down and create a profile on an internet dating site to see what was out there and if I could find someone to settle down with. In all honesty, at those points in my life, I had very low self-esteem.

I want to tell you about one character I met on a dating site that was supposed to screen all their members before they would let them put a profile up. The screening this dating site did was interviewing two friends and family members of the person wanting to put up a profile to make sure they were real and genuine in their endeavors to meet someone special. Those friends and family members would then have the option of putting a character testimonial up about the person who wanted the profile up on their site to help prospective partners see what the type of person in the profile was. This would then help the people looking through the profiles select the best of them to chat with and possibly date. I was told about this dating site by a very close female friend of mine.

I remember coming across a profile of a guy who lived in England who was the same age as me. He had some pleasant pictures and some outstanding character testimonials, and his profile seemed similar to the type of person I was looking for, so I sent him a message. We chatted on the site and found we had a lot of things in common.

We sent messages to each other on the site for at least three months, then we swapped numbers and email addresses. We texted, rang, and emailed each other almost every day for a further three months. He even sent me gifts like a valentine's basket of chocolates, champagne, a dozen red roses and a massive stuffed white teddy bear. He would send me photos of himself. When we spoke on the phone, he had a British accent.

Our conversations were deep and meaningful conversations about what we thought of things, how we felt, what we wanted out of the relationship, for example how many children we wanted, getting married and living out the rest of our days together and how different life would be for both of us.

These conversations made me feel loved, as though I was enough and as though I belonged. It was because of these conversations that I used to bounce up out of bed in the mornings, keen and eager to see what the day had brought me in the way of his calls, texts, and emails. I used to be so excited to start the day like I was a child again, having that childlike innocence about me. Do not get me wrong I loved my life but having someone there who you can share everything with and be there for you to just simply talk to when you were feeling flat or down and in need of a shoulder to cry on and to cheer you up because of a bad day, was amazing and something I had not really experienced much of in my life. So, to me, he was "it."

I know to you it seems like a silly internet romance but to me after speaking daily for hours at a time, texting and emailing really long deep and meaningful emails, it was something to be cherished and I cherished it with all my heart as I never would have thought I could have ever felt something as strong as this since the love of my life left to die in the USA eighteen months earlier. I completely let him in, let my guard down, and became completely vulnerable with him.

My feelings for him grew over that time and so did my trust. By nature, I see everyone as innately good until they prove me otherwise. He used to talk to me about what he thought it would be like when we met in person (face to face), and it was so exciting for me to speak to him about it and he made me feel as though he felt the same way about me as I felt for him. He sent me gifts for my birthday, and Valentine's day when he knew I wanted nothing from him. He said he did it because he cared for me and wanted me to feel loved and special. He told me how he felt towards me.

Then after around the eight-month mark, he asked me to pay for something for him that was over here in Australia as he was going to be here for three months from Christmas. It was a course he wanted to do, but his bank would not let him pay for it himself as he was told he had to wait for another credit card to come through as his old one had been stolen, maxed out and the bank cancelled it on him. The course was $800, and he promised he would pay me back when his new card arrived. Since I had his word that he would pay me back, I paid it for him because that is what you do when you care for someone.

Two weeks had gone by, and we were still talking on the phone via WhatsApp every day, which made me feel like he was legitimate, as he did not just leave my life after I paid for the course for him. He told me he was buying something special from Australia for his mother for Christmas and that he did not want her to know about it. He convinced me that it would be cheaper on postage for him if he got it sent to my place and then for me to post it on from my place. He said he would pay me the $800 he owed me and the money for the postage of the parcel after I had sent him the receipts for postage and handling so he could pay me it all in one lump sum, which to me at the time made sense. So, I agreed to it.

Two weeks later, after he had purchased it and had gotten the retailer to send it to my address, I got a phone call from the police. They wanted to know of a time they could come and speak to me, but they did not say what it was about. I thought it odd, but I gave them a date and a time. That day came, and they arrived at my door. They explained to me how he had purchased the goods with a stolen credit card and had purchased several other gifts with that same card.

The Jeweler who he had bought the item from cottoned on to

what he was doing as the jeweler was an ex-police officer and so he alerted the police about the purchase and gave them my name and address. Before they visited me, they said that they had traced the purchase he had made of several items over the past few months, all on that same credit card. The person who owned the credit card had reported it stolen the day he purchased the item he had addressed it to me. And that was how they found me.

They asked me if I had received any other goods of that nature from him in that way before. I told them no, but I received a valentine's day and a birthday present from him but that they were not really big and expensive items, and I did not know he was purchasing items on a credit card that was stolen. And that I no longer had them as they were perishable items apart from the teddy bear.

They asked how I became involved with him, and I told them exactly what I told you in this chapter, through a dating site that was supposed to be fully screening people before letting them on to their site with a profile. I told them what we spoke about, showed them his emails and text messages and all the logs on WhatsApp of the days, times, and durations of our calls. They then told me I was the victim of an internet dating scam from Nigeria and that I was not to contact him or even help him out again and that if he tried to call me to let them know. I gave them the phone number he would call me from.

I explained to them how stupid and silly I felt about it all, as I did not know, and they told me that many women fall for these scams all the time. Even really smart women who are CEOs, general managers, and powerful smart executives. They told me about one woman at the gold coast that got scammed for hundreds of thousands of dollars from one of these scammers. They said that these scammers prey on women's vulnerability for a living.

I felt so violated, angry, guilty, shameful, lost, confused and sick to the stomach after the visit from the police. So much so that I took two weeks of emergency leave from work to recover and went and stayed with a friend miles away from home to regain my strength and recover from the ordeal I had been through. It took me approximately eighteen months to recover from it fully.

What I learnt from being the victim of this internet dating scam was that:

- I needed to do a search online and really investigate men on dating sites and apps.
- When I meet people from the dating sites, I should ask to meet them in person before becoming emotionally involved with them.
- Not everyone is innately good at heart.
- I need to choose more wisely who I should and should not be putting my trust into.
- If they ask me for money or favors that I need to ask a lot of questions first before agreeing to do anything.
- Only speak to local men on the dating apps and sites so that I can insist on meeting them in person to see if they are really the person in the photos and who they say they are.
- At the beginning of courting, I need to stay guarded and not to open up too quickly to the other person.
- That falling prey to one of these scams is not my fault, and that I was not stupid or dumb for falling for it as really smart women worldwide also fall prey to these scams all the time.

Luckily, I had my holistic health support system in place, which helped me to bounce back enough to go to work the following week after my leave ended and move forward with my life.

The Clingy Drug Addict

*"There are always plenty of fish in the sea.
If the fish you caught, turns out to be a Piranha
(flesh eating fish) run for your life as your life
is worth more than the Piranha's dinner is."*

I once dated someone who was a drug addict. I did not know he was one at the time dating, when looking back at his mood changes, clinginess, and arrogance later, after we stopped dating, it all made sense. That and his friend, who ended up becoming one of my closest friends, told me he was on drugs the entire time we were dating.

We met at work, and he was nice and friendly. Kind of laid-back sort of person. When we got talking, we had the same sort of interests like karaoke, singing and dancing. We had the same occupation in IT, and we were both contractors. We had the same taste in music and movies as well, which was good.

After a few weeks of working together, he asked me to go to dinner with him and meet one of his friends. I agreed, and we made plans to go to dinner on the Friday night of the following week. I quite liked the idea of meeting new people and making new friends. He offered to come and pick me up, but I said no, I was ok to get there on my own.

Friday came around so quickly. And the day also passed very

quickly. I met him and his friend at an Indian restaurant a couple of suburbs away from my place. He introduced me to his friend who was a really nice girl who I also had a lot in common with. After dinner, we all ended up going to a karaoke bar a suburb away from the restaurant. It was a really fun night. His friend told me how she met him. He was in a relationship with one of her friends and that was how they met. She also told me he had tried to crack on to her a few times, but she clarified that all they could be is friends, and so he respected this.

A few weeks went by after that night, and we all became really close and caught up a couple more times for dinner and drinks. Then one night he asked me to go on a date with him and because I knew him as a friend first and thought I knew what he was like, and I liked what I saw, I said yes and so we started dating.

While we were dating, he became very clingy, which I found quite odd and restrictive.

We were dating for a few weeks, and he got really paranoid around me. This was both at work and in our own time. He used to go out drinking every second night and because I lived closer to the city than he did, he would crash at my place even when I was not out there partying with him.

One time, he told me he was adopted, but he loved his adoptive parents very much.

That day, something happened with his parents, and he would not tell me what, and he became furious. And it seemed like every second day his mood would change from happy and fun to be around, too angry, paranoid, and obsessed/jealous. A month went by, and he lost his job, but he did not tell me he had lost his job, our mutual friend told me. Apparently, he became furious at work, and he told them to get stuffed, so they fired him. During the two days after that, he became extremely clingy, more so than normal. And he was sending me text messages every ten minutes and expecting me to answer them even though I had work to do. I could not answer them, because I did not answer them straight away, he then tried to ring me several times. I answered a couple of his calls and let him know I could not talk as I was at work and that I would speak to him after work.

When I got home from work on the second day, he rang and demanded he come over to my place. I was so exhausted, and I told him I was too tired to see him. I spoke to our mutual friend not soon after that and she let it slip that he was not only drinking himself silly, that he was also a drug addict and when he got severe mood changes like it was because he was coming down off his high from the drugs he was addicted to.

I decided that because he did not tell me himself; he had lost his job and that he did not tell me he had a dependency on drugs that he was not the sort of person I wanted to continue to see as he scared me with his clinginess and mood swings, so I told him I could no longer see him.

He continued for the next month to text me and leave voice messages on my phone and buzz my intercom system, wanting to speak to me, and it terrified me and kept me awake at night. Until one night he just completely stopped, and I never heard from him again until our mutual friend got married and he came up and spoke to me at her wedding. He mentioned he was engaged and happy, but he complained about how our friend who could not afford a big wedding would not let anyone bring a plus one to the wedding, that she did not know because he wanted to introduce his fiancé to our mutual friend at her wedding.

When he spoke to me, I just felt numb. And that was when I realized I did the best thing for the both of us by breaking things off with him as he got to meet someone new, and I got to live my life hassle free and also free to meet other people too.

He told me he realized after I broke things off with him, he needed to face his problems and sober up from the drugs and alcohol, as he realized he was running away from his problems and running away fixed nothing. I think this was one of the hardest lessons he had to learn in his life. He had apparently been like this for a good ten years with drugs and alcohol.

When we were dating, he was very dependent on me and the alcohol and drugs to help him cope. To me, it seemed like he was running away from his true real-life problems and escaping them with the drugs and alcohol. I could not be with someone like that, as I am the sort of person who faces their problems head on without the aid of drugs and alcohol to help me feel better. I also had a few issues of my own I needed to deal with back then as well and could not deal with his issues and mine at the same time.

I was glad to hear he had met someone new, and that they were planning to get married. I told him so and I went and spoke to others I knew at my friend's wedding after that.

The key to a situation like that is to remember to look at the signs with the mood swings and the patterns in behavior the other person is exhibiting and make a judgement call on what is right for you and whether you can handle being with someone so dependent of substances, or whether it is better for you to simply walk away for your own health and safety. It is not a simple decision to make, but you have to make it as it will affect your health if you let things continue the way they are with the other person.

Dating A Man Who Stayed Friends
With His Crazy Psycho Ex-Girlfriend

*"If you are a person too afraid of what others will think
and do when you tell them the truth, then you don't deserve
to be happy as you need to get over your fear of being judged
and live your life as your true authentic self as the truth will
always set you free."*

Here is another dating disaster for you. As you can see, I have had my fair share of crazies and I have gotten through each experience, learnt my lessons, grown and changed from those experiences.

So, I met a guy when I was looking for my next project management role as my contract was ending. He was a recruiter. I had applied for a role that his agency advertised. He invited me to come in for an interview at his agency to speak about the role and my experience to see if it was a fit.

I went to the appointment and met with him, and we got along really well, we spoke for over an hour about my experience and his client's needs. At the end of the interview, we knew I was not a match for the role, as it was very clear. He then told me he would like to stay in contact with me as they have other jobs on the radar that would suit me better coming up. I said that was fine.

We caught up for a cuppa a few times and spoke about other roles they had going and about my resume and what changes he wanted me to make so that it was more appealing to their clients. The second time we caught up for a cuppa, we spoke about other things, and he invited me out to dinner on a date. As a rule, I normally keep things very professional with the recruiters I network with, but he seemed like a very nice guy, and we had a lot of things in common.

The date went well, so we started to see each other. Four weeks after we started dating, he asked me to come to his housewarming party at his new place and meet his new friends. As I recall, it was on a Saturday afternoon around 3 or 4pm. I got there at about 4:30pm. I drove there from my place to his place as he lived over the other side of Brisbane city. We had arranged for me to stay the night there, as we were all going to be having a few drinks.

We were all sitting around a large outdoor dining table talking and one of his friends, who was curious, asked me who I knew at the party and how I knew them. I answered, saying I was seeing his friend Nate, and that Nate had invited me. Everything at that table then went quiet and Nate came and asked if he could speak to me privately for a moment.

So, I got up and walked with him upstairs to one of the rooms and he told me how I should not have told his friends that I was seeing him as his friends were mutual friends with his ex-girlfriend who was crazy. He told me some horror stories about her slashing people's car tires with a knife and threatening to stab him several times. He then explained to me he stayed friends with her out of fear and that his friends were not told that he and his ex-girlfriend had broken up and that he did not tell them out of fear of what she might do to him if they found out.

He also explained that she was out of town on a business trip and that he wanted me to meet his friends and had deliberately planned to have his housewarming party while his crazy ex-girlfriend, Jess, was out of town so that they could meet me. He explained now they knew we were seeing each other. It was best if I just left and went home so that he could fix the situation.

I expressed my disappointment in him and told him I was upset, hurt and angry, that he would dare even bring me into a situation like that and I also told him I was not sorry for exposing his lies to his friends and that I really did not think he should stay friends and keep the charade going any longer as I deserved to be with someone who is emotionally and physically available for a relationship with me and how I felt the situation was completely disrespectful to me and that he should never have put me in that situation. I agreed to go, but not without telling him what I thought of the situation.

The next day I got a Facebook friend's request from one of his friends and I thought nothing of it. Two days later his crazy ex-girlfriend messaged me on Facebook threatening to slit my throat and run me off the road whilst driving as she had heard from one of the other people at the party that Nate was seeing me, and she still thought that they were together. She warned me to stay away from him.

The next day he texted me, apologizing for getting me into that situation and to see how I was feeling and I told her she tracked me down on Facebook and what she had sent me and I explained to him I could not see him anymore as it would put my health and safety at risk as it seemed like he was leading her on by staying friends with her as she thought they were still together. I then told him to leave me alone. He sent me a few text messages throughout the week which I did not respond to and after that; I heard nothing from him again.

The lessons I learned from this situation was that:

- My health and safety must always come first.
- If the person you are seeing is still friends with their ex, then in some way, their exes think they are still together or will get back together.
- If they have mutual friends with their ex, then they need to tell the truth about things to them and not hide breakups etc. from their friends.

- I deserve and am worthy of better than that from those I am seeing as that situation was completely disrespectful to me and to his friends.
- I really did like him but if he is too afraid to stand up for himself and to let his friends know that they had broken up, then he obviously was not the right person for me.

The Threesome

"Know that you are worthy of and deserve so much better than partners and best friends that so obviously are in things for themselves and have very low morals and standards than you do."

This is one of the worst ways that Ange betrayed me, and it was the last straw. I still remember the pain, disappointment, and anger I felt when it happened, like it was yesterday. Throughout the years, I thought I deserved what I got dished out to me by my friends, especially Ange, as she was my best friend. I had in the past been betrayed many times before by her and I kept going back for more, as I had such low self-esteem. I thought if I wanted a best friend that I should put up with all of her betrayals, lack of morals and values, just so she was in my life.

I remember it so clearly. I met my first serious partner at the age of seventeen. I met him through my long-time best friend Ange, who I let move in with me after I had secured a rental unit in the outer western suburbs of Brisbane. He was the best friend of Ange's boyfriend Nigel and seemed like a very nice guy, and we got along very well.

He was not much for looks, but because of my low self-esteem and low opinion of my own looks, I aimed lower than the type of guy to which I was attracted to. What he had going for him was that he could make me laugh and he was dependable, and we had Ange and her boyfriend in common. His name was Davies.

When my lease was about to expire on the unit, Ange had just up and left without helping to clean the place before leaving. He was there for me, and he helped me clean the place so that I could get my bond back. At that stage we had been seeing each other for about a year and so we moved in together.

When he moved in with me, something seemed off about him, but I ignored my gut instinct, and it somehow went away. We found we had a lot in common and there was also a lot we did not have in common, like the fact that the only music he liked and would ever play was Kiss. I hated their music, and he knew that, but he continued to play their music, so I just put up with it. He had no respect for his mother, which was a terrible thing, and he used to play video games morning and night and stopped spending any quality time with me. A mother figure who would cook and clean for him all the time was what he wanted. He used to play an electric guitar, and he was terrible at it, and he used to have the volume up as loud as he could, and it used to really get my neighbors angry at us.

We were great for a while together, and we had fallen out of contact with Ange and her boyfriend as we moved a forty-to-forty-five-minute drive away from them and it was too far to travel all the time, especially since I did not have a car or a license. One day, unexpected, Nigel rang Davies and told him Ange and he were getting married, and he invited Davies to their wedding but not me, saying that they only wanted close friends and family at their wedding even though I was supposed to be Ange's best friend. That really hurt me.

Davies went to their wedding and told me all about it and how he had recognized Ange's matron of honor and he told me what she looked like. It was the girl I had introduced to my group many years ago at school, Amanda. Sure, as soon as I had moved far enough away from Ange, Amanda had strolled right in and taken my spot as her best friend as Ange was not a very loyal friend to me because she was always lacking in morals and values.

Before the wedding, Ange was apparently pregnant, and Nigel's parents were not thrilled with that as they were very strict religious people and did not believe in sex before marriage. Nigel's parents did not like Ange because of that. They thought she was the devil incarnate. It seemed simple apart from the fact that Davies did not always have a good relationship with his mother, and he used to have fights with her on the phone and hang up on her. They were a dysfunctional family and his father had run out on his mother when he was very little, so the closest thing he had to a father figure was his uncle Darren, whom we used to visit often.

Davies and I eventually got engaged and all his family were happy with our engagement, as his family really liked me. His mother used to visit us often, and we lived a few suburbs away from his sister in Logan city. We had a nice private rental house with two cats and a dog.

Davies stayed connected with Nigel for the next three months after their wedding, and one night Nigel invited us to dinner at their place and to stay the night there. Their house was one of the best houses in the housing commission area they lived in, in Brisbane's far western suburbs. It was a bit rundown and rickety, but it was ok.

We drove forty-five minutes to get to their place for dinner and then Ange spoke about one fantasy she had. I do not even know how the conversation got to that subject at the dinner table, and she then propositioned us for a foursome. I said no, and I thought that was the end of it because it was late. I went to bed. We were staying in their spare room, and you had to go past their room to get from the spare room to get to the bathroom. A couple of hours went by, and I had a sore stomach from drinking too much wine before bed and had to go to the bathroom. Before I got up out of the spare room, I could hear noises coming from somewhere in the house. I thought it was odd at that time of night to hear noise as it was really late.

I got up and walked out of the spare room, only to see out of the corner of my eye, the door open to their room and the three of them naked and having a threesome on their bed. When Davies realized I had seen them, he pulled out of Ange and came after me. Ange seemed perfectly comfortable and at ease with having the two of them going for it with her. From the way Davies pulled out of her when he realized I had caught them in the act, it looked like he did not use any protection, which made me feel sick. He came after me and we fought in the lounge about it. I told him I wanted to go home and went down to the car and waited for him to get dressed and return to the car so that we could leave. He came to the car fully clothed, and we fought as he drove us home that night.

I remember feeling so hurt, betrayed, angry and was in shock after what I had seen as he was supposed to love me and suppos-edly wanted to spend the rest of his life with me as he had proposed six months earlier. This made me feel like he did not care about me at all, as though I was just a piece of dirt under his shoe. I had never felt so hurt and angry. I also felt extremely sick to the stomach from having seen what they were up to, and it made me think that maybe when Davies went over to Nigel's place prior to that many times before and spent the night there, that maybe this was not the first time they had all had a threesome together.

When we got home in the early hours of the morning, we continued to fight, and I ended up flushing his op shop engage-ment ring down the toilet as I was that mad at him. He slept in the lounge room on the couch that night and the next day I went and stayed at his sister's place until I had found another place to live.

It was really hard for me to get another place to rent soon after I had moved out, he and his mates had a party and smashed holes in the walls and one of his mates stole the dryer that belonged to the house. The real estate agent told me they would take my name off the lease, and he would be the sole renter on the lease of the house before I moved out. The real estate agent lied and never took my name off the lease, they came after me for six months of rent and damages to the property after he had abandoned the house.

I ended up getting the Rental tenant's authority in Queensland fighting the real estate in small claims court for me as they knew the entire situation and I gave them proof that the real estate did not remove me from the lease when they said they were going to and had done the wrong thing by me. I won in court, and they had to remove my name from the tenancy blacklist. After that, I could rent again, and I found a nice unit and moved into it.

I remember it taking me over eighteen months to get past this experience and deal with it so that I could move on. Getting over this was one of the hardest things I had ever done in my life. He tracked me down three months after I had moved into my new place, needing a place to stay, and wanting to get back together again. I gave him a last chance and after a couple of months I could not get past it with him there, so I asked him to leave. He went and stayed at his sister's place. I never heard from him again after that.

From that experience, I learnt:

- Not to ignore my gut instincts.
- That giving people multiple chances to change and make amends does not do a thing if they do nothing to change and make amends and they only continually hurt you repeatedly.
- To look for people to be around that had a closer match to my morals and values to be friends with.
- That those that are selfish and take you for granted are not the ones to be in relationships with.
- That selfish people don't change unless they hit rock bottom.

- That you can be in a relationship and still feel alone as though you have no one to be there for you when you need them.
- That no matter how much you try to please someone they can still take you for granted.
- That this was not a reflection on me as a person as it was their story, and I was just collateral damage in the whirlwind of their dysfunction and broken maps of the world.

The Betrayal Of A Best Friend With A Partner

*"Never believe a man who is afraid of commitment when he
says he will never hurt you and that you can trust him on that.
In the end he will hurt you the most."*

Sixteen years ago, I was in a really long-term stable de facto relationship with a boy who ended up cheating on me with my best friend. This really hurt me as this relationship was the one, I thought would last until the end of time, but it turns out he had been having an emotional affair with my best friend for the entire time we were together.

I met Martin about a year after I reinvented myself and moved into a new place to get away from the ex that had the threesome with my previous best friend and her husband.

When I first moved into this place, I met my neighbors Carol, who was twenty-three, who had a son Dan, who was nine, and her sister Jenny, who was a sixteen-year-old girl. Carol's husband died because of a mishap with some mining machinery at work and so it was just the three of them in the unit next door. I became great friends with Jenny, who introduced me to Melissa, her best friend who lived just down the street from us with her mother.

A couple of months after that, Jenny and Carol had a party at their place and invited me to come. So, I went, and that was how I met Martin. Martin and I got along extremely well. Martin knew Jenny and Melissa because they were friends with Carlton. Carlton had some mental issues and so he was either drinking or taking drugs to get away from facing them. Martin tried to help Carlton the best way he could, as he loved him like a little brother.

What I did not realize at the time of meeting Martin was that he and Melissa had deeper feelings for each other than friendship because they told no one, including each other, how they felt about each other. Melissa had issues with her thyroids being over-active, so she gained weight from that and constantly had mood swings. After a short time, Melissa and I became the best of friends and Martin and I saw each other. But Melissa and Martin were always very touchy-feely friends whenever they saw each other. They would give each other a kiss on the cheek and a long and connected hug which I asked them about a few times but they both denied that anything was going on between them so each time I would turn the other cheek and move forward with my life where Martin and I were a couple and Melissa was my best friend.

A few years went by, and Martin moved into my place and introduced me to his family. His family was delightful, and I got along with his father, stepmother, and brother's girlfriend very well. I remember the first time going over to his parent's place and them telling me how they thought he was gay as he had never brought any girls home, let alone to meet them before.

After the last relationship, I was at first afraid of getting hurt again and Martin knew this and to put my mind at ease; he told me about why he was not very close to his father and why he was closer to his stepmother. He told me he would never hurt me in the way my ex hurt me as he saw what cheating did to his father and stepmother and he said he would never hurt me like that. So, I believed him, and we got closer and closer.

As time went on, I became like a part of Martin's family, as his parents treated me like I was one of their daughters. It felt great, as though I finally belonged to a family that loved me for who I was and wanted me around.

A few weeks before mine and Martin's 3rd year anniversary, we had planned a weekend away in an expensive hotel in the city to celebrate. His parents had a Timeshare that they gave us that would give us massive discounts on the hotel room and food at one of the hotel's restaurants, so we booked the Saturday night and the Sunday night of the week ending the 30th of September. Martin had to work with his stepmother for a half a day on that weekend, so we planned to go to the city after he had finished work. I booked in with a friend of mine who was a hairdresser for her to color and cut my hair that Saturday morning. I wanted to look fantastic on our anniversary. Before going to my friend's place to get my hair done, I had to go to the shopping Centre ATM to get some money out. That morning I was abducted by a stranger from the shopping Centre car park and raped and had my life threatened by the monster, before being dropped back at the shopping Centre. It was the most horrific thing I had ever experienced in my life.

As soon as I could, I drove over to my friend's place and collapsed at her front door when I told her what happened, and she called the police. I became depressed and withdrawn from things for a year while trying to recover from this on my own without medication. The Psychiatrist and I agreed I did not need medication for depression at the time.

A year went by, and I slipped further and further into depression and finally I spoke to the psychiatrist again and told her about the flashback and dreams I was getting, and she put me on medication. The first lot of medication made me seriously ill, so she prescribed another lot that did not have those side effects but made me very lethargic and tired a lot.

Martin and I would fight as he wanted me to help him more around the house like I used to before the rape and abduction happened, but between the medication and work, I was constantly lethargic and needed to sleep when I got home from work. We still managed to have some great times together, even when I was on medication.

We even bought our own first house together. I picked it out because it was an amazing house and when I first saw it; I fell in love with it. Because Martin at the time was making less money than I was when we moved into the house, I paid for all the utilities and the mortgage on my own as I was a contractor and earned maybe 30% more money than he did, as he had only just finished an engineering graduate's degree and had taken up a junior engineer's role with a local company and he was not earning much at all.

I wanted to do a course to help me progress my career further, but I had no money left after paying for all the utilities and mortgage, so Martin volunteered to pay for my course. It was only between $1k and $2k in cost.

Melissa had moved to the beach and found herself a nice man to be with. I think they were together for four years. Martin and her fiancé also had become friends and got along really well. They would stay at our place for a weekend or come over for dinner and we would visit them at their place regularly.

We were in the house I was paying off for over four years, when, unexpectedly, Melissa called me and told me she and her fiancé had split up and she was feeling very down about it all. The reason they broke up was that her fiancé had cheated on her behind her back with the girl next door and got her pregnant. It was strange that she felt the way she did, as Melissa was also cheating on him with a fellow from her work, and she used to tell me about her cheating exploits.

Melissa had moved back into her mother's house and her mother had gone out for the night, leaving her alone, and this made her feel even more depressed. So, me being the loyal and caring best friend; I had invited her over to spend some time with

Martin and myself, so she did not have to be alone and so that we could cheer her up. I felt terrible for her.

She came over that night and we got fast food and had a few drinks, did some karaoke, played some pool, and then finished the night watching some movies.

I was feeling exhausted, as antidepressants and alcohol did not mix all that well, so I excused myself and went to bed. They continued watching movies on the couch in the living room that night until the incredibly early hours of the morning.

I sensed something was awkward between them the next day as Melissa left my place quite early to go home to her mother's place. I heard nothing from her for the rest of the weekend.

I went to work on Monday and when I got to work and read my work emails, there was a lengthy email from Melissa telling me the night she was over at our place. They got together on the couch after I had gone to bed. She also explained how they were having an emotional affair on and off behind my back with each other throughout the time I was with Martin. I went home sick for the rest of the day as I felt sick in the stomach from reading her confession of it all. When Martin got home from work that night, I showed him her email and confronted him about it, and he said he probably would never have told me about it as he thought what they were doing as nothing and innocent.

I found myself a rental to move into a couple of weeks later and moved and while I was feeling vulnerable and alone, heartbroken by what he had done, he served me papers for my house. He gave me the papers three days after I moved to the new place. I signed the house over to him as I no longer wanted anything to do with him and because the banks would not take the risk of lending me the money to buy him out as I was a contractor at the time and too high a risk for them even though technically for four years; I paid for everything.

Later, I found out that it takes three to six months to have papers for the house to be drawn up and so he had to have been planning to take the house from me for quite a while longer than the time we had been apart.

Once I signed the house away, I reinvented myself again, dealt with what had happened with the help of the holistic health support system I put together, and moved forward with my life the best way I knew how to.

- Now there are warning signs I will recognize when it comes to relationships and men that I will not ignore.
- I will never believe a man when he promises me, he will not cheat on me or hurt me in that way, as that simply isn't true.
- I choose those I want to get involved with even more carefully than I did before.
- I go with what my intuition and gut instinct is telling me about people as they are there to help and protect me.
- I choose my inner circle of friends very wisely.
- I won't let people pull the wool over my eyes when it comes to what is really going on.

Confronting My Mother About The Favouritism

"As parents, you should never choose one child over another and favor them all your life, as you risk causing irreversible damage to the unfavored child. Always treat both children with the same level of love and respect, no matter what."

I remember the first time my parents treated my older sister as though she was the only child they wanted. I was five or six at the time.

Every night, my parents used to go into the study with my sister and shut the door behind them, leaving me outside the room all alone. I could hear their voices from outside their room, but it was not clear what they were all saying. I also heard laughter coming from the study.

This made me feel unloved, unwanted, and as though I did not belong. It also made me feel as though there was something wrong with me because I was not being included in their nightly get together. It made me wonder why they would do this to me. Was there something wrong with me? Did I displease them or make them not love me anymore?

When this first happened, I would sit outside the door to the study sobbing. I would sit on the floor in the hallway in front of the door to the study holding my knees up to my chest with tears streaming down my face just waiting for them to hear me cry and wanting them so much to come open the door because they could hear me crying, but it never happened. About six months of this almost every night I decided to not care as much about it, every time it would happen, I would go to my room or go outside and imagine I was somewhere else where there were people who did care for me and included me in the things they were doing. This used to make me feel better.

A year had gone by, and this was still happening, so one night I tried and open the door to see what they were doing. Boy, did I get yelled at for opening the door to the study, and I was told to get out and shut the door behind me. I saw them around the table in the study playing a board game. This exclusion continued for a respectable number of years all the way through to my teenage years.

It was not just this treatment that got to me, though. My parents used to buy my sister the things she wanted and when I would ask for things, they would say, no we cannot afford it, money does not grow on trees or that is not for you. I remember they used to offer to pay for her to get private dance lessons and they knew I loved to dance and would have gladly taken them up on the offer, but they never offered it to me. When I asked about getting them to pay for me to do things like that, they would say, no that is not for you or we cannot pay for both of you to do them, or simply that is something for your sister only. They used to say those things to me not only for the dance classes, but a lot of other things. My sister could do things with them, while I was literally pushed out into the cold.

I would always get the same old response repeatedly until I just learnt not to ask them about those things anymore.

They were brilliant at buying her everything brand new and giving me those things once my sister had grown tired of them. I hated getting my sister's old second hand-me-down toys, school-books, and clothes. They did it to save money. Sometimes I wished I were her so that they would love and care for me in the same way they loved and cared for her. They were extremely supportive and caring towards my sister when she needed their help and support or when she was having problems.

For me, if I had a problem or needed their help with something, they did not show me the same sort of kindness. I remember one time I told them I was being bullied and picked on at school and they just told me to go away and handle it for myself. So that was what I used to do.

My parents were so encouraging to my sister and her hopes and dreams for the future. When I told my parents about my aspirations for my future, they would say to me I was being silly, that I was aiming too high and that I was not good enough to be what I wanted to be when I got older. They used to put me down quite a lot like that when I lived with them.

They also used to say to me repeatedly why can't you be more like your sister, why do you have to be so difficult, why don't you aim lower, don't be silly you'll never become that, don't be stupid, you aren't smart enough for that; you are a wicked child. Why do you always have to learn things the hard way? Your sister would never do that, you'll never become that. You can't do anything right, can you? You never listen, you will never learn, and the list goes on and on.

They saw my sister as an angel who could do no wrong and me as the wicked child that they used to yell at abusively and smack with the wooden spoon or the strap when my sister did naughty things. I tried to tell them that my sister was doing terrible things, including stealing my mother's rare coins and going and buying things with those coins, but they would never believe me.

This made me strong, independent, and grow up quickly. At the age of fifteen, I moved out of home. I went to counselling with them, but the counselling did nothing as they were not willing to see that the way they were treating me was wrong and that things had to change. Repeatedly I forgave them, thinking that this time they would try to change, and we could rebuild our relationship and become closer, but they just continued to favor my sister and put her needs above mine, which drove a wedge between us all.

In the year 2008 at Easter time, I invited them to my place for lunch and I confronted them about their treatment of me as I wanted it resolved so that I could move on with my life and be happy. They were shocked at first, then they told me that there were no books on how to be a good parent back then. My mother then told me it was because my sister needed more attention than I did, as she had a learning disability.

My sister having a learning disability was new news to me because I grew up thinking that they simply did not want me and did not care about me and that was confirmed by an extended family member telling me when I was fifteen the only reason I was born was because my mum did not know how to use the pill properly and that I was a mistake, an accident, and that they never wanted me. It made me feel like they were searching for an excuse to pin their behavior on, and that was the only thing they could think of to blame. If it were true, then they did an excellent job of hiding this secret from me for about thirty years, which was most of my life at that point in time.

My parents apologized for the way they treated me throughout my life and promised they would change that day, but they just kept treating me the same way they used to. I guess old habits die hard or never really die at all. So, I just distanced myself from them throughout the years to protect myself from getting even more hurt by them.

The biggest lessons I learnt from all this is that:

- Empty promises mean nothing.
- People's apologies aren't worth squat without actions to back them up with.
- Change must come from within and if people do not know what to change or why they need to change, they never will change.

- It only hurts you to give people too many chances, especially if they are the ones closest to you that are hurting you.
- One day, you will have to draw the line and do what is best for you and not what society thinks you should do.
- Excuses do not make up for the pain people cause you, nor do they fix or excuse the way you treat other people.
- Putting in and holding people to healthy boundaries early in a relationship is the best way to protect yourself and to make sure there is minimal damage done to you later on, and it also enforces a level of respect between parties.
- No matter how much you want to forgive people and give them chances to change, they will not change unless they are really wanting it deep down inside themselves.
- Change and forgiveness is a two-way street. All parties concerned must be willing to forgive and enact a strategy to change for a relationship to rebuild and become strong from whatever broke the relationship to begin with.

Be Grateful For The Relationships You Have

"To be happy, you have to cut toxic people out of your life if they are continually doing the same things that hurt you repeatedly and are making empty apologies to you without the actions of changing to back them up."

Relationships are frail and fragile. Think of how lucky you are to have a family who love and support you as there are orphans out there who do not have family and it is hard.

How do I know it is hard? Because for so many years I had to go without my family's love and support as they treated me like the dirt under their shoe. I was always second fiddle to them. They may have done their best, but they did not treat me respectfully or lovingly.

Repeatedly, I forgave them when they gave me empty apologies, kept doing the same things repeatedly that they knew would hurt me, and they continually took me for granted.

As per the previous chapter, I was the second child and the mistake, and they would remind me of that repeatedly with their actions. They never tried to change or to work on the relationship or to make things right.

So, for twenty-nine years, I lived life without the friendship, love and support I needed from them. I was practically an orphan who only really could take contact from them once or twice a month and then gradually it became once or twice a year as I could not stand the person I was when I spoke to them because of the way they made me feel about myself.

I always hoped that they would change and see the error in their ways and want to work on the relationship, but they did not. If ever they got to know anything private or personal about my life, they would tell everyone about it, even when it was not their story to tell.

I remember a partner I had years ago when I had been raped telling them about it and the next thing I knew; people from their church were ringing me, telling me that in their testimonials up on the stand that they had told everyone in that church I had been raped. This was my news to tell, not theirs and I did not want strangers I did not know knowing that. It really hurt me they could not keep something that personal and private to themselves and they made it out as though they were the victims. This was the only time I ever let them know anything that was private and personal about me.

Naturally, I confronted them, and they denied it and it drove a wedge further between us. The thing is, though I used to give them chance after chance, and I used to forgive them only to have them repeat what they had repeatedly done previously and hurt me until the final time when they took my sister over to the USA and paid for her to go on my birthday in 2019 and did not invite me. I gave them a choice to stay and help rebuild our relationship for the last time or take her on their holiday on my birthday and remove themselves from my life. They chose to go on their holiday on my birthday and not to be in my life.

I realize their choice was for the best, as they lived in a very toxic little world. It was always negatively geared and, of course, I was, for many years, their emotional punching bag when things went wrong for them, where they would ring me up and abuse me when they were having a dreadful day or week. I do not think they realized they were doing it though, and that was part of the problem.

This became tiring and took its toll on me in many ways, with depression and anxiety hitting me whenever they rang me.

I finally cut them out of my life in 2020 after they filed a false police report on me because I no longer answered their calls and cut them out of my life for the last time. The police at 10pm on a Sunday night came to my unit door yelling my name and banging on my door so all my neighbors could hear. This was very scary for me as I did not know before opening my door who it was yelling my name and bashing on my door late at night.

My parents had told the police that I was self-harming and suicidal, which I was not, and so the police came to my door to check on me. When they came inside my place, they could see that the report was false and an enormous waste of their time. I explained to the police the background story behind why I was not in contact with my parents and the type of relationship my parents had with me and why I was no longer in contact with them. The police then left.

After that I made it very clear to my parents that I never wanted to hear from them again, especially since they had not thought of the repercussions of their actions by involving the police when they should not have, as it was hurtful and disrespectful to me for them to do that.

I have been much happier ever since completely dropping them out of my life. From doing this, days later, I felt like a massive depressive weight had been lifted off my shoulders and my holistic health dramatically improved. I had more energy; I was happier, more self- empowered, and my life is now much less complicated. I had no one making me feel bad about myself in my life anymore.

What I realized from those experiences is that I have made it without their emotional and financial support for such a long time and that I am a strong and capable, loving, kind, and respectful woman with the rest of my life ahead of me. I do not need them in my life to fall back on as I have been doing this thing called life on my own for almost three decades and I have done an amazing job of it. For your life to improve and to heal, sometimes you must part ways with the other person and continue on your life's journey without them. People doing the same things repeatedly will not get them a different result, as they have to work hard on doing things differently to make that change.

Please do not take your family or loved ones for granted like mine did with me as there is only so much that someone's heart can take before they decide they cannot take it anymore and do not need or want you in their lives.

Relationships are difficult and if you really want them to last, you must work hard for them to be strong and healthy and be grateful for those you have in your life, especially family.

Think about the orphans out there with no family for them to fall back on. It is not a simple life they have.

Water Is Thicker Than Blood In My Family

*"Whoever said that blood is thicker than water in family
is completely mistaken. You can choose your family as
they do not need to be blood; all they need to do is to be
there for you when you most need them to be family."*

I remember about three months after I had split up with the
partner I was living with; They invited me on Facebook to my
cousin's 40th birthday party. They added everyone into a group on
Facebook and invited them from there to attend. I not iced that
they had my ex in the group, and he had already accepted the invi-
tation to attend. They never thought to let me know they would
continue to be friends with him after we broke up and did not give
me advanced warning that they would invite both of us to the
party. I really wanted to go, but I was still in so much pain from
only having broken up with him three months earlier.

My cousin was the family member I was the closest to in my
life out of all my family, the one I considered being more of a sister
to me than my own big sister as we were that close.

When I saw he was in the group and had already accepted, I
contacted my cousin and asked her why she had invited both of us
and why she did not think to let me know about it. At the time, my
Facebook profile was locked down to only friends and there were
only about 600 worldwide that I had as friends. I was hurt and

angry, so after I contacted her, I put something up on Facebook about what he did to me and my cousin's husband who only had my ex's version of the breakup attacked me in the comments to my post about it.

This was when I realized that my ex had told them a load of garbage about why we had split up and how he ended up with the house. I paid all the mortgage and bills for when I was with him. This made me feel furious and very hurt as those that were closest to me had sided with him and he was not family to them at all.

I was feeling hurt and betrayed by my cousin because we had, in my earlier years, gone through a lot together and I thought we were very close. I never thought that things would turn out like that with her, as we had so many things in common and we had each other's backs when we were younger. She was more of a big sister to me than my own sister was. It hurt me to know that after everything we had been through that she would side with my ex who cheated on me.

After I saw what my cousin's husband had put up on my Facebook wall, I decided it was time to cut ties with them as they were always going to take my ex's side over mine and things would never be the same even though my cousin now knew the truth about the breakup and what he did to get my house. They still defended him after that, and it was pointless arguing with them over it, as it would only hurt me more.

That day I learnt if people know the truth, but they still do not want to believe it, then there is nothing you can do about it but walk away before things get ugly. Walking away from them was the most integral thing for me to do as I left with my dignity intact. In the end, if people do not want to believe the truth, then that is on them.

That day I blocked them from my phone, email, Facebook, and LinkedIn and I walked away from the relationship I had with them with my head held up high. Even though I was feeling lost, alone, heartbroken, and shattered by the thought that my family would choose a non-family member over me and rip shreds off me publicly on Facebook in front of my Facebook friends to humiliate and hurt me.

Instead of doing the decent thing which would have been to cut all ties with him as he was not family, they chose him over me and deeply hurt me as I thought our bond was stronger than that. Obviously, I was mistaken.

So now when people say that blood is thicker than water, I say no; it is not as you still have a choice who you want as family, blood or not, and I tell them about what happened to me with this situation and how my blood relative chose him over me and the truth. She was the last relative I ever let get close to me like that.

I am much better off now without them in my life as life is simple and uncomplicated and I am now finally at peace with how they treated me and have healed from it. Besides the fact that relatives like that, you do not need in your life as there is no guarantee that they will not hurt you in that way again as they have no loyalty to family at all.

One of the hardest things I have ever had to do was walk away from my bond with my cousin and move on with my life.

Dating The Narcissist Barry

"Be wary of those who are too sweet, as once settled in they will turn and use manipulative games on you if they cannot have what they want."

I dated someone once called Barry. We met on a dating site, and he seemed really nice and sweet. At the start of our courtship, we told each other we would deactivate our accounts on the dating site and exclusively see each other. When I was around him, he made me feel loved, special, and enough, like I was the only woman he wanted to see. I felt amazing when I was with him, and I thought I had hit the jackpot by being with him. Barry would take me to dinner, drinks, movies and special weekends and day trips away. I offered to pay my share, but he would not allow me to pay for anything. I felt like a queen as we had dancing, exercise, movies, food, and music in common. We got along like a house on fire and had some really deep and meaningful conversations about our future together.

He was so close to everything I wanted in a partner. We spoke twice a week on the phone for two to three hours at a time, and he would text me special little good morning and good night text messages every morning and night to let me know he was thinking about me.

One time, Barry told me I was not opening up to him enough and that he felt like I was holding things back from him about my past. He made that entire conversation all about how he was feeling and himself. This made me feel terrible and a little sad as I thought I had opened up to him quite a lot about things and it was early in our courtship together, too. So, I opened up to him more about everything. One particular thing I shared with him was about one of my previous serious relationships. I did not think at the time that he would ever use what I had told him in confidence against me.

I remember I had made plans with a male friend of mine two weeks prior to Barry asking me to do something with him on the day I had the plans to catch up with my friend. We had planned to see a movie together. I told Barry I already had plans to see a movie with a friend and asked if we could do what he wanted to do the next day as I had not caught up with my friend in months and was really looking forward to it. Barry then asked me if it was a male or a female friend I was catching up with. I was honest with him and told him it was one of my closest friends who was a male and that nothing romantic ever happened between us as I did not see him as anything more than a platonic friend and that I was not in the slightest bit attracted to this friend of mine in any way. So that Barry knew exactly where things were at and would not get jealous or feel uncomfortable with my friendship.

Barry asked me to cancel my plans with my friend and hang out at his place with him instead. I said no and Barry then tried to manipulate me and make me feel bad by throwing in my face the things I had told him about a previous relationship and why it did not work out.

It really hurt me, because he had twisted everything I had told him about that relationship and why it did not work out. He made out as though I was to blame for that relationship collapsing. He was mean and cruel about what he said to me.

I was so upset and angry with him and we fought over it. After we had finished fighting, he told me he did not want me to spend time with any of my friends anymore. He was jealous when he had no cause to be. I told him I would not give up my friends just for him and I left his place and went home. He left me feeling as though he did not trust me and that I was a bad person for having friends and wanting to spend time with them.

A few hours after I got home from Barry's place, he rang me and asked again if I would give up my friends. I said no, and he stopped ringing and texting me for three days and it made me feel even worse. Once those three days had passed, he texted me saying he had arranged a special dinner for the two of us. That he would pick me up at around 7pm.

He took me to a fancy restaurant with candles lit up on the table where we were seated, and there was really nice romantic music playing. During dinner, Barry's phone rang every 20 mins to notify him he had a message\text. Barry sat there texting whoever it was back during dinner. He said it was just his manager at work, as he was on the on-call roster for his work. The evening ended, and I thought nothing of it.

Every time we spent time together after that in the following weeks his phone would constantly ring to notify him of his messages, and he would always answer them back to where we could not even sit and watch a movie or a TV show without it ringing constantly. This started to bother me, so one time I asked him if everything was ok as his phone was ringing an awful lot. He then accused me of trying to read his text messages when he was texting, which I did not do as I trusted him, even though his phone was annoying me. We had a few fights over this and then he said maybe we should call things off. I said no and thought everything was fine between us after that.

I was speaking to a female co-worker of mine about him and how things were going, and she asked to see a photo of him. I showed her a photo and her jaw dropped when looking at the photo of him. She told me he was chatting her up on a dating site and she showed me his profile from her phone. Sure enough, he had not deactivated his profile on the site we met on. She also showed me his messages to her, and they were during the time we were seeing each other exclusively.

This explained why he did not like me having male friends and why he was so protective of his phone every time it notified him of new messages, and also why he would turn his back to me or get up and walk away when he was sending and reading messages.

I was so heartbroken by it. It made me feel lost, angry, unloved, used, and confused. He thought by accusing me of not trusting him, it would get me off his back about why his phone was constantly going off. I could not believe that he had lied to me saying that his phone was going off as it was work contacting him as he was on call, and I bought it.

That night I got home from work, and I rang him and told him I needed a break from seeing him for a while and that I would contact him when I was ready to speak to him again. Two weeks went by. It was my birthday, and I hoped he would at least contact me to wish me a happy birthday, but he did not. This hurt me deeply as it showed me. He did not care about me at all.

It was at that moment I realized I needed to make a clean break from him and told him it was over and that I knew he was still on the dating site trying to pick up other women and that I deserved better. He had no comeback to this at all.

The next day I packed up the stuff he had left at my place and took it down to the security desk on the ground floor and told him to pick it up from there as I did not want to see him again. He never returned to pick up his stuff.

From this experience, I now know what the signs are to look out for, as he was a liar, cheater, and a narcissist. I can spot those signs very quickly when seeing someone now and will get out quickly if I ever date someone like that again.

I learnt I deserve and am worthy of better in a man I am seeing, and if they are accusing you of things you are not doing, then they are probably doing those things themselves. If they are very protective of their phone, there may be something going on behind the scenes which I do not know. That if you are truly exclusively dating or in an exclusive relationship with each other that you will share things with each other and not try to hide them from each other. That if you do not give them any reason to distrust you and they still distrust you they are the ones hiding things from you as they are projecting their insecurities about being found out onto you as a protection mechanism to make out as though you are in the wrong and not them.

I am much happier and better off now without him in my life, as his behavior was disrespectful to me and not good for my mental health. I know now that when the time is right, the universe will deliver the right man into my life.

How To Tell If You Are Friends With Or In A Relationship With A Narcissist

"If you are being manipulated in a relationship to do things for the other person, you don't want to do, the good times are not worth the bad times when it comes to your mental and emotional health."

If they are a narcissist, then they have a mental condition where they have an inflated sense of their own importance, a deep need for excessive attention and admiration, a lack of empathy for others and turbulent relationships. But behind this mask of extreme arrogance is a fragile self-esteem that is susceptible to the slightest piece of disapproval.

The narcissistic personality disorder creates issues in multiple parts of life, such as work, business, relationships, financial affairs, and school. These types of people with the narcissistic personality disorder are usually upset and frustrated when they are not given what they want in the way of a special favor or admiration/gratitude they deem they deserve. The relationships they have are usually unfulfilling, and others after a while do not enjoy being in their presence or even speaking to them.

Here are the signs you are in a friendship or in a relationship with a narcissist.

- They are often preoccupied with fantasies of how brilliant, successful, powerful, and wonderful they are and that they are the perfect mate.
- They see faults in others but not in themselves and when they hurt someone else; they do not see that they have done anything wrong, so they do not apologize and accept that they have hurt the other person.
- They have a sense of entitlement and require constant, excessive admiration and gratitude for things that they take credit for doing, even though they may not have done it at all.
- They have an exaggerated sense of self-importance and say things like I got you through this; I did that for you, and you would never have been able to get through it on your own.
- They want you to jump and obey them when they say so.
- They expect to be viewed as exceptional and superior even without achievements that warrant it.
- They say everything is wrong with you, but there is nothing wrong with them and that they have no issues to fix within themselves.
- They over inflate their achievements and abilities.
- They pick out the bad in others, but they, according to themselves, are perfect, and others should be so lucky to be in their presence.
- They dominate conversations and belittle or look down on people they recognize as inferior or less smart than they are.
- They are jealous, envious, and resentful of others and believe others are jealous of them.
- They behave in an arrogant or condescending, snotty manner, coming across as vain, boastful, conceited, and pompous to others.

- They expect special favors and obedient compliance to their extremely elevated expectations of others.
- They take advantage of others to get what they want by making others feel bad about themselves and reliant on them.
- They have a lack of ability or reluctance to acknowledge the needs and feelings of other people.
- They always insist on having the best of everything, no matter what the cost.
- They will not apologize for hurting you, as it is inconceivable to them they have done anything wrong.
- They judge you harshly and tell you their judgements of you.
- They believe they are upper class and upper market people and will try to only associate themselves with equally important people.
- They can spot another narcissist a mile away and will tell you.

At the same time, people with narcissistic tendencies have problems controlling and handling anything that they view as criticism or a threat to their perceived superiority, like the below:

- They have difficulty controlling emotions and behaviors.
- They have significant interpersonal problems and easily feel slighted and jaded.
- They are very impatient or angry when they do not receive special treatment.
- They have hidden feelings of insecurity, indignity, helplessness, and humiliation.
- They react with rage or disrespect and try to put down the other person to make themselves appear superior.

- They experience major problems dealing with stressful situations and having to adapt to change.
- They feel neglected, depressed, and temperamental because they fall short of perfection.

In my time on this planet, I have dated three narcissists and been best friends with two narcissists who drained me and made me feel bad about myself and dependent on them. They think your world (what you write, say, think and feel) revolves around them. They make you feel bad for them to feel good and to get what they want from you. They are expert manipulators and when they do not get their way, accuse you of being a liar and a manipulator. They will do whatever it takes to get their own way, even if it hurts other people in the process. Everything is wrong with you, and nothing is and will ever be wrong with them.

They will never compromise or apologize for anything they do against you that is wrong. They accuse you of doing the things that they themselves are doing when they are feeling paranoid or insecure.

The only thing you can do if you are friends with or in a relationship with a narcissist is get the hell out of there and make sure they know you want nothing to do with them because if you don't they will try to convince you they are good people and that it is all in your head so that you will come back to them and so that their narcissistic manipulations can continue. Being around these types of people is hazardous for your mental and emotional wellbeing. They will constantly build you up, only to shatter you into tiny little pieces to get what they want. They love being in control. The only way you can break that control is to get them completely out of your life as quickly as possible. You are worth so much more in life than to be controlled by an expert manipulator and narcissist.

How I Got My Money Back From Tradewell, An Illegal Crypto Currency Brokerage

"Always do your due diligence and research everything you invest in. If you do not and you believe ads on trusted social media sites, then you could get scammed big time."

I remember being at an all-time low in my life financially and emotionally. I had been between contracts for at least two months and had many interviews but was being knocked back for the roles I was being interviewed for as the market was becoming extremely fussy when it came to what it wanted in the way of project managers in the ICT industry in Melbourne. I wanted and needed so much for things to change for me financially as my savings were dwindling away to next to nothing because I was being forced to live off them even though I did not have much. The government refused to pay me unemployment benefits to keep me afloat, even though I had provided them with all the paperwork they had asked for.

I was fearful of not being able to pay the rent and becoming homeless. As each day went by, I became increasingly consumed with this fear, so much so that I started looking for other ways I could make an extra income stream.

I kept seeing on a few different popular social media platforms ads for this crypto currency broker saying that for $150 people had made thousands of dollars from investing in their crypto currency platform. They claimed they were interviewed on a popular and reputable Australian TV show and that the reporter on that TV show had tried their platform out and so did others from the TV network and that they had made a lot of money. They claimed you could pull your money out at any time if you felt it was not working for you and that you would get a full refund. Their ads kept popping up daily and at first, I ignored them, but as the fear of not being able to support myself got stronger and stronger after a month, I gave it a go. After all, the saying that came to mind for me at the time was that you had to be in it to win it and that nothing ever comes for free.

Let me paint the picture now with some history for you, so you know the emotional state I was in when I made the investment. I was three years in a new city where I did not know many people and I felt bad burdening the friends I had. We had not been friends for very long. I had supported myself financially for fifteen years despite the fact that I had anxiety and that anxiety was triggered and based on my finances. I never got help from anyone to live and survive before. My family was still on their holiday in the USA after being given the choice to leave my life forever or to stay in Australia and work on fixing our non-existent relationship and what got to me the most about that was prior to their trip to the USA.

I invested in the Tradewell crypto currency platform, thinking it would not take me much money to get started and that I would just get triple my money back. I clicked on the link that was below their ad on a popular social media platform, thinking they would not let any place that was not legal or legitimate advertise on their platform. The link took me to their website where they had a couple of videos of their people being interviewed about the massive returns they had received after just a week of investing as little as $150 AUD in the platform. The videos also showed how the platform worked which drew me in, so I created an account and invested the minimum of $150 into it. The next day I got an introductory video meeting scheduled from one of their account directors. He told me how it worked and then gave me a demo on a test account. It looked great and very professional.

The accounts director told me at first, he would do the trading for me, and after a while, once I became confident, they would let me do some trading for myself.

A couple of days went by, and I monitored it at night from my laptop and I could see the trading values on what I had invested were going up. Then it dipped, and I contacted them and asked them to refund my money as per the ad. They told me they could not refund my money until I had invested more money into their platform and once the trade shares had doubled; I had put into their platform. They knew how vulnerable I was as they knew I did not have a job but was looking for one and really needed a second income to keep me afloat and they promised me that with the next investment that they would make me ten times the amount of money I had put into their system. They said it would take them three days to get the investment shares to rise to thousands of dollars. I had sunk thousands of dollars into it already and that money was from my credit card as the investment had knocked out and sucked up what little savings I had left. A few days went by, and the trades were going up and down quite a lot during that time to where it was really stressful for me, and I asked for my money back as they had a money back guarantee and they just kept pushing me for more and more money and playing on my fears and feeding my hopes to have a nest egg and an extra income stream behind me to support me. They even sent me paperwork on their platform and the so-called investment package they had me on and even told me they had upgraded my package for free. But what I did not know about that upgrade was that I could not get my money back at all from them because they did not tell me, and it was not in the account package upgrade documents they sent me.

Towards the end of my dealings trying to get my money back from them, I was so stressed out and the thing was they made it so hard for the bank and visa to trace the money back to them as they had me debiting my credit card into an offshore online money wallet called CXE so my visa had to deal with them to get my money back and not the Cryptocurrency broker that screwed me over for $20k.

I put in a visa dispute with my bank and visa to get my money back and I had to send them a full statement of events, the dates of the credit card payments and transaction reference numbers from my credit card account and the CXE money wallet account details and also records of me trying to sort it out with Tradewell via email to resolve the dispute and their responses, and also the times and dates they rang me and how long the calls went on for and all other documentation I had to support my claim.

A week went by, and I had heard nothing from my bank or visa on the dispute I put in and so I rang them so stressed out as I could not pay my monthly rent and really needed the money back because what little money, I had left went on living expenses like utilities and food. I rang them and put in written enquiries about it and explained to them how much I needed the money back as my credit card was also being charged overdraft fees as it had no money in the account to pay for my monthly account keeping fees, they had charged me even though they knew my situation and had my dispute paperwork going through their system. The fees totaled over $500. They knew I had no way I could even pay the account keeping fees as I had no job or money to do so. They said it would take them a month to investigate and see if they could get my money back, but that I should contact them for a status update on my dispute during that month. So, every two days I would ring and message them about it, wanting to know what was going on and it was so stressful for me.

I eventually got another job, but they paid monthly, and the pay was much less than my normal contract rate, as I just needed to survive until the bank got the money back for me. Even though I had the job, it was the most stressful month of my entire life.

Finally, the one-month period had ended and at that point in time I was not expecting my money to come back to me as I had lost hope and felt depleted. Unexpected a day after that month ended, a deposit for the amount for money I had lost to Tradewell had been deposited back on to my credit card. I noticed it as I was looking at my accounts online to see if my new work had paid me for the month, so I could pay my rent and utilities which had late fees on them due to not having the money to pay them on time. I felt relieved and rang visa and my bank to check to see what it was as I had resigned myself to not getting my money back and they told me they had gotten all my money back from Tradewell by putting pressure on the bank that Tradewell used and held my money in. I was so relieved after hearing this and I jumped up and down and I thanked them several times for all their challenging work in getting my money back before ending the call.

That month had been the most financially stressful time for me as my anxiety was through the roof and I was not sleeping, lying in bed wondering how I would pay the rent and bills.

What I learnt from this experience was that:

- You need to fully research something before investing in it and do not believe what you read and watch on the internet about things as they can be deceptive, and you really need to go digging deep to find out if places like that are legal and legitimate or not.
- Perseverance goes a long way.
- Following up as much as possible on things really helps, and it keeps you in the forefront of the credit card companies' minds.
- Always fully document everything into which you are investing. Keep every communication, transaction record and document on it and journal those events as

they happen. Then you can use that as your statement, and you have the backup documentation they need to move your dispute forward.

- Miracles happen. You just have to believe and put action to that belief to have that miracle manifest.
- Lots of people every day get suckered into these scams and you should not feel guilty or ashamed of falling victim to them.
- Fight for what is yours, do not just walk away. You must fight the battle so that you get justice and your money back.
- Always be grateful for what you have.
- Exhaust every option to get back what is yours if it was taken from you wrongly and deceptively.
- Going through things like this has made me a better and stronger person.

Going Through A Company Takeover And Corporate Restructure

"A corporate takeover and restructure can take its toll on the management and their teams that they manage. Lead by example not through dictatorship, bullying and manipulation to justify why you should keep your job in this situation."

I remember years ago I was in a lower management role, and I was doing a wonderful job for a company that was small, friendly, and cared about their employees. I loved working for them and managing the teams for their projects as they were amazing to work for.

I was with them for six months on contract and because I was doing such an amazing job; they offered me a permanent role. You see, in my first three months of working for them, I fixed up their operations when it came to managing projects by putting a very tailored agile project management framework and structure to their projects as they did not have any in place. They had originally asked two other people who were contractors to do this, but they just kept putting it off saying they had too much work to do so I stepped up, took this task on, and got it done for them alongside managing my own projects. For me this was an easy thing to do as I needed to put structure and a project management framework to the projects I was managing anyway, and I had already done it for my projects, so it was just a matter of scaling and tailoring what I had created for myself to suit a project management office (PMO) with multiple projects running from it.

I did this by showing management what I did up for myself, explaining to them how it could be scaled for a PMO, talking upper management through the templates, processes, and procedures I had created for myself as well as how to manage a project from start to finish in agile and waterfall OneNote guidelines/instructions I had created and stepping them through this. I then gained their feedback and tailored it all to suit their feedback.

And I got another project manager to test it out on a project for a while as a test case and implemented his feedback into the final implementation into the organization. I used it for five or six projects while I was working there, some projects ran very smoothly and a few of the projects even completed earlier than the estimated completion dates with massive successes as the clients could recuperate some of the money that was paid for the project that had not been used and move it to a support arrangement which made them happy.

They made me permanent after the company got sold to a larger global enterprise. I noticed from this the company culture changed from a close net family orientated company culture to a number based, in it for yourself, narcissistic culture. The company continued like this for six months and after my probationary period had ended the company restructured and the company culture became even rougher when upper management felt insecure about their jobs. Anyone who was great at their jobs and were in lower management roles really felt the difference as those that felt threatened above them would publicly try to nit-pick their work and tell them they weren't doing their jobs properly and try to put them on Performance Management Plans and bully them to get them to resign. Which they were implementing with people they were doing it in a way that made the bullying treatment legal. They were giving people warnings about the smallest things that did not warrant warnings or a performance management plan to be implemented.

Some were given redundancy packages, and those they did not want to pay a redundancy package to and who did not want to leave, were given the choice to go on the performance management plan where they were told that they would be treated even worse than what they already were. This would be a very intrusive process where those above them would pick holes in their work and bully them about it and give them two to four months to improve and come up to the impossible standards that were set for them by the insecure upper management above them, or they could choose their mental health and take a small payout called a golden handshake which was not as much as the redundancy to leave and find another job.

Many people who were made this offer chose the second option of their mental health and the golden handshake. I cannot tell you which option I chose but can tell you I found another job three months later.

I heard from those who took the golden handshake and they seemed happier and more settled within themselves for taking that option, and they found it quite easy to find another job after that. I stayed in touch with people that stayed in the organization and was constantly being told of how unhappy they and others were who stayed with the company. Many other people were leaving without new jobs to go to because of the way they were being treated.

What I do not understand about this whole thing is why upper management in that company and other companies going through a corporate restructure would feel insecure and threatened enough by the people in the teams they try to force them out of their roles, and how that even justifies why they should keep their jobs. There is this certain ring of injustice about the entire thing.

I have never really been the type of person to feel insecure about my job, as I love sharing information and communicating to others on improvements that will not only help me but them as well. I have trained, coached, and mentored many people in my entire Information, Communication and Technology (ICT) career and love creating and building up new leaders and helping people find ways of more effectively doing their work. If you are great at the work, then you should not feel threatened and insecure about your job around others who are amazing at their jobs. I prefer to give people the tools they need to succeed in their roles and if they surpass me in the food chain that's fine with me, as I know I have done my job as a leader to help them grow and develop into amazing leaders.

Why not help others become all that they can be and to reach their true potential instead of scaring them by harassing, bullying and game playing them publicly with nit-picking to save your own skin?

I have been through four corporate restructures in organizations in my time and also three budget cuts, and I still cannot see how that would turn a really great manager into an insecure narcissistic bully who tries to push those below them out of the company so that they can hang onto a job which they may not stay at long term. Leaders in upper management roles should work on being the leader that can be proud of themselves by nurturing, growing, supporting, mentoring, and coaching the people below them to also be amazing leaders.

Working For Someone Who Feels
Threatened By Me

*"An insecure and incompetent manager will make a
working environment too toxic for others to work in."*

Recently I have been reflecting on all the places I have worked, and it pains me to say this, but I have come across several really insecure managers in my twenty-two years in the ICT industry and most of those managers were females. I cannot for the life of me figure out why they felt threatened by me or any other female in the organization.

I am trying to figure this out. Is it that if another person is smarter, better looking, more efficient and way more effective in their jobs under them they feel as though that person may make them look bad as perhaps, they do not know enough or aren't doing enough in their own jobs? Do they think that the other person is after their jobs, so they instantly go on the defensive side?

Do they know that the only person who is making them look bad in their jobs is them because of their own behavior towards the other person who they feel insecure and threatened by?

There have been scenarios in my career where I have been set up to fail, terrorized and victimized by the managers above me, purely for doing my job to the best of my ability. They have known me in the industry as the person who gets things done, who resurrects dead sunken projects and gets them running efficiently and delivers them. That is not a straightforward thing to do. Especially when you are hired to clean up the project from another person who managed it before you who did really poor planning and has left the project for dead with little to no documentation on the project, its risks and issues and its status.

One scenario comes to mind when I worked for a government department where the senior manager above me, who was my manager, sat me down on my first day and told me her expectations of me and the role and what I should and should not do. I did things to her expectations. She did not, however, tell me about the most crucial things like the office politics in the department and how I should navigate around that. When I asked her the question, she moved me on to the next question. I thought nothing of it at the time.

Apparently, before the project had started, another part of the department had put in a bid to have it managed by their department and was still angry about not being able to manage it, as it was a big high-profile project.

Because there was no RACI chart of who was Responsible, Accountable Consulted and Informed on the projects processes and the management artefacts for the project, I emailed that part of the department thinking we were all one big happy team to find out about something to do the testing. They asked me why they had not been involved in the sign off for some of the project management artefacts. So, I went to my manager and asked her, and she said that it was because their signatures and feedback were not required, that they weren't really key stakeholders for the project and that they should contact her directly if they would like to discuss it further. I emailed back, letting them know in the nicest, most sensitive way possible what she had said as she told me to respond to them on the matter.

The next thing I know my email was sent all the way up to their General Manager and they had CC'd in the program director and CEO\CIO of our part of the department with some very nasty words and demanding that they be involved in the review and sign off for all the project management artefacts for the project.

Because of this email, she told me not to communicate with the vendors or the other parts of the department directly and if I needed anything from them I was to go to her, and she would ask them for it. I did what she told me to do, which was email her my requests for information from the vendors and the other parts of the department. This was very slow and ineffective as I was constantly emailing, messaging, and asking her face to face for the information I needed and had asked her for weeks earlier, and this was holding up the project.

After that she called meetings in my lunch break when she could see in my calendar that I had back-to-back meetings booked in with the project team and with another project team I had taken on each day. she would bully me and have a go at me about why the project was slowing down. She didn't like it that much when I told her it was because she was not getting me the required documents and information. I had asked her for these documents and information weeks earlier and I was having to chase her every day for the information. She never used to respond to me until she had the information I was asking her for.

She then started booking meetings after hours that she required me for. You could clearly see from her outlook calendar she had free periods during business hours that she could have held the meetings in, so she did not need to book them in over my lunch break or after hours at all, but she did as she wanted to exert her power to everyone. You could see on a day-to-day basis that this manager was all over the place and was very unorganized and did not plan for anything and she would micromanage the team, which was quite frustrating for me and other project members.

She also could see that from the other project I was involved with that I had built up a good healthy working relationship with the Program director and that he was thrilled with my work as he had sent contract extension papers to the agency, I was contracting through for the role with the department for another twelve months. Maybe she felt threatened because of that. All I know is two weeks after I had signed the contract extension papers, she called a WebEx meeting with me and told me I was not doing a good enough job as I was not communicating with the other areas of the department and the vendors to get the information I needed and that I was to finish that day. This contradicted what she had told me two months earlier about wanting me to go through her to get what I needed from the vendors and other parts of the department. So, essentially, I was set up to fail by her because she felt threatened by me and my work and because she held back on telling me vital information; I needed to perform my role properly in the project as a Senior Scrum Master/ Agile Project Manager. I did not mean to make her feel threatened by my work or the relationships I had built up while working there, as everyone who knows me and has worked with me knows I have a very collaborative, open, honest, transparent, and flexible working style.

This situation, with the email going to the heads of department, could have been avoided if she had told me what the office politics were like to begin with and also provided me with a stakeholder analysis and RACI chart. They never had a stakeholder analysis document or a project RACI chart for the project. These were Key project management artefacts that were missing from the project. My manager was the one that started the project and got it up and running but had missed out on some very key project artefacts that every project needs to have, whether it is a Waterfall (traditional) or Agile (new ways of working) project.

These types of people get their jobs through manipulation and prior relationships they have had with the hiring manager or higher in the organization. I hear she had worked in another government department with the CIO and was very good friends with him and that was how she got her job on the project it was not that she had the experience necessary to do the role as she clearly did not as she was in a very senior management level role there and her previous experience in a management role according to LinkedIn showed she only had three years management experience in her career prior to being put in this role.

I heard from other females in on the project two weeks later as we all stayed connected, and they told me about their stories while working for her. They had very similar experiences with being set up to fail in their jobs after she decided they were a threat to her and her job and fired them in the exact same way, using the same reasoning she had used on me.

What I learnt from this scenario was that there will always be people who will feel threatened by you and your work and that you should never stoop to their level. Just keep working at the same high level of standards you have always worked at and if the job is right for you, then it will sort itself out if not then look for another job and get out of there as fast as you can as this sort of management style can affect your emotional and mental health if you stay there and it isn't sorted out.

The Importance Of Dreaming And Visualising Your Dream Life

"If you have a vision for your life and never work towards that vision, then you will never truly know who you will turn out to be, how far you can go and what you can achieve. So, aim high to reach for the stars and take action to make that vision a reality."

Too often we get caught up in the hustle and bustle of normal everyday life and we lose touch with whom we are, what makes us happy, who and what we want to be, what we want out of life, what we want our life in the future to look like, and how far we have come in life already. We do not see what is right there in front of us in the here and now, because we take it for granted.

This obsession with going to work to earn money and then moving up the food chain in organizations to get paid more and more. This often makes us lose touch with whom we really are and what we really want our future to look like. Because of this, we often become blindsided by the outside world and forget to look inwards.

By daydreaming and visualizing what we want our future to look like and how we will get there, we regain alignment with our true selves; it brings us back to our center and core drivers, helps us to recognize what our core needs are, whether that is certainty, connection, variety, or significance. These are our core needs, and they are the things that motivate us, help us get more driven and help us concentrate on what is important to us. Sometimes these core needs are mistaken for money, power, selfishness, greed, jealousy, which are all elements of our ego.

When we let go of our ego on the outside world through visualization and dreaming, we are brought back to our core and back to what will really make us happy, which is not always possessions from the outside world. If we learn to look internally and fulfil our internal needs, we will have a greater sense of achievement, a greater feeling of peace, joy, love, and satisfaction within ourselves and our lives.

If you cannot sit there and visualize your own future by fulfilling your needs, then go on to YouTube and find a good, guided meditation that will help you visualize and dream.

Visualizing and dreaming big are well worth doing as they not only motivate you towards your goals and your dream life, but they quieten the mind and have relaxational benefits as well.

Visualizing the achievement of your goals will also give you the motivation and inspiration you need to achieve your goal of having a fulfilling life.

Visualizing my future and how I wanted it to look like is a good ritual to have and is a part of my holistic health support system that helped me get through a lot of the traumas I went through in life to get me to where I am now.

You know, until the age of twenty-five, I hated reading. I found it boring, and it used to always put me to sleep. It was not until they sent me out to a mine site for a company I worked for, that I really got into reading as there was nothing out there for me to do after work every night.

The first book I read that changed my mind on reading was a book that a medical physician gave me instead of putting me on anti-depressants for a rape and abduction I went through in Queensland which was extremely traumatic for me to have to go through, that I had picked up a book and read it since school. I really enjoyed reading that book. The book was called "The feeling good handbook."

This book completely changed my perspective on reading, and what reading could do for me. This book was all about acceptance therapy and cognitive therapy. It had so many exercises you could use and implement in your life to change how you felt about life. It was that book that made me realize just how powerful the written word really is.

I did not read this book until eight years after it was given to me. Because of that, I went on medication for a few years. I now wonder if I had read that book sooner and went on that personal development journey, I did in the year 2000 just after the rape and abduction had taken place how different my life would have turned out to be for me and how different I would be now. Would I have come into coaching and authoring my book sooner? Who knows! But through the power of the written word, I learnt how to dream, have goals, and aim for the stars, but most of all, how to get out of my own way so that I can achieve my goals.

I am not much of a visualizer on my own but when guided in a meditation or visualization I get into more of the feeling of the emotions that are attached to the words the person is saying during the guided meditation\visualization, which is truly powerful because once you felt the emotions attached to the words it completely changes your perspective on yourself, your life and everything going on around you.

Therefore, when I coach people, I love guiding them through the visualizations and seeing how their posture, psyche, tone of voice, change and how their faces light up and their expression changes when they are in that visualization and how they can connect with those emotions and feelings they are seeking. This is what inspires and motivates my clients to want to act and transform to be better versions of themselves.

The Art Of Gratitude

"Through making gratitude a ritual forming habit, you attract more positives into your life and become more powerful in the things you do. Living in gratitude is the best attitude you can have."

Sitting here in lockdown, I remember back to my first experiences in the world where everything was new, positive, and encouraging, from the day I first cried to the day I learnt how to walk and did my first 2sie in the potty. Such fond memories. Those experiences were exciting, inspiring, and encouraged a mindset of growth, determination, and resilience. They were exciting times, as there was no discouragement. Those days were newborn to three years of age. They were exciting times, fun times, and times of exploration.

Do you remember how you felt when you first realized that you could get around on your own by crawling? Weren't you excited and wondering if one day you could get around on two legs like those who were older than you? Of course, you were and so you tried it and you were not afraid of falling down and having to get back up again or of being judged for it. You were determined to walk, and nothing would stop you from trying to do it. Little by little, day after day, you tried, failed, tried, and failed some more, but you always got back up and tried again. A little piece inside of you was excited about the complete experience and that was what motivated and inspired you to keep trying.

How did you feel after you took your first couple of steps? You laughed and giggled, and you loved the challenge and every day you would find that you could increase your steps on your own without anyone's help.

The day you did it on your own, didn't you feel proud of yourself and what you had accomplished? Of course you did. Then once you had accomplished that, you wanted to try your luck at running, so a little at a time you tried to run, and you found it easier than walking, as you already had your balance, stability, and strength to do it. Of course, it was a bit of a challenge, but that did not matter. You really wanted to do it and so you did. That's right, you did. What a marvelous day it was when you accomplished this goal.

What about the first time you heard a sound, like you really heard it? Maybe it was the sound of a bird chirping or maybe it was one of your parent's voices. Didn't you find that exciting and amazing too?

And then to find out you could talk by saying your first word, well, everyone cheered and encouraged you to talk some more when that happened. That made you feel invincible, didn't it? Once you had mastered your thoughts, you would have a crack at singing. You were not worried about being judged for it, as you only wanted to see if you could do it. So, you tried on your own for a little in private with your radio louder than you are singing so no one could hear you. Once you had mastered it, you then sang in front of family members and, depending on their reactions, you would if the feedback was positive, sing around with your friends at school. It felt great, didn't it?

You learnt how to do those things from your own strength, will power, tenacity and resilience for life. There were no manuals on how to do that stuff. They were life lessons you needed to learn by doing them repeatedly and practicing them, and you were very excited and grateful to do those things. The world was at that age a massive place full of fun and exciting to be in, with wondrous adventures to dream about and achieve. The gratitude for what you could do, and experience was there within you.

As we grow older, we lose some of that gratitude and take for granted the big things we learnt to do when we were little, as they are not that big a thing to us anymore, they come automatically to us now and that is sad. We now live in a world full of discouragement, judgement, fear, and shattered dreams, which makes it sad and negatively geared. We are now less willing to face our fears and overcome them, riddled with shame and guilt. We are less spontaneous, less kind, and less positive towards others.

We now see the world through tainted lenses instead of fun and exciting. We see it as judging, cruel, hard, and cold and so we learn to be more guarded, more judging of ourselves and others and err on the side of caution because of the negative experiences we have had throughout our lives. Some people will become bullies and be selfish and try to change others while other people will become people pleasers longing to be loved, belong and to be enough for others not realizing that in order for us to be truly happy we must go deep within ourselves and find the deeper meaning behind why we are this way and explore this and ourselves fully, so that we can know and truly love ourselves.

Gratitude is a big part of this process. When we are in a place of gratitude and truly felt that gratitude, we then felt self-love and with self-love comes that boldness of daring to be ourselves around everyone else.

I only hope that throughout the pandemic we are going through that we go back into a place of gratitude for who we are, what we have done and can accomplish and the journey we have travelled during our lives to get to where we are now. That we have gratitude for all the small things and the bigger things in our lives, even if it means remembering back to our first steps, the first note we sung, our first of firsts when it comes to doing and experiencing things as there is so very much to be grateful for in our lives and out there in the world we live in today.

Practicing gratitude every day is the key to living a truly satisfying and fulfilling life. It gives us back the ability to be bold, try new things and it gives us more excitement and zest for life and the world around us, so that we are encouraged to step out of our comfort zone and really experience what life is about.

Interview Discrimination For Being The Wrong Gender

"In a world where everyone is different, whether or not we like it, there should not be any form of discrimination. We should be able to put our differences aside and live our lives with others, no matter what."

The last thing you would think of having done to you in this day and age with all the laws around regarding discrimination is to be discriminated against when going for a job because of your gender.

Well, it happens. It's not fun to experience when it happens.

It happened to me about three years ago. At the time, the projects I was managing as a contractor were close to completion and the company had no more projects for me to manage as it was coming toward the end of the financial year where they did not have the budget to extend my contract. I was a career contractor with over 19 years of experience at the time in the ICT industry, which is a heavily male dominated industry. I did what all contractors do when their contracts are ending and that is apply for and interview for other jobs elsewhere.

They asked me to go in for an interview with a global company for a job they had vacant and needed to fill. I psyched myself up for two days, going over my resume and possible interview questions and scenarios in my head, and researched the company online to prepare for the interview.

I had the interview, and it ran smoothly, way better than others I had had previously that month. I went out of the interview smiling and feeling extremely happy and pleased with the way the interview went.

I got a call two days later saying that they absolutely loved me in the interview, but they had an all-male team and that they could not and would not hire me for this position because they wanted to put a male in the role. They also said that by law, they had to interview both male and female candidates. I asked the person giving me the feedback for more of an explanation on this and they would not give me one and hung up the phone.

I was so mad, angry, and hurt with the reason they gave me about why they would not give me the job. It took me a while to change my mindset to be able to see that it was for the best that I did not get offered the role, but I did it just in time for another interview that had come up with an even better company where I smashed the interview out of the park and got offered the role then and there on the spot. The money for this role I was offered was heaps better than the money for the role with the company, where they rejected me due to gender bias. Every cloud... and all that.

Have you ever been made to feel so small for being who you are and discriminated against for it? If so, how did you handle it? How did it make you feel? What did you do to stop feeling bad about it so that you could move on? Did you change your mindset quick enough to get offered an even better role elsewhere not long after you were rejected and discriminated against?

If you are still struggling with it now and are stuck with not knowing how to get the anger out and how to change your mindset, then look up my coaching Business Dare To Be You: https://daretobeyou.net.au and contact me about this as I have specialized coaching techniques I can use to coach you into a more positive, healthier mindset and ready for that next job interview. Also, watch my YouTube video via the link below.

YouTube link: https://youtu.be/aZ0BeBFmt6I

Facing My Fear Of Singing Out Loud

*"You will never really know what you are made of or
what you can accomplish or become without facing
your fears. Fears are only challenges in your mind that
you can overcome if you want to badly enough."*

When I was little, and my parents were out of the house, me and my sister used to play loud music upstairs and sometimes even downstairs in the carport and dance to it. Those were truly fun times. I miss those times.

One song that came up quite a lot was "The greatest love of all" by Whitney Houston. It is a brilliant song, and I used to love it for what it used to mean to me and how it used to make me feel when singing and dancing to it.

Back then, until I heard this song, I did not even know that to be loved fully and truly for who you are, you first had to love yourself. I wondered for years what that song and the words really meant. Why would the greatest love of all be to love yourself?

My childhood was not the greatest of childhoods that a child could have as they constantly made me feel unloved, unwanted as though I did not belong and as though I was never good enough by my family and the people around me. My childhood was an incredibly sad and lonely existence and I thought that love was what you got from or received from others when you fit into their perception of what perfect was. So, I learnt to push all my feelings deep down inside of me and I never spoke up about my own needs in the fear of displeasing those around me.

I was never perfect, although in my eyes I tried to be and that was where my journey of being a people pleaser began. From the age of eight through to thirty, I was continually seeking love and approval from others to feel better about myself because the way I saw it was if others could love me then I could love myself. Those that I sought it from always took advantage of me and the fact that I wanted to fit in and be loved/liked so much.

I thought at the time that it was just me being kindhearted. People saw my good nature and how I did not want any form of conflict, and they exploited it for their own personal gain. Even the two girls I considered being my best friends took what they wanted from me, including having affairs and cheating on me with my partners. They thought it was ok to do so as I would be ok with it. I would not mind them trying to take what I held dearest from me because they could not see me objecting to what they were doing. They saw me as a doormat.

It was not until my thirties when I was single that I truly realized what the true meaning of that song was as I explored every part of me (physically, mentally, emotionally, and spiritually). This was where my personal development journey began. I was depressed, having gone through so much in my life and having nothing to show for it other than being taken advantage of by others.

Sure, I had a career, dated, could support myself financially, but that just was not enough for me. I wanted and longed for something more out of life, a purpose and meaning to my life that I could not find. I was sad, depressed, and withdrawn from the world around me in many ways.

I even had my sixty-year-old neighbor tell me that when I first moved into the unit next door to her, she could see I was in a dark and withdrawn place, and she was frightened to say hello to me. However, a couple of years into my personal development journey, we became great friends. She told me I had changed and opened up so much to the world in those couple of years that I was almost like a different person.

A few years after that, I started up a personal training and life-style mentoring business, which made me happy, but I still felt that something was missing and so I continued down the personal development path until I knew fully what that song meant. I experienced so many things that made me happy, that helped me to face my fears and find out who I was and absolutely love myself for who I was without having to search for love externally as I loved myself truly and knew who I was and what the meaning of my life was that gave me joy.

I work in an industry where I help organizations improve technologically now, and I have opened a coaching business and am constantly helping others with their lives and learning, growing, and changing within myself all the time. The point to life and the lessons that life teaches you is learning those lessons you are being taught through experience and transforming to be a better version of yourself so that you do not repeat the same mistakes repeatedly.

In 2019, I started authoring my book and articles and I have been getting some really positive interaction from my articles about my life and what I have been through. Many people have told me publicly on social media that my life stories inspire and give them hope that life will get better and that they can make it through the traumas they are going through, as I did. My articles/blogs give people the desire to continue living and moving forward with their lives in the darkest of times.

The meaning I have for my life now is to make a massive impact on other people's lives through my coaching, writing, and speaking, whether it be on video or otherwise. My purpose is to one day buy an orphanage and give the orphans the love, support, and personal development education I never had so that they can grow up to be the world's future leaders and do not have to feel as though they are not loved, not enough and do not belong.

The Mindset Of Looking At Fear As A Challenge To Be Overcome

"If you are constantly living in fear, you are not living at all, so you might as well just stay in lockdown for the rest of your life, being too afraid to go out in case you catch something."

Let me tell you why I look at my fears and see them as challenges to be overcome rather than letting them rule my life. You are going to want to sit down for this, so get yourself a large glass of water, sit back and relax, and I will begin.

I remember when I was twenty-two, and I was going to spend the weekend away for my birthday with my partner. I was so excited as it was a birthday present, and I was in a fabulous mood that day. It was a Saturday morning, and I had arranged for a friend of mine who was a hairdresser to do my hair before I went away.

That day was also my mother's birthday, so I rang her that morning to wish her a happy birthday. I then drove to the super-market as I needed to get some money out of the ATM at the supermarket. I parked my car in a very easy to see place, got out of the car and got the money out of the ATM.

I went back to my car, not noticing anything that was going on around me. I got in my car, put the key in the ignition and did not lock the door as it was 10am on a Saturday morning and I thought it was safe. I was about to put my seat belt on when my car door beside me on the driver's side where I was sitting opened. There was a man crouching down with a syringe full of blood with a shirt over his head pointing and waving the syringe at me, telling me to move over to the passenger side of the car and get on the floor.

I did what I was told to do as the syringe horrified me. More importantly, the sight of blood made me sick and squeamish inside at the best of times. He kept telling me the syringe had AIDS and HIV infected blood in it and if I did not do what he said, he would inject me with it. He then told me to tie a long football sock that was lying on the floor of the car around my eyes and not to scream.

He drove me to his place, got me to get out of the car and guided me to a room where he forced himself on top of me and raped me. I told him to get off me several times and tried to wiggle and move, but it was pointless as he was bigger, heavier, and stronger than me.

Once I realized there was no escape, my body went into shock, my brain froze up and I could not move. I did not know whether I was going to make it out alive. The fear I felt that day was the worst fear I have ever felt in my life. Nothing ever compares to the fear you feel when you have your free will and liberty taken away from you. I remember my heart pounding like crazy and needing to scream but not being able to. Being paralyzed by fear of what was going to happen to me and not being in control of it. All of my life I have always been in control of what happened to me, but this time I could not control it and it threw me into shock.

Not having my eyesight meant that my other senses were heightened. I remember smelling cigarette smoke in his breath and feeling the roughness of his touch on my skin and the horrifying roughness of his voice. I wanted to throw up. I wanted to scream and run, but had no control over my body. My body went into shock to protect me. If I could not move or struggle, I would not get hurt from struggling.

I still to this day have objections to people calling me pretty as he kept saying whilst raping me "You're a pretty little thing aren't you," "I'm going to enjoy this" repeatedly. The best I could hope for at the time was that it was over and done with quickly and painlessly and that no further harm would come to me.

After he raped me, he guided me to a shower and made me wash the DNA away. He dressed me in my clothes and while he was driving me back to the supermarket to drop me off and run; he had a look at my driver's license from my purse and told me if I ever told anyone about it, he would hunt me down and kill me as he had seen my license and knew where I lived. Just after he had parked the car in the supermarket car park, he made me count to one thousand and told me not to move until I had reached one thousand. If I did, he would know.

I did as I was told. Once I reached one thousand, I untied the football sock from around my head and eyes and drove over to my friend's house and collapsed at her front door. She then called the police. I was reluctant at first to tell the police but knew I had to, as I did not want this to happen to anyone else. So, I then told the police what had happened. They took me to the station and got a formal statement and got a physician to do a lot of blood and swab tests on me.

It traumatized me for a very long time after that and I started going to a rape support group where everyone told their stories about what they had gone through. There was a difference between me and the other survivors and that was they felt guilty and blamed themselves for what had happened to them, and I didn't as I did nothing wrong and did not know the perpetrator. I knew inside me it was the monster's attempt to feel powerful by doing what he did to me, a power play of sorts.

I lived in fear for many, many months after that and had nightmares every night and at work. I had terrible flashbacks of it. At work sometimes, I would stare at the computer screen and break down in tears. I got counselling which did not help, and my parents were less than supportive with my mother telling me over the phone a couple of days after the rape had happened that it was my fault as I had moved out of home at such a young age.

Myself and my partner moved to a new house soon after that so I could feel safe again because living where we were was not allowing me to heal and move on with my life. After a month, my brain had deleted everything that had happened to me out of my head, and I moved on with my life. Not once, however, did I play the victim.

At work, I arranged self-defense classes for the women in the government department I worked for, giving myself and the other women an education on how to defend ourselves if anything like that ever happened again. It was through doing this that I decided that being the victim and living in fear was not for me. I was better than that. I had the rest of my life to live, and I intended to live it.

I did not go on antidepressants until six months after it happened, as I thought I could handle all the emotions, nightmares, flashbacks and fear I was feeling and experiencing on my own. The only reason I went on antidepressants was because the nightmares were getting too much for me and I needed a way of not having them anymore. I was diagnosed with depression and PTSD not long after that. That was one of the most traumatic and horrifying experiences of my life and I lived through it, built myself up to be bigger, better, and stronger than before and moved on with my life without ever playing the victim and blaming myself.

Years later, because of the anti-depressants, my relationship ended as I was not the same person anymore and had pushed him away. He cheated on me with my best friend which hurt me more than the rape did as the two people I trusted more than life itself had betrayed me and hurt me so deeply while I was at my lowest point in my life and trying to recover from it.

I moved out into a rental and three days later he served me with legal papers for the house that I was paying the mortgage for. It seemed he had been planning to take the house from me for weeks if not months, as legal papers like the ones I was served with cannot be drawn up in a couple of days. He knew that if he served me with them soon after I had found out about his indiscretions with my best friend, I would sign the house away to him and not put up a fight. That is exactly what I did as I did not want to have anything to do with him ever again, as I was extremely vulnerable and was not thinking straight.

The sad part about it was that I had put so much of my money into paying off that house. I put half of my compensation money, which was about $30k from the rape and abduction, into the mortgage.

Anyway, that seems like a lifetime ago now and the only thing I had left to do was to pick myself up, reinvent myself, and move on with my life, and that is exactly what I did. It took a lot of energy, strength, and courage to do it, but I did it and I am so glad I never gave up on myself after all of that.

As I was picking myself up off the ground from what had happened, I started putting my holistic health support system together to get me through the troubled times after those events and it helped me so much to become the person I am today. From building up my system I changed my views on my fears and became daring and maybe a little bold by facing my fears head on by jumping out of airplanes for my fear of heights, getting a professional photo shoot done to find out if I really was as ugly as others in my life had made me believe I was, and getting driven around a V8 supercar racetrack to face my fear of being out of control once again. I even went on holidays overseas to face my fear of being stranded in a foreign country and not being able to find my way home again.

Now I no longer have depression, but I have anxiety and know exactly how to make the anxiety work for me so that it drives me and moves me forward in a positive light to where I am now as senior project manager and digital scrum master and I handle stress and have managed multi-million-dollar projects for global and international companies, and I am bloody good at it.

The anxiety makes me an excellent project manager who plans things thoroughly and makes sure that there are mitigation plans in place for all the risks and issues the project may encounter. I now believe that fear is a challenge that can only strengthen you if you choose to take up the challenge to face it and overcome it.

Yes, I still have fears and tell people what they are, but I have never let the fear overwhelm me and I have always found the courage to face my fears as they are just challenges to me that only make me a better and more resilient person.

Beauty Is In The Eye Of The Beholder

*"Your entire world will change when you look at
yourself in a more compassionate and positive way.
Every day look in the mirror and be grateful for at least one
thing about yourself and see how your world changes."*

Looking back to when I was in primary school and how I used to get teased and bullied by the popular children and thinking to myself now about how much I have changed and if only those children could see me now. For you see, I was not always like this. As a child, because my home life was not the best and at school, they bullied me a lot. I had a very low opinion of myself and continually wished I could be someone else. This led to low self-esteem.

The popular children used to call me fat, ugly, odd looking, dumb, and stupid. This happened throughout my primary school years. I did not know whether I was those things, or if it was because I was different, or because of the way my parents used to dress me. My parents used to get my haircut really short like I was a boy and dress me in my sister's hand-me-down clothes.

To this day, I still do not know what made them be so cruel to me, but I remember I was damaged by the teasing, taunting, and bullying that I went through back then for a very long time. This bullying continued to happen to me throughout my high school years until I moved out of my parent's home and changed schools. I went to three different high schools trying to fit in, but never did.

My parents let my sister grow her hair long, but they always had mine cut like a little boy, and I hated it so very much. My parents, over 85% of the time, used to dress me in my sister's hand-me-down second-hand school clothes that were too big for me even though I was chubby. The only new clothes I remember getting were when my aunt told my mother she needed to get me some fitted clothes and so because my mother loved to sew my sister dresses, she would sew me a dress or outfit every now and again. In those years, I used to wish so very hard that I would become beautiful and smart one day because I hated what I looked like.

My parents used to compare me to my older sister, who was their chosen child all the time, and it would really hurt my feelings. My parents made me feel emotionally abandoned, unloved, and unwanted and I moved out of home into my aunt's house for a while.

I had to get the living away from home allowance/Austudy for youth and they assessed me psychologically to find out why I could no longer live at my parent's place. They found I had been psychologically abused, and they made me go to family counselling for a while as a condition of getting the payments from the government. The counselling did no good as my parents could not see how they were doing anything wrong and so they just never changed. They were always twisting things to suit themselves. I guess that was a product of their own upbringing.

I used to get belted with the strap for no good reason except that my sister would be naughty and blame me for the terrible things she had done. Because of this, they saw no good in me and always saw my older sister as the chosen child who could do nothing wrong.

How I wished I were her at times. As they gave her all the love in the world and had no time for me. They offered her dance classes, self-defense classes, and sports group memberships, and they offered me none of those things. I was simply told that "money did not grow on trees" and that "they could not afford to do it for both of us." Regularly, I was told by my father I was worthless, useless, had a heart of stone and that no one will ever be able to love me.

I remember getting rejected many, many times in high school by the boys I liked, and it really hurt. Even the boys in my youth group at church rejected me. I could not figure out what was wrong with me. I ended up thinking it was because I did not fit into the stereotyping and that I was ugly, unlovable, and unlikeable, like the school bullies and my family used to tell me.

I left school close to the end-of-year eleven and got myself a job. At that point in my life, I was sad, lonely, and a little depressed. Throughout my young adult years, I was in emotionally abusive and narcissistic relationships where the men in my life would build my self-confidence up to a certain level only to smash it back down again and manipulate me so that they could get their own way. The first one ended up having a threesome with my best friend from school who was married and had only just had a baby, and the other one had an emotional affair with the best friend I had for three years prior to getting involved with him and he tried to keep it from me as he said it meant nothing to him which showed exactly how much he really thought of me to do that to begin with.

During this timeframe I was also raped and abducted and dragged through court (trial) twice only to have the rapist get eight years behind bars for what he had done to me, his cousin, and a fourteen-year-old girl. The police told me he died in prison of lung cancer three years after he was convicted and sentenced. I would plan birthday parties for myself and none of my friends would turn up as they always went on holidays on or before the week of my birthday, so they did not have to attend my parties, but they expected me to buy them birthday presents and attend their birthday parties when they invited me.

Because all these things happened in my life, I had very low self-esteem, no self-respect, and always thought I was ugly and believed what my father had said, that no one could ever truly love me.

It all changed, though, when I fell deep down into the depths of despair and had a breakdown. When I looked in the mirror every morning getting ready for the day all I could see was an ugly Golem like creature looking back at me and that person to me was really ugly and it often used to pain me to see this creature looking back at me, even the photos my friends took with me in them portrayed a golem creature standing in the spot I was supposed to be in. When I had reached rock bottom, the only way forward for me was up. And believe me, I had hit rock bottom pretty badly.

This was when I realized I had to change my life. I started getting into personal development and built my holistic health support system up. This holistic health support system saved my life, and it completely changed my lifestyle. I looked at myself in a different light. It was not an instant thing. It took a lot of time, effort, and perseverance on my part, but I really wanted my life to change, and I would have done anything for it to change.

Christmas in 2008, I bought myself a professional photo shoot to see how photos would turn out when they were taken by a professional photographer as all the nonprofessional photos had made me look ugly and I looked like this odd golem shaped creature in those photos. I hated getting my photo taken by my friends because of this.

I was very surprised to find that the star shots photos in 2008 made me look amazing and through those I realized I was not ugly at all and that the way I saw myself wasn't the same way that other people saw me. I saw myself through dark and dreary tainted lenses because of past experiences and had let those experiences dictate my thoughts, feelings, and actions for a very long time.

These professionally taken photos showed me an exquisite side to myself I had never let myself see before.

Because of the programming, I had had from childhood and the limiting beliefs I had formed as a child and had let overtake me, those negative experiences and the programming I had from childhood I had perceived myself to be completely different as I was filtering out all the positives I had about myself because I did not know any better. All I could see before getting those photos done was a hideous woman who did not know who she was and could not see the positives or how other people really saw her.

I was so impressed with those professional photos that I put them up on Facebook and my entire world and views on myself changed from then on as I got so many compliments and likes on my photos which made me feel good about myself and the way I looked for the first time in my life.

Since that time, I became friends with some photographers in Brisbane and did amateur modelling and now have a stash of amazing photos of myself throughout my thirties and have an amazing system that holistically supports me in my life's journey and helps move me forward from the many other things that happened in my life that were negative to where I am today with self-love, self-respect and enforcing boundaries for how others treat me in my life.

Making The Impossible Possible

"Break free from the shackles of the past and become that truly amazing and wondrous person you dreamt of being who is bold, courageous, daring, and strong. Dare to be YOU and all of YOU out there in the world, no matter what NOW."

Before I started coaching, I was not the same person I am now. I let my fear of being judged override parts of who I was. I lived a mediocre life, not wanting to rock the boat by saying what I really thought and felt. So behind closed doors I was me, but out in public I was someone more mild, placid, afraid of offending others and being mistreated for it, and so for many years I hid my true self from the rest of the world.

I became what everyone else wanted me to be. I was a doormat and let everyone else tell me what to do and how to do it. On the outside I was ok but, on the inside, I was a mess, angry, upset and dissatisfied with the way life was going. I pushed all my feelings and needs deep, deep down inside of me and it took me over twenty-years to break out of that life. That life crippled me. I ended up being this person who just went through life without opening up to others without truly knowing who I am.

Deep down inside me, there was this energy wanting to get out to be seen, to experience life, to stop hiding from the world. This energy was way below the anger, disrepair, and dissatisfaction.

I did not really know how to let those emotions out fully until two years ago when I became a coach and learnt a lot of different techniques that when coupled with what I already knew on emotional release, helped me to get past and process all of those deep dark emotions and let that beautiful energy underneath it all out. Once I had done that, I built up enough courage to go on my journey of breaking through one of my biggest fears of being judged by others. I ventured in front of a video camera and made a few private videos and then ventured on to do Facebook live videos and now I am on a public speaking course to become the best version of myself I can be in front of an audience in person and online with a video camera.

I am genuinely excited about this new journey I am on and pushing myself outside of my comfort zone to improve and grow and change along the way. I know that there will be obstacles and hurdles along the way to the new transformation. Some of them will be good and some of them will be bad, but I am ready for them.

In life, you must have the courage to go beyond who you are now to become the person you are proud of being and can share with the rest of the world, warts and all. If you want to succeed in life, you must have the mindset to make the impossible possible and to live true to your values immediately and do all you can to succeed. You must break free from the shackles of the past and become that absolutely amazing and wondrous person you dreamt of being who is bold, courageous, daring, and strong. You must Dare to be YOU and all of you out there in the world, no matter what.

What Being A Project Manager Has Taught Me

"Live life like a project manager and see how planning and being driven, motivated, disciplined in life can change your entire world and the meaning of that world."

Looking back to many years ago where I was not as organised or on top of things like I am now. I remember I was a little scattered, but do not get me wrong, I was very good at what I did. I just did not have a plan for what I would do and when, and that was frustrating.

It was not until I became a project manager that I learnt what the meaning of being efficient, organised, and focused really meant. I got my first project management job over eleven years ago and I am so glad I got that job as it taught me so much about the person I wanted to and needed to be to be successful at achieving my goals.

I have been a project manager now for over twelve years and I have learnt, grown, and changed quite a lot. I have had to, as I have managed projects and mini programs of works for small to global organizations with budgets ranging from $2K to $35M.

Being a project manager taught me all about the following things:

- Schedule and time management and how most people do not keep to schedules if they do not have something or someone to remind them of their goal and what they need to achieve and how to join the dots to see the bigger picture.
- Planning and how if you do not plan ahead then the project and the goal you are working on can go south and die a slow and painful death as you have not taken into consideration any risk and issues and how to manage and mitigate them any time, cost, and quality constraints you may have. When you do not plan in advance for these things, then you are essentially dooming the project from the very start.
- Tracking and monitoring tasks so that you stay on track regarding your milestones, budget and resources, and any risks, issues, dependencies, major decisions, and other constraints you may have.
- Being more organised and how when you are, you are far more productive, effective, and efficient and you are completely on top of things.
- Being more focused on the work you are doing and the end goal and bringing others in the team along on the journey so that they are focused and know what they need to do.
- Being more resourceful and how this will help you achieve the milestones and if there is an obstacle in your way, you can quickly use your resourcefulness to navigate around it or find a solution to fix it so that the project can carry on moving forward at a rapid rate.
- Being driven and disciplined for success when you have the drive and discipline to succeed you are less likely to become disinterested and far more likely to succeed by inspiring others and pushing yourself to get things done

as you are less likely to become distracted by other things.

- People/resource/stakeholder/client expectation management plans. When you have clear and precise plans that shows a clear process on how to do things, there is less confusion and more clarity and everyone knows where they stand.
- People/resource/stakeholder/client communications strategies. These strategies give people on and involved with the project an idea on how you think and what you expect regarding the team, stakeholders, clients, and vendors.
- Budget management is one of the key elements of being a project manager.
- Knowing what you are forecasting/estimating to spend and what your actual spend is and why you may not have kept to the budget is great so that you do not overspend and so that you are not constantly raising change requests on budget as you simply weren't keeping track of it, and it also shows you financial budget constraints and trends within the project.
- Quality management plans and strategies speak for themselves as they tell you what standards the work needs to be at and what the definition of done/acceptance criteria. If the work is up to standard and meets the definition of done and the acceptance criteria, then there will be far fewer bugs/defects and rework further down the track and the client will be happy with the work and the product or service being produced.
- Changing communication skills to suit the audience. This is important as you do not want to speak to detailed with upper management as they will probably not understand you and they really only need a high-

level view of the project and where it is at whereas the team you can be as detailed as you like as they dig deep into the details of the work to be able to do the work properly.

- How to design, test, and implement the entire project management governance framework for organizations who had none. Working in chaotic situations with no governance, processes, procedures, templates, guidelines and frameworks is a nightmare and throughout the years I developed my own project management frameworks and governance structure for the projects I have managed in waterfall and agile environments which has made me far more effective and efficient with how I manage projects and I have managed to upscale it for Project, program and portfolio management offices to help them regain control of their projects and bring a certain form of uniformity to the management of their projects which has made these organizations far more cost effective and have far less resources leaving them for other organizations because of the ineffectiveness of the management of the projects. This has made the team far more transparent and collaborative in their work and more initiative-taking in solving their own issues as they occur before escalating to management for a resolution.
- How to manage my time and other people's time more efficiently so that we reach our project milestones and stay on track to the end of the project.
- How to delegate and how to manage upwards regarding issues that cannot be resolved at my level and require delivery managers, commercial managers, contracts managers, General manager, and Chief Information Officers help to get resolved in a timely manner.

- How to collaborate better with others through various communication tools like project team chat groups, MS Teams, Skype, phone calls, emails, and meetings.
- How to be flexible and adapt to change because projects and the work involved in the projects change so rapidly/frequently, especially in Agile and Scrum projects. This is also about asking questions and listening for the answers and often digging deeper to get to the root of the issue. Being flexible with communication styles in the team, client, and internal stakeholders for the project.
- How to motivate and inspire teams to deliver projects by connecting them with the project vision and goal and thought being easily accessible and approachable and relating to team members on a person-to-person basis to build up a good solid working relationship with the team.
- Picking my battles wisely, sometimes in projects and organizations there are political battles at play, and it is best not to get in the middle of those battles and only fight the battles you have backup and support for and know you can win.
- Personal and professional development are important because if you have a learning and development mindset you will pick up work on the job a lot quicker and this also shows you are serious about what you do and wanting to improve on how you do it.
- How to resurrect a failing project and make it a successfully delivered project by analysing the project and what it does and does not have and putting plans and strategies in place so that you can get the project up and running properly.

These things that I have learnt over the twelve years in project management have contributed to the person I am today. This has gained me an amazing project management reputation within the ICT industry.

I have been told over the course of my life that I am inspiring and admirable for the characteristics and traits I have. I have been through so many things in my life that giving up is not an option and nor should it be. My life has been exceedingly difficult and because of that, I am in a very fortunate position to coach and mentor people through their life's journey and the turbulence in their lives.

Ever since I can remember, I have loved helping people. I got into ICT support many years ago because I wanted to help people and organizations with their problems. I got into project management so that I could deliver transformational projects and systems that would help change how people and organizations operate for the better.

Now I am embarking on a coaching journey as I can delve in deep into people's subconsciousness to help them repair, change and transform their internal relationships which will trickle down to their professional, personal, and business life.

Until the internal relationship of a person with themselves is repaired and transformed, that person cannot transform their relationships and communications with their partners, family, friends, co-workers, bosses, managers, leaders, and team members. There is a saying I like to say and change a little, which goes like this:

- Do unto others which you would have them do unto you.

I really do believe that the above saying should go like this instead:

- Do to and for yourself that which you would do to and for others as your outer world reflects your inner world and do it with the best of intentions, as your intention in doing things people see and notice the most.

People will not and do not change on the outside if they have not and are not willing to change on the inside. So do personal development, learn, grow, and change from it, and let your inner beauty shine through on the outside. Once you do this, you will see a remarkable change happening in your outer world. Be all that you can be! Dare To Be You!

Take Ownership For Your Life, Your Decisions, And Your Actions!

"Preaching forgiveness to others and then not forgiving people for something that has been said or done to you will not win you friends. You will only look like a hypocrite."

You cannot blame the other person for a failed friendship or relationship as it takes two to make and or break a friendship. Look for the lesson and how you can change/improve through personal reflection and development if you want to move on and not repeat the same patterns as you did in the past. Figure out if staying in that friendship is affecting you in some way, either positively or negatively, and do not continue to fight with the other person involved, as it will do you more damage than good.

Be prepared to either walk away or take a break from communications with that person if you notice it is affecting your health, either physically or mentally. Be the bigger person and do what it takes for you not to be drawn back into that cycle of anger and pain caused by fighting with the other person.

We need to take ownership of our past and how we got to where we are now. We are the only ones responsible for our thoughts, emotions/feelings, actions, reactions, and decisions that we make and do. The hardest part of taking responsibility for our lives is admitting that we have problems and issues and admitting that we are flawed by taking ownership of our lives and where we are, owning up to and taking responsibility for our mistakes in life.

Because we are complex beings and are layered, we all have issues and problems in our lives. It is not a sin to be ashamed of if you have made a mistake or taken a wrong turn and you own up to it.

Taking ownership of things can be scary, but also quite empowering at the same time. Once you have taken ownership of your life and decisions you have made, then and only then can you work towards improving and positively fixing things.

Have you or a friend of yours ever been in a situation where you have repeated the same patterns repeatedly and wondered why these patterns are repeating?

If so, was there a specific thing you did to break the repetitious cycle and move positively forward or in a different direction?

I have made many mistakes in my life from the people I spent time with, who were bad influences to taking the wrong job with the wrong company where the culture was toxic, to giving people too many chances to make up for hurting me and to change, to trusting the wrong people.

For me to change, I had to dig deep within myself and do some self-analysis to figure out why I was being and doing the things that only caused me heartache and grief and figuring out what the positive lessons were in those situations. In doing so learning those lessons so that I did not repeat those patterns again. Sometimes I would fail at changing course and would have to go through similar experiences again and relearn the lessons until I implemented the correct strategy to move me forward.

It is not a straightforward thing to be digging deep into your subconscious after a bad or traumatic experience and figuring out what you could have done differently so that you don't repeat the experiences. It is exceedingly difficult to do. In this process, you must remember that you are human and that humans make mistakes and not be too hard on yourself so that you can learn the positives from the experience and move forward.

I have learnt through experience that being too hard on yourself is sometimes the thing that makes you your worst enemy. When you are hard on yourself, you will never see the positive learning from the experience as you are too busy beating yourself up negatively to see that there are positive learnings to gain from the experience. I know that seeing the positive in a negative event in your life is difficult, but it is well worth it. From learning the positives from experiences, I have moved forward and let go of what would usually hold a person back far more quickly and efficiently than I could when I was in depression.

I now look back on how far in life I have come, and I am so enormously proud of myself for learning all those lessons and implementing far more resourceful strategies that serve me to move me forward towards my destination and achieve what I want to achieve. I could not have done this without personally developing and having a mindset of continual improvement.

How To Break Out Of People Pleasing

"Stop being too nice a person and stand up for yourself.
Tell people what you need, want, and put healthy boundaries
in place so that those you have in your life will love and respect
you for the person you are and not for the person they want you
to turn into."
"Respect comes from others when you respect yourself."

Are you constantly feeling as though you are a puppet on a string?

When other people say jump you jump and when they say sit down or go for a walk you do it. Are you constantly thinking and doing the below things?

- Constantly walking on eggshells so that you do not upset anyone and be abused for it.
- Constantly putting other people's needs above your own needs so that they will like you.
- Constantly being disappointed by others' actions, reactions, and words to you and about you.
- Constantly feeling as though you are not good enough for some people, as they always act so high and mighty.
- Constantly staying in unhappy and unhealthy romantic and platonic relationships because that is what society and family tell you to do.

- Constantly thinking that if you tell people how you feel and what you think, they will not understand and will judge you for it.
- Constantly feeling bad for doing things with good intentions that get taken out of context and with negativity by others.

The above are all symptoms of our three universal fears of not being enough, not being loved, and not belonging.

Continually being this way must really drain you.

For me, I was doing all the above things for others day in and day out and it got really draining over the years. It depressed me as I could never make them happy and because they did not respect me, they just kept treating me the same way all the time. Truthfully, they treated me like a doormat or a piece of scum under their shoe.

This got me to the point where I was so depressed, low on energy, and could not function properly in what is called "Normal everyday life." I wanted to just belong, be loved, and know that I was enough for just being myself rather than being a too nice person who felt they could take advantage of and someone I was not.

I felt misunderstood, taken for granted and used by people constantly when they took things the wrong way and let me down continually and because of this, I felt lost, broken, and depleted.

I just wanted to be myself and not have to worry about thinking of and doing what other people wanted me to do, but I was afraid the change would leave me with no one. I continuously felt that life was just too hard with everyone else's conditions about life hanging over my head and deep down inside I did not feel that loved, good enough or that I even belonged even though I was being and doing everything that others wanted me to.

Because I felt this way, I was constantly erring on the side of caution where I got the least amount of conflict and where I would not be judged. The inability to endure conflict made me want to continually please others and put my own needs below the needs of their needs, thus attracting the wrong people into my life.

There will come a time in your life where you will hit rock bottom because you have been doing everything for everyone else for such a long time, you will not recognize yourself in the mirror anymore, and this will shock you. This will be the turning point in your life where you will wonder where your life went and what you achieved in life. You will wonder why you are not happy and why, when the chips are down for you, none of your friends and family are there for you when you need them.

This will be the time for you to dig deep within yourself and figure out why you are not happy, who you really are, what makes you happy, what you want and need out of your life to achieve fulfillment. You will need to put a plan together and implement that plan to achieve your goals, which will give you the fulfillment, meaning and purpose in your life that you so desperately crave.

Remember, though, without a clear and precise plan of action and implementing that action plan, you will stay stuck in endless where you are currently, doomed to repeat that endless groundhog day cycle that you currently call life.

I dare you to take the next step towards being your true self and living a life of purpose and meaning today!

How To Have A Positive
Mindset In Uncertain Times

"Sometimes a positive mindset of personal and professional development is what will move us forward the most when it comes to getting outside of our comfort zone into something that really scares us. We grow and change the most when we have faced our worst fears head on with this mindset."

It is important when you are going through uncertainty to keep a positive mindset. Many people in times that are uncertain struggle.

Why is that you may say? Let me answer that for you. People forget that through uncertainty, change and adversities come many things:

- We can see other options that we could not see before.
- We can create our futures the way we want to, by changing our mindset and improving on processes and procedures that have become outdated and redundant.
- We are the creators of our own destinies, so we get to create our lives in a way that is more closely aligned to our dreams and values.
- Through uncertainty, change and adversity comes personal growth and the ability to learn from previous mistakes or the mistakes of others.

- Through uncertainty, change and adversity comes more flexibility. We are less rigid and strict on the way things are done and we change and adapt with the times.
- Through uncertainty, change and adversity comes self-realization and life-changing moments, so we get to re-evaluate what is most important to us and cut out the things that no longer serve us positively
- Through uncertainty, change and adversity comes a new perspective on life because we are no longer about to look at our lives in the same way as we grow and change from the experiences that throw our lives into turmoil.
- Through uncertainty, change and adversity comes a new perspective on what really matters, so we get to take a good hard look at our lives and work out our highest priorities and change or move them around if we need to.
- Through uncertainty, change and adversity comes positive change and the ability to experience new and exciting things if we are open to them.
- Through uncertainty, change and adversity comes evolution because of the experience we evolve as humans to become an even better version of ourselves, one that is more resilient and capable of bouncing back from traumatic events and we become stronger people.
- Through uncertainty, change and adversity comes possibilities you would never have thought of before because these experiences open our minds up to the other possibilities that are out there that we would not have been open to before.
- Through uncertainty, change and adversity comes pure strength and determination to move forward. This is done when our natural ability to control and manage things becomes activated or triggered by the event.

- Through uncertainty, change and adversity new doors open for us in our romantic, business, and professional lives as the old doors we went through previously end up closing on us, so we must choose a new option to move ahead with as these experiences force change on us.

Instead of focusing on the above things, people tend to focus on the negative things like the lack of, loss of things, or what you cannot do or where you cannot be.

In these times, we need to, now more than ever, focus on our internal dialogue with ourselves, and the things we can control, which are our thoughts, emotions, feelings, actions, responses, and reactions to things.

We need to be focusing on getting more positive, more secure, more certain, and stronger within ourselves so that we have a mindset that when things do not go to plan, we pivot, and we look at alternative solutions to the roadblock instead of going straight into the roadblock and smashing in a downwards spiral by dwelling on the problem and worrying about the negatives and the what ifs in this world.

Why not have a mindset of "if because X happened, we now get Y which is really positive," or "when A takes place, we get B which is also really positive" or "if we do H, we will receive G which is really positive." Through problems and roadblocks, we now become more creative, more daring, more grateful, more flexible, and more courageous with life. And when there is a pothole in the road, we now find ways around it and so we become problem-solvers and are more likely to create and go after the lives that we really want.

This is when our true selves come out to play, and we flourish and grow the most. I remember my move to Melbourne five years ago, like it was yesterday. This move was scary for me, and I was very uncertain whether I could do it on my own. Instead of focusing on the negatives, I focused on the positives, like all the many possible doors that would open up for me with regards to personal and professional life endeavors. Such as the fact that Melbourne has a lot more jobs which meant variety of experience and career progression and growth, the possibility of meeting a nice man and having a great love life as there are thousands more men in Melbourne than there were in Brisbane. And a better social life as there were plenty of places to go and things to do to meet new and interesting people who aligned to my values and interests. These things excited me and so I put my fears aside and managed the move like a true project manager by planning for the move and how I was going to do, afford and approach it. I planned for the budget, timeframe any risks and issues that may have come up during the move and implemented that plan. The move was the biggest thing I had ever done in my life as I used to be a creature of the comforts of my comfort zone and played it safe often except for when I felt daring enough to face a fear like heights or being out of control; they were big fears to me and I had them all my life but I overcame them by doing little things like jumping out of airplanes.

The move was a massive thing for me as I had a massive fear of being stranded in a new city or country on my own and feeling lost and so far out of my depths as I did not know the place or what the people were like. The first five months in Melbourne terrified me as I was battling financial anxiety because I could not get a job because I did not have a reputation in my industry for the work I did, and I really needed to get a job so that I could support myself and get a place of my own.

To get that first job, I had to drastically lower my pay rate. I ended up getting my first job here in Melbourne at a small consulting firm that hired me permanently and because their clients were not wanting a project manager, they could not place me with any of them, so three weeks after I started with them, I finished up with them. It then took me three weeks to get another job with a large Australian telecommunications giant where I was being paid almost half of what I was worth until another contract opening came up with them in a different area where I got paid almost double the money. I then moved around in the same organization to another role and finally got paid the money my work was worth, and I have stayed on that pay rate or above ever since. This process took me about a year to get put on the correct pay rate for someone with my experience and qualifications.

It took a lot to stay positive when I first moved to Melbourne, as I did not have the stability I had craved for so much and that frightened me. To stay positive, I put together a professional development plan for myself and upskilled myself in Agile and waterfall project management and on the different project management tools that I would need to use on the job when I got one.

I would say this plan and implementing this plan was what got me my first job and subsequent jobs after that. My learning and development mindset made it possible for me to make the plan and implement it. I do not know where I would be right now if I did not.

I remember the predicament I was in when I first move to Melbourne as I had to rely on the kindness of someone, I hardly knew for a place to stay and after a while that got difficult as he wanted more than friendship from me and made it difficult for me to stay there. When I got my first job, I found a place closer to the city and moved there.

Although having to finish that first job so quickly scared the hell out of me as I now had rent, utilities and living expenses to pay but had no income to do it so I was extremely glad to have gotten the contract after that which gave me a little stability and eased my financial anxiety quite a lot.

I have now been living here in Melbourne for over six years and am loving it and have little to no problems at all finding and getting work and I know I can support myself when push comes to shove. I had to adjust to being in lockdown and working from home for eighteen months because of the COVID-19 pandemic where I had to get used to the sound of my own voice most of the time because I live on my own, but at times I most enjoy the peace and quietness as I know myself very well and built my life up around myself here in Melbourne and not others. I still love living here in Melbourne and I am eager to see where life takes me after the pandemic is over.

When the pandemic and all the lockdowns are over, there will be a new way of life for all of humankind, which will be very new and exciting. With the new norm, we will pave a new way of living and being that is different and not like the normality we had been given over the past number of centuries that were handed down from generation to generation from society and its dictatorship, so I am very excited about that.

The HBFK™ Model And How To See The World

"One must first have hope that they can do something and then believe that they can do it, then have faith that they have and can again. After that comes the knowledge and trust in themselves for the action to become automatic for them."

I find coaching and human psychology interesting but at the same time extraordinarily complex to work with, so I developed the HBFK model (Hope, Belief, Faith, and Knowledge/trust) which is a thought process and human behavioral model and is simple enough to understand and link back to our thoughts and behaviors.

This model is in every strategy ever used by humankind, although this model did not exist until I developed it a little over a year ago. I created it so that you could see where it is used in strategies as it is common sense and not in coaching language, but in normal everyday language.

The model shows you the links between the four distinct levels. These four levels I have matched up to my coaching programs and have been using it in my coaching ever since I developed it to help my clients understand themselves better so that they know the level at which they are currently operating.

Please keep in mind that fear and limiting beliefs will pause the progression up through the different levels and that we must act fast in removing the fear and replacing the limiting beliefs with empowering beliefs that will help us keep the momentum going all the way up through all the four levels of the model to the 4th level which is the Knowledge/trust in ourselves level because it has become automatic to us and therefore, we know we can do it and have trust in ourselves that we can do it.

An example of this is of a baby and how the baby learns, grows, and evolves as they get older.

Babies, when they are little, crawl around and they see these people that are bigger than they are who can talk, sing, run, walk and who most of the time seem free to them because they are crawling around on their hands and knees and some babies are too little to even be able to speak yet. Some babies are even too little to be able to even comprehend what it would be like to be older and to be able to walk, run, jump, and can play properly and challenge themselves.

Younger children challenge themselves more than older children and adults at times. Do you know why this is? It is because they don't have that sense of fear. They see things as a challenge and as an adventure because it is something new for them to try to do and, through trying to do it; they change from that experience. Babies are very fearless because they haven't lived their lives enough to be able to go through traumatic events and defining moments, and so they have not yet developed those types of fears.

Wouldn't it be awesome to be able to go back in time, and to have a fearless mindset that a baby has, where everything is adventurous, everything is fun, everything is exciting? To be able to challenge yourself to walk, challenge yourself to say your first word or sing without being afraid. Wouldn't that be amazing? And that is where my coaching model came from. It came from thinking about how babies and little children are. They had that spark of hope within them first and that they can be like others that are older and bigger than they are one day. Then they try to do a little by standing up and then once they are stable and steady on their legs then they think to themselves "I think I can do it."

So, they start to believe they can do it once they have stood up on their own for three to six times because they have experienced doing it unassisted repeatedly through their actions. Once they have mastered the art of standing up unassisted several times without falling over, they have faith in themselves that they can continually do it without a problem so they do it repeatedly until it becomes like second nature to them and that is when they really know and have the knowledge that nothing will impede them standing up unassisted. They then trust in themselves that they can stand up strong and stable automatically, as it is second nature to them. Then this cycle of Hope, Belief, Faith, and Knowledge/trust starts again by them wanting to walk and run. Babies are far more adventurous than adults are when there is uncertainty, and they employ the HBFK model in everything they do which challenges them to do more things and they become inspired by people older than they are doing the things that they hope and want to do.

Level 1 = Hope: Everything we do and think stems first from hope and our expectations of what we want to happen and how we want it to happen.

Level 2 = Belief: Then we go to belief where we try a baby step and build our beliefs around that. Then once we have the beliefs in place, we try to do and be more.

Level 3 = Faith: This then brings us to faith. Faith is where we have done it before, and we have faith that we can do it again, so we do it again, but we do it more often.

Level 4 = Knowledge/trust: This then builds up the knowledge that we can do it because we have done it in the past. Through knowledge that we can do it, we then have that trust in ourselves that we can do it, as doing it has now become automatic to us.

Faith does not necessarily have to be a religious thing, as you can have faith in yourself and humanity, which has nothing to do with God or any religion.

The above should show you the links between hope, belief, faith, and knowledge/trust in our lives. This model is a simple coaching model to use and understand when it is explained correctly.

Dating In The Modern World

"It is not easy to be single and dating in the modern world as there are so many people out there who are only after what they can get from you. Choose to be with a man who will love and respect you for who you are and who will support you in your personal endeavors."

I used to be a very nervous and anxious person. I was very shy and withdrawn from the world in my childhood and early adult years. It was not until I learnt who I was on the inside and let my inner child shine that I came out of my shell and showed people who I really was.

I was so introverted and withdrawn; it was not funny. I was the very awkward little child, a good child who was treated poorly by family who developed a deep-seated consciousness about myself though being told by family and other children at school that I was dumb, stupid, would never amount too much, that I had a heart of stone and that no one will ever and can ever love me, that I was fat, and I was ugly. The other children at school took great pleasure in teasing me about my appearance because they could see I, was different to them.

The teasing, taunting and bullying words from my childhood years ended up being limiting beliefs of mine all throughout my teenage years until I was in my early thirties. I dated a couple of guys in my teenage years who weren't the nicest people to be dating as they had their own issues and did not know how to treat women in general and so I would get dumped for the next best thing or cheated on.

When I ended my ten-year de facto relationship when I was twenty-nine, it was because he was having an affair and cheating on me with my best friend. I then had to pick myself up and start again from scratch with extraordinarily little in the way of friends and family to support me. I told you about this in the chapter called "The betrayal of a best friend and with a partner of ten years."

I started dating a couple of years later. I first started chatting to people on an internet dating site called "Meet My Best Friend." This dating site was recommended to me by a very close friend of mine.

I chatted to one guy there for two months then we exchanged numbers. His profile was very well written, and he had recommendations from his friends on his character on that site, so I actually thought he was legitimate. I have written about this in a previous chapter called "The Internet Dating Scam"

The next year I thought I would give internet dating another go. One guy arranged to meet me at a coffee shop that was local to where I lived but then never showed up and did not even ring to tell me he could not make it. Another guy turned out to be completely different from his profile and profile photo. He was a weird, awkward looking Egor like fellow who was so dark and negative in life. I just wanted to run, but I was still a people pleaser back then, so I stayed a little while, then made an excuse to get out of there and left. Another guy I got along really well with, and we had dinner and then he told me he had forgotten his wallet and that I would have to pay for both mine and his dinner. This was so rude, of course. He had not left his wallet at home at all, but as soon as he had found out what I did for a living, he figured I could afford it.

I had other guys on the internet dating sites who would invite me to meet them, but it would be at their places, and I would say no as you could tell straight away that all they wanted was sex and I would not put myself in an unsafe situation with them. Others would pretend they wanted a relationship only for me to find out later that they only wanted a friend with benefits or a sex buddy, and so I broke things off with them. Some guys were womanizers and some of them looked completely different to their photos, and some did not even speak the same way to me as they did on the dating sites.

I used to constantly be approached by men for sex, casual sex and one-night stands and I turned them all down.

It used to drive me nuts, as I used to get hit on by married men at work and at clubs and bars. And I also had a lot of my male friend's asking about me. They were formidable guys, just not my type.

I remember though before every single date I would work myself up into a nervous, anxious frenzy as these guys seemed really impressive online, and I hoped they would be the same in real life and I wanted to be in a relationship of substance. And so, the nervous anxiety would kick in before the date, with me thinking things like what if this happened, what if that happened, what if they dislike me and then what if they do like me? So many thoughts of the unknown future ran through my head. These were the things that made me feel nervous and anxious, as well as the limiting beliefs I had developed as a child in my childhood about myself. These limiting beliefs did not serve me at all. They gave me little self- love, no self-respect, and a very low self-esteem.

It was not until I got really annoyed with what I was attracting in my life that I realized that what really needed to change was me and my internal relationship with myself. I had to woman up and build up my self-love, self-respect, and my self-esteem.

Now because of that realization and the work I did on myself I am attracting a better quality of people into my life, and I have put standards and boundaries in place that help me with my self-respect, self-love, and self-esteem and when I go out on dates now, I am not nervous or anxious anymore. I am just being me, calm, cool and relaxed and at the slightest hint of something being off with the other person I leave immediately as my relationship with myself, and my safety are the most important things to me in my life apart from my health.

I now see dating as another opportunity to make another friend that is single. Of course, I still dress up for dates and I would hope that the guy does too, if he wants to make a good impression. I expect for the first couple of months that if we make it that far that we go out for dinner and drinks and that the guy is old-fashioned and will volunteer to pay for dinner and or drinks as my good male friends do and they are not even interested in dating me. After those couple of months, if it gets serious, then I will pay my own way with things.

One guy once let me pay for everything and when I wanted to go out to dinner where he was to pay, he told me he did not believe in going to dinner and spending money on restaurants and that we should stay at his place all the time. I dropped him like a hot cake as that meant he was only interested in a sex buddy that would pay for everything for him. I have more self-respect and dignity than to stay with someone like that. He rang me a year later, wanting me back as apparently the other girls he had dated were not up to the standard I was, and I simply said no thanks and left it at that.

It is important when you are dating to have a mindset that is not on the what ifs but on the making a new friend space as then you can be yourself and be comfortable around the other person. I have coached a couple of my clients on how to be in the right head space when dating and they have told me that my coaching has helped them quite a lot with the dating scene. Remember, dating and good relationships all start with you and your relationship with yourself. No one can do this internal work for you, as it is all within you.

Remember, if they want to meet you, then you already have met some of their criteria for a partner and they are curious about you and the person you are in person. Please also remember that on internet dating sites people and their profiles can be deceiving as they are behind a phone or computer talking to you and you cannot see their body language and can't sense anything apart from what they write if anything is off mentally with them. There are also fake profiles out there on internet dating sites, apps and on social media and you never know when you may be chatting to a Nigerian internet dating scammer. These scams are very easy to fall for, as I have been told by police and read up on the web that even the smartest of people like CEO's, CIO's, General managers and directors have been scammed by the best of them for hundreds of thousands of dollars. These people are cunning and deceptive, and their aim is to make you fall for them so that they can scam you for your life's savings.

Social Anxiety And The Things You Can Do To Manage And Minimise It

"It is not the end of the world if people dislike you. When you love and accept yourself, you will succeed and be happy in life. Acceptance must come from within first before others will accept you, so be confident in who you are."

Have you ever felt really anxious when around other people that your hands would shake, your palms would go clammy, and your heart would race a million beats per minute?

If so, do you remember how that felt? For many years, from about the age of seven to my early thirties, I was this person. Fearful of judgement, of doing or saying the wrong thing in the presence of others. So, I would psych myself up into an anxious, nervous mess, all because I wanted to fit in, to be liked and accepted by others. This was the worst feeling ever for me.

I remember an experience I had when I was seven years of age. I called a girl at my church thinking that the thing I called her meant something else. It was terrible because the next thing I knew, her parents spoke to my parents, and I got the hiding of a lifetime from my parents when I got home from church that day. Not to mention, while at church, my parents scolded me in front of the entire congregation.

They said some of the meanest hurtful things to me and everyone around us looked on at me with very mean, judging eyes.

I wanted to run and hide but had nowhere to run to, so I stood there and took the abuse while deep down I was so deeply embarrassed, ashamed, and afraid. I knew exactly what they would do to me when I got home that day from church, and it terrified me.

After my parents finished having a go at me and walked away. I walked past many people to go outside and be alone and as I walked towards the crowd, I could hear them whispering to each other about me and they didn't even have an ounce of empathy in their voices as they whispered judging and horrible things about me. Not one of them even bothered to ask me if I was ok. They shook their heads at me in disgust as I walked past them. Apparently, the other girl's parents had gone around telling everyone they could that I was a wicked and nasty child and that I called their daughter an unforgivable name, which made her cry.

I felt so very alone, angry at myself and my parents, embarrassed and mixed with a lot of negative low-level emotions. I really wanted to find a small dark little hole in the ground and crawl into it and hide away from the world and cry. I wanted to be so far away from judging eyes.

Once I got outside, I took my shoes off and ran away from the church in my hand-me-down clothes. I kept running for about an hour to calm myself down. When I got back to the congregation, we were getting ready to leave the church as the church proceedings had finished for the day.

After we got home from church that afternoon, my parents verbally abused me and hit me several times with the strap, saying repeatedly that I was possessed and that I was wicked and that I needed to be punished. My dad then dragged me to the bathroom and forced me to wash my mouth out with soap.

From that day forward I was this very shy withdrawn and frightened little girl who whenever she was around people spoke little and tried to please everyone as I had attached emotions and memories from that one event to being around others socially.

This made me socially nervous and anxious and too afraid to speak up and be myself around other people.

When I was around people after that, I would feel nervous, a little lightheaded, my heart would race, my palms would go clammy, and hands and arms would shake because of nerves and being overly self-conscious. I was too afraid to speak up and be myself around anyone but my sister and those I knew really well because of a fear of being judged and punished for it.

I felt like that for many years around people I did not know. This added to the depressive state I was in as a child because of the way I was treated at school by the other children and my family behind closed doors.

It was not until my late twenties to early thirties when I turned my life around and dragged myself out of depression from being raped and having to go through trial in court twice that I got this social anxiety under control. My holistic health support system which I implemented was a big part of me being able to face the fears and replace the limiting beliefs that no longer served me from that past experience and move forward to where I am now and who I am now, as I learnt to, know, love, and accept myself for the person I am now that will speak her mind and be herself around everyone. Part of my holistic health support system are the really awesome techniques below that helped me to tackle my social anxiety.

- Be yourself.
- Be confident in who you are.
- You do not have to interact straight off.
- It is okay to observe others and see how they interact with each other first.
- Do not change to fit in or to be what others want you to be.
- Take deep breaths in and out slowly for 2 to 3 minutes.
- Go for a short 10-to-15-minute walk.

- Meditate with a future pace meditation for 10 to 15 minutes.
- Get to know people slowly. If they like you, they like you. If not, it is their problem and do not take it personally, as there will always be people out there that won't like you, no matter what you say or do.
- Listen to an uplifting song.
- Do some emotional frequency tapping for social anxiety.
- Stay calm by visualizing how you want things to turn out.
- Be coached on it. I have coached people with anxiety before and do it very well as I have lived with anxiety and now manage it very well now in public.
- Shift your thought and perspective on socializing and think of the positive that can come out of socializing with other people, especially those you do not know.
- Research natural remedies for anxiety and try them out. Experiment a little with them until you find something that works for you.

When Being Compared To Others
Change Your Perspective

"Comparisons made by others can really hurt, so shift your perspective to one of empowerment and be the best leader that memorably stands out from the rest of the leaders out there."

I remember this like it was yesterday when I was told that someone else that is doing the same job as me in another state was made permanent that he would set up the processes, procedures, and templates for the projects. Keep in mind that this is something I did months ago for this company when I first started working for them.

At first, I could not understand why they would get him to do something I had done months ago for them. I got a little defensive and upset and I felt as though my work that I had done for them was not good enough for them, even though deep down inside I know I did an amazing job for them.

I spoke to one person a couple of hours later that could change my perspective on the way I looked at it as I felt like they had deliberately sidestepped me into a support role, as they did not have my particular type of work because of COVID. He shifted my perspective on it but there was still a little pain there as I wondered why they did not sidestep the other person and get him to do the support role so that I could revamp the Project Management practice procedures, processes, and templates as I knew them best as I had designed, developed, and put them in place for the company in the first place.

I reached out to someone else in the office who I thought I could talk to only to have her compare me to the other person and it triggered something in me that was extremely painful. It was painful because all my life as a child I was constantly being compared to my sister and being asked why I could not be more like her when they knew I could never be like her. They then psychologically abused me for not being like her.

This brought up feelings of not being enough and not being loved for who I am. I took myself through a defining moment visualization of the very first time it happened in my childhood. I visualized myself as an adult there comforting my seven-year-old self, who was sad, hurt, lonely, upset, angry, insecure, and afraid. In this visualization my adult self-told my child self that she is loved for who she is that she is enough, that she is special, unique and amazing and that she should not take on board the comparisons that other people make of her as she is different and deserves to be loved for the person that she is and that she will grow up to be an amazing young woman, that she should be strong and believe in herself and her abilities and know that she is capable of so much more.

My adult self also told her the comparisons that other people make of her, and others is a reflection on them and not her and that she should not take those words on board, so whenever people compare her to others in the future, she is to know that it is a reflection on their insecurities and nothing to do with her personally.

After the visualization finished, I immediately felt better, stronger, more confident, and secure within myself as a person, my abilities, and my unique qualities that I have that make me stand out and be different to everyone else, that make me who I am, and I love how different and unique I am as a person. I now have a sense of clarity in my thoughts and how I feel about things. My perspective has now completely shifted from woe is me to that of confidence and strength in my uniqueness and my ability to stand out and be a leader for others.

I may not have been able to clear this up with myself if I did not go through those things previously and so, now I am grateful for that and being compared to others doesn't seem to bother me only empowers me to stand out even more.

I have also realized that sometimes people do not realize that their outer world reflects their inner world and that they are trying to shift their own insecurities onto other people to make themselves feel better. They do not realize that their words, no matter how well intentioned they are, hurt others and that they need to be mindful of that.

The Journey From People Pleaser
To Living And Speak My Truth

*"If you seek to please others all your life, your own needs will
never be met and you will never feel fulfilled in your life as you
need to have your own needs met, to feel loved, wanted, accepted,
as though you are enough and that you belong as the person you
are and notthe person you turn into, to please other people.
You are amazing just the way you are!"*

Why is it so important to me to help people who think they are not one and have no voice, find themselves and know that they have a voice?

Well, the reason for this is that when I was younger, no one ever listened to me and every time I tried to speak up and say what I wanted and needed to say I would get shot down bullied and told that I did not know what I was talking about and that I was supposed to stay in a dark corner hidden away from the world. I was told regularly what I wanted and that my opinion did not matter and that I would never amount to much. I was told that I was stupid and dumb and that no one could ever love me.

This made me withdraw from the world into a dark and unloving place inside of me where my insecurities would get fed day and night, eating away at me. All I really wanted in this world was to be loved, acknowledged for who I am, and encouraged to grow and change. I desperately wanted to belong, to know that I was enough, and I wanted to be heard and to be seen for the beautiful person I was on the inside.

Because of this treatment, I lived in a world where I was a people pleaser because I wanted to be loved and to belong and I thought that was the only way that people would love me and want to be around me. I became particularly good at pushing all of my hopes, aspirations, wants and needs so far down inside of me I became this shell of a person who did not know who she was or what she was about, did not have any boundaries and could not speak up when people hurt me. Because I did not know any better, I would forgive people only to have them do the same things to me repeatedly, which hurt me deeply. People treated me like garbage and took advantage of my kind nature and my inability to speak up repeatedly. That was a familiar way of living for me as I did not know any better and I became very comfortable being in my comfort zone for a good number of years.

Then something inside of me snapped and all the anger, pain and sadness all came pouring up and out of me and I became depressed and negative. There was one time that I have never admitted to anyone, and I hate admitting it to myself, but I just wanted to die. At that point in time, I thought the world would be better off without me, as my fiancé had only just had the three-some with my best friend and her husband. I thought I deserved what they did to me, and I hated myself for it. The only way I could escape from the pain was to take antidepressants and drink. My life was so full of drama and very dramatic people who were angry, disrespectful, and did not know how to treat others because their relationship and internal dialogue with themselves was shocking.

It took me many years of soul searching to realize that what they had done was not my fault and that I deserved better, that I deserved and was worthy of love and respect. The day I realized that my journey of self-love, self-discovery and independence began. I learnt to speak my truth; I learnt to sing my song. I learnt to love and respect myself. This journey I was on was a very lonely journey, although I would never have admitted it to anyone at the time, as I did not know who I could trust to respect me and love me for who I was.

I learnt to become someone new, someone that I never knew I could be. That was the first time I had completely reinvented myself. I learnt what made me tick, what made me happy, what made me sad, where I needed to improve and the parts of me, I really loved and would not change for the world, I learnt to sing my own song and dance to the beat of my own drum and to be original and I loved it. I learnt to say goodbye to the familiar and the comfort zone that was holding me back and keeping me in that dark and lonely place and to say hello to the early morning sunrises, 4am meditations, 5am exercise routines and found out about everything I really loved about myself.

So now I say hello this is who I am and where I am at in life, and I will not apologize for being me and if other people dislike it, then that is their problem not mine as I love the person I am now and the person I can become whilst moving towards being the best version of myself I can be in my life. I deserve and am worthy of being seen, heard, respected, and loved. If you break a boundary of mine and disrespect me, be warned that I will not tolerate it and I will speak my truth, and you may not like what I have to say.

A link to a YouTube video of a song that has helped me on my journey is below. It is more the lyrics in this song that I connect with, not the actual video. This is who I am, and I love myself! https://www.youtube.com/watch?v=CjxugyZCfuw I now want to help others on this journey break out of the shackles of the past and be true to themselves by helping them shine their own signature light on the world and become all that they can be.

How To Get Your Money
Back From A Business Con-artist

"Stand for truth and what is right and fight for what is yours. Never let a con artist get away with taking your hard-earned money as there are ways to get it back if you fight for it. Be resourceful when looking at your options on how to get your money back. Even after you have been knocked back by one means, another way should be there. You have a right to get it back."

Have you ever felt manipulated, and peer pressured into buying a service only to not have that service delivered at all because you trusted the wrong person and they took advantage of your trusting nature and the situation you were in at the time? It sucks, doesn't it? So now you feel you can't even trust yourself, as you trusted, and looked up to that person who manipulated you as a parental figure.

I got upset in front of a lot of other people many years ago and that is a side of me I generally like to keep hidden as I am a robust person, and I rarely like to fall apart in front of anyone. My story that got me down is the story which is below. But before we get into the story, here is a bit of background on me.

I always like to see the good in people and it takes a lot for me to give up on people. I believe you should do unto others what you would want done to you. I treat people with honesty, respect, and hope that people treat me the same way in return.

Unfortunately, there are people out there that are only after your money who will lie, scheme, and deceive you to get it. Not all people are honest, kind, and trustworthy.

I did not know that there were people out there that were like this and so I trusted someone a little more than I should have, and that person used me for the money they could get out of me and that really hurt me.

This person told me stories about who and what they used to be over thirty years ago and told me about their large network of friends from the good old days to lure me in further and further and then used my dreams of helping lots of people and impacting the world against me. They promised me a service that I thought they were good to deliver on as I was being manipulated. She was an expert in manipulation, which I did not know. She built up a friendship with me that was strong and that I thought was genuine. So, I bought the service. She told me she had delivered to many people in my industry that made their businesses successful.

There were times where things did not add up and when I called her out on non- delivery of specific parts of the service, she used to blame other people and things and promised that she would make it right. When I said no to her or even questioned her on things. She would try to change my mind by throwing in extra bonuses like a gift here and there to shut me up and to get me to agree to pay more money to her so that she could deliver an improved service to me.

She was so good at sweet talking people and sales. She was very narcissistic and manipulative and would send me text messages every morning, telling me to have a blessed day and that I was loved, with little smiley faces and purple hearts to make me feel all warm and gooey and doubt myself.

I looked up to her like a parental figure and that was why I gave her the benefit of the doubt many times when asking her about the next event for my business or why I was seeing the same people online at my business zoom events time after time after time with no new faces.

She promised me that there were many people in her network that would be interested in my coaching services and that things would only be slow for a couple of weeks until we both got our grounding on the events and got better at hosting and running them virtually.

She would never give me an honest opinion on how I could improve my pitch in the events. She would always say I was amazing, that I did splendidly, that I did fabulously.

This should have been a warning sign when she begged me to do a video testimonial for her. But she looked so helpless and so I did one broad one for her business networking group, but it was not specifically for her personally.

She was so upset that I only did one for her business networking group and not one for her other business where I had bought the service package from and so she told me she could not use that one and begged me to do one that was specifically about her and her services as a paying client of her services. Because that would help her attract more people with money to her business so that she could then refer the new people on to me for my health and wellbeing services.

Of course, I did the testimonial as I did not like to hear a grown woman beg and grovel and I was a little naïve in believing her about the referral of more clients that she would attract with my testimonial. To this day I am not proud of doing the video testimonial because she pressured me into doing it and I lied in it. The truth was that I was not getting the service I had paid for from her. In fact, her service was terrible. You could not reach her on the phone very often and she was very slow to answer emails and she would not answer text messages until hours and hours later.

It should have been a second warning sign when she begged me to help fund her app development for her business networking group which was supposed to go global and would help her attract many people that she would then refer on to my events and for my health and wellbeing services. She also promised they would feature my business as a sponsor on her App which never happened. Being manipulated into paying for this app's development cost me thousands of dollars.

What I am trying to get at here is that yes, I am human and that some people out there will pull at your heartstrings to get you to do things you do not want to do. You must be wary of these people, research them thoroughly and get a list of the people they say they have services with and contact them first before handing over any money.

I think throughout our lives we have all felt that sort of peer pressure from someone in our lives that we trusted and looked up to. Where we had given those people the benefit of the doubt when we should not have and later on been made to feel sorry for doing so. This con artist was a local in the state I lived in back then and had been conning people like this for a good number of years before she conned me.

I gave this con-artist a year to rectify things as I am a generous person and she continually promised me that things would turn around and that through various things she could generate sales of over $500k by the end of that time for my health and wellbeing business. So, I believed her, and I looked up to her as a kind of parental figure, but she was not even able to generate one sale over $150 for me. So, I complained to her in writing and asked for my money back and she refused to refund my money insisting that she had delivered the services paid for, but the bank records never lie, and they told a completely different story. So, I proceeded down the path of trying to get my money back within the boundaries of the law and below is how I did it.

I went to a lawyer in Queensland and sought legal counsel, where the lawyer wrote a letter of demand to the con-artist. When faced with a letter of demand, she fraudulently created evidence to prove that she had delivered the services I paid her for, even though my bank account showed a different story. When I saw all the lies and fake evidence, the con-artist sent to my lawyer trying to get out of paying me any money back, I was furious.

The lawyer I had was pressuring me to take it to a barrister and get the barrister's legal opinion on how much I could take the con-artist to court for in the way of damages as she had caused me a lot of stress, time and pain battling with her. I knew that getting a barrister to look at it and advise me would cost me more money than the entire refund and there was no guarantee that I would win in court either.

I then told the lawyer I could no longer afford him and that I would deal with the con artist and her lawyer directly. For months, both the con artist and her lawyer tried to bully me into just walking away.

However I was smart, and I went to Visa and put a complaint in as one of the payments was made via a visa. Visa has a three-month buyer's protection policy where they will if you have enough evidence that you did not receive the goods and services you paid for, try to get your money back for you. This took a few months for them to investigate and get the money back, but they eventually got the money from that payment back. As this was the last payment I made to her, and it was within Visa's three-month timeframe.

While waiting for visa to complete their investigation, I went to my bank as one payment was a direct electronic funds transfer. I did not know that it had passed the deadline with my bank to complain to try to get that money back until my bank told me. My bank still tried without guarantee to get the money back by going directly to the con artist's bank and investigating the situation with them where they sent her a series of letters asking for a response and for the refund, the con-artist's bank said they could not give the money back without the con artist's consent to take the money out of her account and transfer it.

Meanwhile, the con artist was legally being told not to respond and that it would go away soon by her lawyer.

My bank got back to me after three months, they told me they could not get the money back as the con-artist's bank needed her approval for the funds to be refunded, which is preposterous as she had illegally conned the money out of me to begin with.

This made me so furious, and I was so disheartened with this, but it did not stop me. I was still very determined to get all of my money back. My next point of call for the third amount of money she conned out of me was to go to PayPal and my bank together. After a month of papal not really trying hard to get my money back I had another word with my bank and they did an investigation on their side of things and found that PayPal had incorrectly processed the money and taken it out of my credit card instead of my bank account that was attached to the account I had with them and this meant that the bank could get that payment back to me within thirty-days.

I was so grateful to my bank for their wonderful efforts in getting this payment back, as it was almost half the money that I had paid the con-artist. This only meant I was waiting on Visa to get some money back from PayPal, which Visa promised they would do their best to get back as I had a powerful case.

A few months went by, and I wondered what I could do to get the money back from the Electronic Funds transfer, which was the amount the bank could not get back for me. I then decided from speaking to a wonderful, business savvy friend of mine to take it to mediation.

I did not expect for the con artist to agree to go to mediation, but she did. However, she thought that since I no longer had a lawyer that she would use a bullying tactic by telling me her lawyer would be there in mediation with her. This information stressed me out a little and so I investigated getting another lawyer to go into mediation with me, but they were just too expensive for me.

Through speaking to people in my social media network, a fellow who had helped several people prepare for and win court cases agreed to help me with my case. He coached me through putting a witness statement\affidavit together for the mediation case and I sent that to the mediator the night before the mediation happened.

I stated my case in mediation, stood firm to the truth and the con-artist and her lawyer agreed to refund the final amount of money to me, minus some legal expenses.

The biggest lessons I learnt from that experience was:

1. Standing firm to the truth and not playing dirty will set you free.
2. You only become stronger from standing up for what you believe in and what is right.
3. There are lots of ways around things, and you just need to see all the avenues and options to be able to choose the correct course of action.
4. You have a right as a customer to get your money back if you did not receive the goods or services you paid for.
5. Never ever do Electronic Funds Transfers to people or businesses for goods and services you are buying from whether it is a business or person you do not know as you cannot get your money back if you do not get what you paid for unless you take it to court or mediation.
6. Always pay with visa, PayPal, and stripe, as they have buyer's protection policies for three to six months where you can put a complaint in and get your money back if you did not get what you paid for and have proof of it.
7. Never trust someone who uses your hopes and dreams to guilt trip you into paying them more and more money.

8. Be careful who you trust in the business world, as there are a lot of dodgy people out there who will scam you for all you have if you are not careful.

Always look for the three warning signs I wrote about, as they are precious warning signs and should not be ignored if you decide to pay for goods and services from a business, you know little about.

The process I went through above was incredibly stressful and there were times I thought about giving up and did not and I was so glad I fought for my money, and I did not give up. Going through this has strengthened me and I can now coach others in situations like this and what their options are for getting a refund of their money.

(Disclaimer: the timing, gender and location of the above were changed to protect the identity of all parties involved)

Being A New Business Owner
And What To Look Out For

"Do your due diligence and research every business and person you decide to pay for goods and services. Reference check them, look them up on the internet, speak to earlier customers and clients before ever employing them to provide you with goods and services for your business. If you don't, you will regret it."

I still consider myself new to business even though this is the second business I have had. The first business I had was a personal trainer/lifestyle mentor business. In that industry, however, people do not want to take advantage of you like they are in the coaching industry. My previous business was a Sole trader business, and I set this health and wellbeing business up as a company, so tax etc are different for the two different business entities. One, you have to do a BAS every quarter, and the other you do your business tax once a year with your personal tax.

As I did not know any accountants because my previous accountant had moved elsewhere, I went off the advice of someone who I thought I could trust who I wrote about in the previous chapter of this book. As it was at the beginning of my friendship with her, I paid someone she recommended interstate to set up my health and wellbeing business as a company. This person told me his rate for setting up my company and told me the postage and handling of my actual company register was included in that price. There were no legal contracts, just a verbal agreement and an invoice I paid after receiving my company registration certificate and the expectation that he would post my company register to me once he had received it, but this never happened.

I emailed, rang, and texted the so-called accountant, as did my new accountant, for many months, trying to get him to send me my register and he never responded to either of us. He completely ghosted us for the entire time.

I put a complaint in with his accounting governing body about his behaviour and they did nothing about it, even though this so-called professional was keeping something that legally belonged to me.

After two months, I got a text from this so-called accountant saying that he would not send me my company register unless I paid him an extra $300 for it. In his text, he said if I did not send the money to him, he would deregister my company and pursue collections. The thing was, he never told me or even sent me any invoices for this extra $300 over those six months he had my register, even though he had many opportunities to do so.

He could have at any time in those six months replied to me on this because I was contacting him about it. He could have responded to me in a text message, phone call or email, but he did not because I did not owe him any more money. He was only trying to extort me for more money. It was a really desperate attempt on his part to extort more money out of me.

This all felt bad and completely wrong to me so I responded to him saying I would go to the police if he did not send it to me and that never did, he at any time tell me I owed him any money as I paid him in full the money to set up my company and for the register via a bank transfer of funds and I had the proof of it. And that in the six months, me and my new accountant were chasing him for my company register and he never even mentioned any outstanding amount because, as I said before, I paid him in full for his services and for my company register.

I thought his blackmail message to be strange, so I rang ASIC and told them about it, and they told me I did not need my company register as single directorship companies with only one director/owner do not need to have a company register at all and that I could if I wanted to take him to consumer affairs for not rendering the services I paid for.

ASIC changed my company login details on their system and sent them to me so I can manage my account on their system myself. I then blocked this person who was holding my company register for ransom as he can't do anything to my company according to ASIC as he would need my written consent which he does not have and therefore his blackmailing efforts were in vain.

So here are the lessons you need to learn from this situation.

- If someone is trying to extort you for money, they say you owe them, go back through all your communications you have had with them in writing and check it first before continuing anything with them.
- Don't overreact and take it personally as there are lots of shonky businesses out there.
- Do your research on the businesses you get involved with (internet, verbal on the phone references etc…)
- If it feels wrong go with your gut and research what they say, especially if it is something legal to do with your business (speak to governing bodies, government agencies and solicitors that will know about these things and will give you an honest answer).
- Never, unless you know they are a legitimate business, or you have done your homework on them, or you have dealt with them before, hand over more money to them

if there is no evidence in writing that they are telling you the truth.

- There is no use continuing a conversation with a dodgy business if you don't legally need the thing they are holding for ransom. Just block them as they are not worth your time of day in arguing with them.

Breaking Through My Fear Of Being
Judged When I Sing And Dance

"Who so ever judges others and acts upon their judgement should expect the same treatment in return by those they judge and hurt by their actions. The young and impressionable should be allowed to believe in themselves as much as possible o that they grow up to be a positive force to be reckoned with."

When I was younger, I was raised in a strictly religious family. I was a shy little girl where fitting in and belonging was all I wanted to do. I was always the outcast in that religion as I was the only female of my age in that branch of the church that was born in 1977 and all the other children in that religion were older or younger than me and the children there constantly let me know I was an outcast and odd.

I so desperately wanted to fit in with them and to be accepted by them. They were constantly judging me, and it wasn't just the children, it was the grownups and my family members as well. I thought I had to be perfect to fit in, and I tried so hard to be what they all wanted me to be.

There was one thing that I still hung on to that gave me joy and hope while being around those people and that was my hopes that one day, I would become an entertainer as I enjoyed singing, dancing, and acting so very much. When I was doing those things, I did not have to be what everyone else wanted me to be as it was a land of make believe where anything could happen, and you could be whoever you wanted to be without judgement.

My father used to sing as a soloist before me and my sister were born, and we used to get told all his stories about how he would go up on stage and sing.

I practiced my singing quite a lot. And it took a lot of courage and strength to put myself in front of those people and sing, but one day I had built up enough courage to be comfortable enough to sing upon the stand at my church. When I went up to the stand to sing, I was so nervous that my stomach was churning, but I did it anyway. I remember singing and somehow, I missed a verse in the song, but I continued to sing the rest of the song, anyway.

When I missed the verse, I saw the look on the people's faces in the audience and it was horrible, and it made me feel terrible, like I was a bad person, like I wasn't perfect and as though I was not good enough. They had very sour looks on their faces and they were shaking their heads in disappointment.

When I had completed the song, I came down from the stand where people pointed their fingers at me and laughed at me, and my family pointed out that I had missed a verse and they wouldn't stop going on about it. There were no words of encouragement from anyone, including my parents. They made me feel so ashamed of myself for missing that verse.

I was a little girl, so innocent and in need of comfort and words of encouragement. From then on, I became extremely hard on myself and wouldn't sing in front of an audience for years. During those years, I practiced singing on my own in my room, where no one could hear me. I immediately stopped singing every time my sister or anyone would enter the room, as I did not want to be judged and teased about it.

One day, I had built up enough courage and confidence to want to give singing in front of people another go as I didn't want to let what happened in the past detour me from giving it another go, so I tried out for a female lead role in the church roadshow. The roadshow was where the youth would every year perform an in house written play, which were musicals.

I remember a couple of hours after I tried out for the part, hearing the ladies in their meeting who were judging people's auditions for the parts in the musical and selecting the youths that would perform the roles, talking when no one was there. These ladies all had such a high opinion of their children, as their children were the children that I was up against for the lead role.

The reason I was there was that I had left something of mine backstage and needed to get it as I needed it for school. Anyway, I overheard them saying that they would never pick me for a lead role as their daughters were better than me with their voices and that I should probably stop singing all together. They laughed and brought up the past where I sang in front of the church a few years prior and how I missed the verse in the song and how their daughters would never have missed a verse like I did and that even if my voice was better than their daughters voices because of that performance years earlier, they would never put me in a lead role. They said such mean things.

After hearing that, I walked out of the back door to the stage area broken and in tears and from then on, I felt even more ashamed of my singing voice and never sang in front of anyone who I wasn't very close to ever again.

Well, now I am in my forties, and this is now changing. I am facing my fear of being judged and made fun of head on with a recording I did on YouTube of me singing, as I feel it is time to face this fear and let go of the pain and shame, I felt inside from those two childhood experiences and move forward in my life. Here is the link to the recording on YouTube https://youtu.be/7xfiMrhXl8E

I am now fine with people judging and remarking negatively on my singing voice and if I miss a few words here and there while singing along with the vocal artist of this song.

I am now putting my voice out there for the first time since my childhood and those two negative experiences that shaped how I felt about myself and my singing many years ago I have dealt with and do not affect me anymore.

Sure, my heart is pounding just now while writing this, but I will get over it and the only way of facing my fear of being judged is to just put it out there. I am not that same shy little girl anymore and I am done with having those limiting beliefs and fears I had back then, making me feel the way I did about myself and my singing.

Feel free to comment, tell me my voice is terrible, that you hate it, whatever, I do not care as I am a strong, confident woman now and have vastly different viewpoints of myself and the world now to what I did when I was a little girl. Remember, this voice has not been let out and heard for many years and is totally untrained.

Another experience that I remember that influenced the way I felt about my singing and dancing was when I was ten to twelve years of age whenever my parents used to go out and leave me and my sister at home alone, with the neighbours down the street watching us. We would go into the lounge and move all the furniture that was in the middle of the floor, to one side of the room, and we would put on some loud music like ABBA, Elvis Presley, Kylie Minogue etc and we would sing and dance around in the lounge until we got tired.

We would spin each other around and make up dance moves and pretend as though we were professional dancers and singers, yelling and screaming the words at the top of our lungs. I swear it scared the neighbour's dogs, as not soon after we started, they would join in. It was so much fun, though.

My father did ballroom dancing lessons and I think he mentioned some competitions when he was younger, and he also sang soloist for a few years at some events and so forth. I guess that may have been where I developed my love for singing and dancing from.

The two terrible experiences when I was younger that I just

mentioned to do with my singing made me believe I was a dreadful singer and I should not have been using my singing voice in public ever again, instead of hiding it away.

The children in my street used to have dance competitions in the garage of one of their houses and I used to pretend I was a dancer and dance in those competitions. I found it so much fun but then the other children became very critical of me and my dancing and started picking on it and telling me when I didn't do something the way they would have done it, so I stopped dancing after a while as they said some really hurtful things to me, and I never won the competitions, anyway. So, the only person who would see me dance until I moved out of home was my sister, who really didn't care about my dancing anyway, as she was just as bad as I was at it, so she never judged me for it.

My parents offered to pay for my sister to do ballroom dancing classes, but never even gave a second thought about asking me if I wanted to take up dance classes. This gave me more evidence that I was terrible at dancing and that I should not do it in front of anyone.

When I started renting for the first time, I remember moving my stuff out of the lounge to make an area to dance in and I used to dance on my own for hours and hours at nights and on weekends, and it felt great. Then when I was old enough to go to nightclubs, I would go, have a few drinks and dance as I figured that the people there would not be watching me anyway as they would be way too drunk to care about my dancing. It turns out I was right. Little by little I would dance at the clubs to the music. I would practice my moves at home first, then go to the clubs and dance with my friends on the dance floor which was so much fun.

I paid for and tried ballroom dancing lessons in my thirties but the people at the class had their own clicky little groups and would not dance with me and would not invite me out, so I stopped those classes after a couple of months. This was another thing that gave me evidence I was terrible at dancing.

- When I moved to Melbourne in 2017, I had no friends here, so I started salsa classes as a nice recruiter I knew suggested I do that, and he told me about the salsa foundation in the city. I started going there and the staff and instructors were so nice, welcoming, and friendly, and I have been going there ever since. I know I can be a bit of a klutz on the dance floor, but they still encourage me to keep coming back, practice and to continue giving it a go. Eventually, after a few years, I made a few good friends there, and that was great. My friends are the ones who go to the level two classes constantly as the level three classes are too late at night for us. Not once did I ever receive a word of discouragement from my friends or the instructors there at the Salsa Foundation and to that I am grateful.

Being in the pandemic and lockdown now, I really miss going to the Salsa Foundation, as it was like a second home to me, and it made me feel good about myself. I had so much fun there. Diane and Jai are amazing instructors and I feel so blessed to have learnt salsa from them.

The reason I like to sing and dance is that I could express myself artistically, just be me and have fun. There is nothing on earth like the feeling I get when I sing and dance. And now because of the pandemic, I have had to become gutsy and sing and dance in front of my Facebook community in front of the camera in a Facebook live video. I built up enough courage and guts to do it from my coaching and my Facebook community love my singing and dancing videos and are incredibly positive and encouraging.

So, I guess I can't be all that bad at singing and dancing after all. If it weren't for the pandemic, I probably would have not faced my fears of doing things in front of the camera and breaking through those fears and the limiting beliefs I had about singing and dancing. So, for me there is another upside for me with this pandemic and that is now I know I am not as bad as I thought I was from those bad defining moments in my childhood for singing and dancing.

I have now sung for my Facebook community four times and danced twice on camera. I feel so grateful to be able to do that now. This just goes to show how young and impressionable children are easily influenced negatively by other words and actions and that we need to be more careful with how we act and talk around children so that we do not instill negative limiting beliefs and fears into the young and impressionable. We should also teach our children to be less negative, judging, and critical of other children.

Please check out my Facebook profile for the Facebook lives of me dancing and the Dare To Be You YouTube Channel for videos of me singing. Due to copyright laws, the music may have been removed from the videos and they are only small recordings.

What Do We Really Have?

"Happiness is an inside job, and no amount of money or physical possessions can ever give you the happiness you seek if you are not happy within ourself and are grateful to be alive. When you find happiness from within yourself, then you will have true fulfilment and enlightenment. When you over analyse things, you paralyze yourself because you are not seeing the simplicity and beauty of what you already have."

About a year ago, I sat at the beach all on my own at lunch time. There wasn't anyone there, as it was a reasonably cool and overcast day.

I felt the need to do a self-assessment of things, so while I was there, I asked myself the below questions to get a grip on life, where I was at and where I want to be.

- Who was I in the past?
- How did I get to this point in my life?
- Who am I now?
- Who do I want to be in the future?
- Where has my life to this point taken me?
- Where do I want life in the future to take me?
- What do I need to get me there?
- Who do I need help from to get there?
- What will I need resource wise to get me there?
- How am I going to get myself there?

- When do I need to start taking action to get to my destination in life?
- What am I to people right now?
- Why is this destination I had chosen in life so important?
- Am I on track or have I somehow veered off course?
- If I have veered off course, how will I get back on course?
- Do I still use the same goals I created last year, or do I create new goals and a strategy to reach them?
- What parts of myself do I like and are working well for me?
- What parts of myself aren't working so well for me?
- With the parts of my life that I wanted to change as they weren't working for me what would my strategy be for changing and improving them?
- What people and things in my life am I grateful for right now?

What hit home for me was that we are all perfectly imperfect, we all have our strengths and weaknesses, our positives and negatives, our own sense of what is good and bad, right, and wrong. We are all a work in progress, as everyone has flaws and a past. There are people who love us and there are people who hate us. We all experience life in different ways, therefore we all have our own realities that are shaped by our past experiences, fears, and limitations. It is all a part of being human to constantly learn, grow, change, and evolve.

What I also realised is that we should not be living our lives in the past and dwelling on it, we should not be overthinking what will happen in the future as we should all be living life and being in the here and now, because in the here and now time stands still for us, and we have exactly what we need.

What this means is that we aren't living in the past and getting depressed about what has already happened, we are not worrying about the future and what may or may not happen and getting anxious about it; we are just simply in the moment and enjoying living in the moment. That, to me, sounds bliss.

Too often we let life overtake us and steer us down many fast-paced winding paths, and going down these paths may not necessarily be the best thing for us. We need to sit down, take a step back, relax, take a few deep breaths, and just experience the here and now, for the here and now is really all we have as the past has gone and the future is yet to come.

These realisations have made me grateful that I am alive and can breathe. The gift of life is the most important, most precious thing in the universe, and the ability to breathe is what keeps us alive.

Have you ever come to the same realisations I did on that day with regards to life?

Have you ever over-analysed things?

Have you ever been grateful just to be able to breathe and to be alive?

If you have never felt grateful for being alive, then perhaps you should start now as life is a gift and what we do with that gift of life makes all the difference. Therefore, monks teach meditation and breathing and live in a world where physical possessions are minimal and meaningless. They have figured out the true meaning of life and how to be happy. As the quote I have at the top of this chapter goes, happiness is an inside job, and no amount of money or physical possessions ever give you the happiness you seek if you are not happy within yourself and aren't grateful to be alive.

The Transformation

"To become the beautiful brightly coloured butterfly on the outside, you must transform how you feel on the inside so that you can let your inner light shine so brightly on the outside for the entire world to see, this is what true transformation really is. All the clothes and possessions in the outer world won't make you beautiful or truly feel good about yourself if your inner world is selfish, bitter, twisted, and broken."

For many years, I thought I was tough, as though I could make it all alone. That I didn't need anyone's help. And for many years, I was right, until one day my world collapsed in front of my eyes. I had so many things going on in my life that weren't going right for me. I couldn't understand why everything I had spent so much time on building up would crumble and fall apart.

Even when they crumbled and fell apart, I couldn't cry, as that was a sign to others that I was weak. So, I kept all my feelings bottled up and locked away. I had this persona to others that I was tough and that I wasn't to be messed with, so much so that it scared and intimidated them.

I couldn't work out why for many years people would steer clear of me and not want to be my friend because:

- I was successful in my career
- I had a nice place
- I had a nice car
- I dressed really well

• I thought I was a great person to be around.

Then, through talking to my neighbour one time on a chance passing, I realised that the tough, strong persona I was putting out there was what was making people not want to be around me. People perceived that persona of me as trouble and me being in a dark place.

In realising this, I realised I had to change if I was to make friends. So, I asked the loveliest person I knew at work to help me change. She thought it was an outside makeover that I was asking her to help me with when, in fact, to me, it was much more. It was something that would change the way I felt about and saw myself so that I could continue to change and attract into my life what I really wanted.

So, she sent me pictures of outfits, shoes, etc. that she thought would look good on me. She even sent me pictures of what hair colours would look good on me because at that point in time I had really dark blood red to black hair. And apparently, my hair was very standoffish, out there and scary to many people. People perceived me as an angry person because of my hair colour and the dark clothes I wore.

We went shopping and bought a lot of new clothes that were stylish, fresh, and light. We went through my wardrobe and threw a lot of my old clothes out and replaced them with the new clothes. I got the hairdresser to gradually take my hair lighter. They did this in two sessions to get it blond, which was a three-month process so that we did not damage my hair too much.

Over the next three to six months as I became more and more comfortable with the clothes, the fashion, colours, and styles. More and more people complimented me and wanted to be around me. So too did my own views on myself change from "I can do it all on my own' to "let's make friends and see how the friend-ships pan out." I learned so much about myself through that transformation, and it felt great. As the year went by, I learned more and more about myself and other people.

I caught up with someone I knew back then a couple of years ago and they told me they hardly recognised me anymore as I had grown and changed so much. To them, I was a completely different woman. As I had changed from being closed off, angry and overly protective of myself, to being very engaging, easy to be around, easy to talk to, lighter, happier, and more comfortable with who I was as a person.

Now I realise that:

- Sometimes it is ok to ask for help.
- It is ok to let your inner light shine.
- It is ok to want to be happy and to be happy.
- It is ok to let people in and be vulnerable.
- It is human to make mistakes as long as you learn from those mistakes.
- Everyone sees the world differently because of their past experiences.
- It is perfectly fine to be me and to love myself for who I am.

I am happy with this. Transformation on the outside for the sake of it isn't my thing but if it helps me to learn about myself, change and grow internally from it then it is something I would definitely recommend to others.

I trust you can relate to this sort of transformation and the positive effects it has on people.

- Can you relate to the positive effects it has on you and how you feel about yourself?
- If you have had an internal transformation, how did you benefit on the inside from the transformation?

Healing And Speaking Your Truth

"To be able to heal and speak your truth, stand up for what you believe in with conviction and courage and let the truth speak for itself, forgive from within you and release all the negative built upemotions that you have from the situation and move on with life."

Being the victim of three fraudulent scams in twenty months was not exactly the way I wanted to spend the last couple of years. I judged myself pretty harshly for falling prey to all of them, but then I remembered something my bank had told me when I was scammed out of $20k the first time by a crypto currency scam. What they told me is that these scammers do lots of courses and are very heavily trained to scam people, that at one point or another, everyone gets scammed, some for only a few dollars and others for thousands and even millions.

These scammers are extremely good at scamming people. The way they do this is at first, they will either advertise themselves as legitimate companies or people on the internet and social media platforms. Stalk you for a bit to get to know what you are like as a person on social media. Once they think they have figured you out they will then contact you, either inviting you to join a free event, sign up with a free account to trial their system or platform or start talking to you about a post you have put up on social media about a product, service, or business you are developing. Once they have gotten to know you and what you are interested in developing, they will make you an irresistible offer.

At first it will be for minimal down payment then later they will push you or beg you for more money for an upgrade or an app or something that is supposed to help you develop your products and services and generate a faster return on investment. If you say no, then they will offer you something a little less risqué to reel you in.

The police told me something similar except that a lot of very smart and intelligent people fall prey to their lies and deceit. That some people have also been conned out of hundreds of thousands to millions. It is nothing to be ashamed of and it is best to report these scams as soon as possible so that your bank or the authorities can investigate and possibly get your money back for you.

Remember that it is best if you are going to pay for goods and services on the internet to do it via visa and or an organisation like PayPal, where they have buyers' protection for three to six months after you have made the purchase. If you pay them through direct transfer over the internet, you can never get your money back unless you are willing to take them to mediation and or court, which can be costly.

I recall extremely well how I felt after realising these types of places scammed me. One scammer even pretended to be my friend for almost a year, pretending to be a famous author and ghost-writer who wanted to help me with the writing of my book. We spent almost every day on zoom for two to four hours talking about my life and what to put in the book and how it was going to help so many people, and I let him get close to me during the pandemic when I should never have let my guard down.

I was so heartbroken when he refused to refund my money and give me the intellectual property for my book back. I really could not do much about it as I had sent him $11k via a direct deposit via the internet and he was in the USA so the local authorities couldn't get to him or even be bothered to investigate it. I did, however, fill out an internet complaints form for the FBI over there to investigate it as it was internet fraud he had committed, but I heard nothing back from them. I was so angry with myself. I felt so ashamed of it and disappointed that I didn't see through his scam until it was too late.

The only thing I could do was to let it go. In the end, it took me almost a year to get over that and start authoring my book again, and I had to write it from scratch. I had very little confidence in myself and my abilities when I started to write my book on my own and it was a lot for me to put behind me, but with a little support and help from a friend and another coach, I started writing this book and my online articles and blogs again. I am now more than ever determined to write this book and to reach as many people as possible with the experiences I have had in my life and how I got through them and well now I have an extra chapter which I added into my book about the best friend book writing scam I went through to make people aware that these things do happen and that these people are really out there, and only after your intellectual property and your money. You really need to be careful who you tell your hopes and dreams to and who you trust when it comes to the internet and social media and those people that contact you offering to help you with your book or your business.

These experiences were big lessons for me to learn as I was naïve and didn't realise that these sorts of people and businesses were out there until I experienced it firsthand. Please heed my warning if you are starting a business and investigate everyone offering you service to help you build your business that you don't know and that has not been referred to you by a friend or family member before investing money into their goods and services.

If these people are not willing to at least get you one or two paying clients or part of the results you are after before you hand over your money, then don't invest in their products and services even if they have a networking group that you can network in and build up connections in, because some of those people in that group may be in on a scam to get money from new joiners. If you want to network and do it with other genuine people, then go to groups like BNI, as they have a great reputation and they screen their members.

As per the previous chapter, check them out on Scam watch and report any scams you come across there so that others do not fall prey to their deception and lies. One particular scam had a website developing company, accountant, and a business coach/mentor in it. It was local, and it really hit me hard, as I never knew that people in my state would do such a thing to other people. The web developer broke all my links and took all the website plugin licenses away that I paid him to use on my website before I took my website away from him.

The accountant kept my business register and tried to extort me for more money when I asked him to send me the register that was legally mine and that I had paid him in full, months earlier to set up my business. When I rang the Australian Securities and Investments Commission about it they told me I could take him to fair trade as he did not deliver the full service I paid for and that I'd did not need the Company register as I am the single owner and director of the company "Dare To Be You" and that the register is only a bit of paper and as long as I have given my new accountant authority to act on my behalf then I would be fine.

The business building coach/mentor scammed me out of thousands of dollars and did not deliver the services she promised. She promised me she would get me paying clients to the value of over $500k in eighteen months and could not even deliver a fraction of that in eight months. The business builders' package she sold me was a load of garbage because for eight months I did exactly what she advised me to do and still could not get a single playing client over the amount of $150.

So, I had to learn to release and let go of a lot of things and my expectation of how people should treat each other, which is with respect and honesty. I learnt from those experiences that there are very few people in this world who you can truly trust. Be wary of people out there promising you what they say they can deliver. Do your due diligence and thoroughly research every business you are looking to do business with so that you don't get scammed out of your hard-earned money.

To truly heal and live your truth, stand up for yourself and what you believe in with conviction and courage. Let the truth speak for itself and forgive from within you. Forgiving does not mean you have to tell them you forgive them; it is a way for you to deal with and let go of what other people have done to you so that you can move on with your life and heal.

There are a few different techniques you can use to forgive and release things that I will tell you about in the later chapters of this book.

The Ovarian Cyst

*"You must make self-care your number one priority today
before it becomes too late with physical, mental illness and
or a burnout breakdown manifest into your life."*

Have you ever really felt like you were in that much pain you were
going to pass out?

My personal experience of being in that much pain was about
eight years ago. It was an hour after I had gotten back from a run. I
lived in Milton Queensland at the time and a friend had dropped
by for a chat and a cuppa.

Before my friend turned up; I had a small twinge in my lower
left abdominal area. I thought at the time it was just a stitch and it
would go away, so I did nothing about it. My friend turned up, and
we chatted for about ten minutes and the pain just kept getting
worse and worse and it had gravitated down my left thigh. It was a
crippling type of cramp. As I was sitting down on the couch at the
time, I bent my upper body over my knees, as the pain was getting
too much.

It worried me as the only pain I ever felt that even came close
to that physically was my period pain where the cramps were so
hideous in my lower abdomen and gravitated down both legs so
that it was very difficult to walk. Lucky for me, I normally get

those pains at night. Anyway, coming back to this pain now, I was bent over my knees in so much crippling pain with my left hand on the area of my abdomen where the pain was worst for me.

I was lucky my friend was there, as he rushed me to the emergency area of the royal Brisbane hospital. I can't even remember how I got down the stairs of the unit block and into my friend's car, and I truly felt like I was going to die. I had developed a fever, and I thought maybe it was my kidneys or liver or something but wasn't sure. It was like someone had stabbed me repeatedly in a critical artery or organ.

When I got to the hospital, they took me in straight away, as they could see just how much pain I was in. They ran some tests and took some x-rays and then knocked me out with some kind of liquid painkiller through a drip for a bit. It put me to sleep for an hour while they ran more tests. When I came through, they told me it was an ovarian cyst and that it was too small to cut out.

They showed me the x-rays of it and explained a bit about it to me and then gave me some extra strong painkillers and told me to monitor it for a couple of days and if the pain got any worse during that time, I would need to see them again as that meant the cyst had gotten bigger or even ruptured. I received a prescription for strong over-the-counter painkillers. They told me generally cysts like mine will go away in a couple of days and they got my friend to take me home.

I headed to my friend's car, and he drove me home. When I got home, I went straight to bed and didn't get out of bed for the next two days until the pain subsided enough for me to get up and walk again. I remember being on painkillers for the next two weeks after that.

It drove me nuts as I am a very active person and not being able to go for my 5am run or exercise during the day really got me down, but I had to rest and take it easy. I remember for the first couple of days the pain was the worst, and I just wanted to curl up somewhere and die, as it was so intense and crippling.

While I was taking things easy, I practiced gratitude when I woke up in the mornings and also tried to meditate to calm and clear my mind and focus on recovering. The thoughts that ran through my head were things like "It could have been worse," "I'm lucky my friend was there to take me to the hospital," "I don't know how we women can give birth if the pain was anything like the pain I experienced with the cyst."

I really was lucky that the cyst wasn't a big one, and that they did not have to operate. The pain eventually went away, but I've never forgotten it, and I never ever want to feel such agonising pain again for as long as I live. To this day, I am extremely grateful that the cyst has not come back.

What I realised from this was that life was trying to slow me down as I lived such a very busy and rushed life and so the cyst was there to get me to relax, take it easy and to give me a gentle nudge to do some self-care. Throughout our lives, we must schedule in time for some self-care so that we do not burn out or have a breakdown. Self-care should be our top number one priority. Without it all kinds of illnesses, physically and emotionally, will manifest into our lives.

I Am A Woman, But I Am Not Just Any Woman

"If you don't love who you are, then you can't fully ove someone else and you can't expect anyone else to fully love you in return. Be proud of who you are, stand strong on your morals, values, and beliefs as you are extremely powerful."

I never really knew what it felt like to unconditionally love myself until I went on my journey of self-exploration. Whilst exploring what made me happy and what made me tick, I discovered many sides to myself I have never really gotten to know or even thought of exploring before. Since a very young age, they made me feel unlovable, worthless, useless, as though I wasn't enough and didn't belong and as though there was something wrong with me because I stood out, was different and not a crowd pleaser. People made me feel like I had to always please them and turn into someone else just so they would accept and love me, so I did.

I started my journey of self-exploration just before I turned thirty years of age. This journey helped me to see that being me and letting my inner self shine was the best thing for me. That being single isn't a curse, and that love from within oneself is far more important than the love you get externally from others. Because of this journey, I now know the following things which make me unique and powerful:

- I am loved and loveable .
- I am enough.
- I do belong.
- I am healthy.
- I am special because I have unique qualities inside of me that make me who I am.
- It is ok to do the things I like doing which includes singing, dancing, and exercising.
- I am strong.
- I love my life.
- I love to learn grow and change from the lessons I have learnt in my life personally and professionally.
- I am an amazing survivor having been through a good many things in my life and lived to tell the story.
- I am a lover and a fighter.
- I have emotions and its ok to let them show and be vulnerable and I am not afraid to be vulnerable.
- When I get hurt, I find the lesson in things, and I learn from them break the cycles of the past and never look back.
- I let my body deal with the emotions as and when they come up as bottling them up can cause physical and emotional illness.
- It is not easy to pick myself up put my big girl britches on and move forward with my life, but I do in the best way that I know how to.

I love that I have survived and lived to tell the tale of having been through a lot in life and how I have:

- Picked myself up from heartbreak.
- Reinvented myself a number of times.
- Moved out of being a people pleaser into a life full of self-love and self-respect.

- Dealt with massive amounts of trauma in my life as a child and an adult.
- Lived through harassment, bullying, rape, abduction, and abuse.
- Survived financial hardship.
- Survived a scare with cervical cancer and an ovarian cyst.
- I worked in highly political and volatile workplaces.

I am daring and bold as I face my fears head on. Some examples of me doing this are below:

- I have faced my fear of being out of control when I went in a V8 supercar ride where I wasn't the driver .
- I jump out of an airplane to face my fear of heights.
- I do Facebook live videos to move me out of the fear of not being enough, not being perfect, being judged.
- I went into floatation tank to face claustrophobia.
- I go into large crowds at concerts etc when I was agoraphobic.
- When I am afraid of getting and being lost, I go on holidays on my own to foreign countries.
- When I am afraid of being and getting hurt emotionally, I get really vulnerable with people.
- When I was afraid of not belonging, I show people who I am as I am very beautiful on the inside and if they don't like me too bad for them.
- When I believed I was Ugly I bought myself a photo shoot that change my perspective and outlook on my outer appearance.
- In my twenties I used to hate reading now I read all the time

- When I was afraid of being alone, I don't jump from relationship to relationship I go through a phase of self-exploration where I am alone for long periods of time.
- When I was emotionally lost and did not know who I was I spent large amounts of time by myself finding out who I was and constantly surprise myself with the things I found out about myself on this journey of life.

What I have learnt from all of this is that life is so very precious, and you cannot make anyone else happy unless you can love and make yourself happy first. Therefore, I face my fears head on, and I look at things from a different angle or perspective.

I am and always will be a work in progress, but for me, the learning, growing, and transforming is exciting, and it challenges me in a good way. To me, if it doesn't challenge me, then it isn't worth doing. I constantly push myself out of my comfort zone and don't mind if others give me a little nudge as well from time to time.

In the end these things make me unique, different and special and for now just daring to be myself, knowing and loving myself is more than enough for as I am an amazing woman with a heart of gold and if you get to know me, you see that I don't do things because I have an agenda; I do things because I genuinely want the best for myself and those around me.

I love being a strong, bold, and wonderful woman.

What Equality Mean In A World Where Societal Views Are Still In The Stone Ages

"Equality of the sexes still isn't there in society yet as we still teach our daughters to want to become wives, make our husbands happy and be stay-at-home mothers and wives and to put family first above ourselves. Whereas we teach the men that they need to go to school, get good grades, get a good job so that they can support a family by being the breadwinners. Who are teaching children at such a young age to give us equality in life?"

So, to give you a little history on how things have been for many years, I have done some research and written it up below, which fits in well with how I was raised in an unequal society.

According to theweek.com, the first recorded evidence of marriage ceremonies uniting one woman and one-man dates from about 2350 B.C., in Mesopotamia. Over the next several hundred years, marriage evolved into a widespread institution embraced by the ancient Hebrews, Greeks, and men.

From way back then, we have been teaching girls to diminish themselves to make themselves less significant than men within society. Every culture within society as we know it today, instructs girls they can have ambition but not too much of it, that women should aim to be successful but not overly successful otherwise it becomes threatening to men.

Because I am female, I am expected to aspire to marriage and to be a single woman is wrong and not really accepted within society. I have experienced this firsthand as have some of my female extended family members who I used to be close with years ago.

Once immediate family members know you are single, they ask you to the point of harassing you every time they see and speak to you "when are you going to settle down, get married and have a family of your own?" Some will even try to set you up on a blind date and or make jokes at your expense about how you are single to make you feel bad for being single.

In my family, when growing up from a very young age, they taught me that they expected that I make my life choices, but always keeping in mind that marriage is the most important thing. They taught me that marriage is the ultimate goal for a girl and that it will bring about joy, love and mutual support and respect.

The question that I know of many women these days is why we get taught to aspire to marriage and the boys don't get taught the same thing. If there are equal sex opportunities in the world, then shouldn't both boys and girls get taught the same thing, whether that is marriage or a career?

Girls are raised to see each other as competitors in life with regards to men and dating. Girls are not taught this for what they accomplish or what they do for work, although a lot of women feel threatened extremely easily in the workplace by other women because of their insecurities. If girls were emotionally intelligent and taught how to be more secure as children, then in their adult years they would not feel so threatened by another successful woman in the workplace. They would see them more like equals and feel less insecure.

I have had some female friends that were employed in some pretty powerful roles in upper management of some companies that say they are employers of choice and have equal opportunity in their culture but the men below them end up making things so difficult for them to stay in those roles that they end up leaving.

Society teaches boys to embrace their sexuality, but girls are taught that they cannot be sexual beings in the same way that boys can. We teach girls they should keep their sexuality and sexual orientations to themselves and that they should not speak up about these things as it is shameful for their families. Men, however, can go around telling their friends how many women they have slept with and make a competition out of it.

When a girl or woman is sexually harassed or bullied in the workplace, or sexually abused and raped in general, we teach girls it is their fault that they must have worn or done something to provoke the man and that they should be ashamed of themselves, like the man cannot control himself in those situations and if the girl reports it then they get treated in court like the predator and not the victim. The lawyer of the accused in trial will stop at nothing to get the man off the hook and to prove the woman was the one in the wrong and she provoked him. Oh please, what a load of garbage. A woman does not twist the man's arm behind his back and make him rape her. Therefore, fewer women report that they have been sexually assaulted and or raped every year. There is a tiny percentage of women who report these acts being done to them each year as they are afraid of judgment, afraid for their lives and do not want to relive the experience in trial and so they would rather walk away with their dignity intact and pretend like it never happened.

I know what trial is like for a woman who has been raped, as I have been to trial three times in my life, and it definitely makes the woman relive what they went through in the rape because the defense lawyer will bend and twist things around to make the woman break and to get the predator off the hook. It is one of the worst experiences I have ever had to go through in my life next to the rape itself. In that way, the justice system is really a joke. They would be better off putting the predators on trial with a lie detector on them and asking them what happened than to drag the poor innocent woman through the victimisation of trial where she is treated like the guilty party. In trial, I was strong enough to send both rapists to prison, but they weren't sentenced for life like they should have been. They sentenced one for less than two years and the other one less than eight years for three rapes.

269

According to https://www.rape-dvservices.org.au/news/the-truth-about-sexual-assault website:

"girls\women have the right to go anywhere, wear anything, and do anything just as men do. The person who does the raping and assaulting is the person who does the assaulting - no one else."

"Choosing to sexually assault or rape someone when drunk is just as much a crime as doing it when sober (just like choosing to rob a bank or hit a pedestrian in a car when drunk)."

Yes, that is right. It is a conscious choice they make to do these acts. And it is disgusting that people get off on the technicality of being drunk and not in their right mind when doing it. Like the alcohol forced them to do it. Of course, the alcohol took their free will away. What a load of shit!

They label you a feminist if you are a woman who believes in the social political and economic gender equality. There are still women today who are amazing at what they do, being knocked back by equal opportunity companies for jobs not because they did badly in the interviews but because of the way they look, sound and because those companies are still predominantly male based, and the interviewers would rather hire a man for the role as they don't think a strong, competent professional woman can handle being in a male dominated environment. I have had this happen to me by a global and well-known company several years back and it was not fun. When it came to giving me a reason, they would not hire me, they told me the truth and did not hide it.

I can tell you right now that those views are biased, as I have worked in a male dominated industry for twenty-two years and am still in that industry now. Yes, I have come across difficult situations in my time, but they have not stopped me from working in this industry as I have learnt how to adapt my approach to every situation to come to the best possible result for my employer.

Therefore, I say that the beliefs and views of society are still in the stone ages or caveman era and need to be changed. Females are not less than men in the workplace and or in the home. You are allowed to be happy and single for as long as you like, and we should teach girls and boys the same morals and values in life regarding their choices, whether that is career oriented, or family and marriage related.

Please listen to the words of this YouTube video, in particular the lyrics that are in the middle of this video around one minute and twenty-six seconds into it as you will find it also points out some inequalities in the modern age and the person talking also asks some relevant questions. https://www.youtube.com/watch?v=IyuUWOnS9BY

Women should be treated as equals everywhere in society, including the home and workplace at all times.

You Are Limitless And Amazing!

"Stand tall, stand proud of who you are and know that you are powerful beyond your wildest dreams. All it takes is self-love, self-respect, and self-belief to touch the lives of others, for you are limitless and amazing, just as you are."

Sometimes you have to stop looking for what's not there in yourself because other people criticize you and say that it is there. Don't beat yourself up over those things that aren't there.

Know who you are, have faith, confidence, love, and respect who you are because you are amazing and awesome. Others only see what they want to see as they do not see a true representation of you, but simply what is in their own map of the world which is limited to their past experience, limiting beliefs and fears.

You are limitless in who you can be, what you can do and have, if you only just believe in yourself and your own value/worth. With belief in yourself, you find you can do and be anything in life.

Never let others put you down or judge you when they have not walked in your shoes or lived a day of your life. It is really none of our business what other people think of us anyway, so why bother wasting time worrying about it?

There are always going to be critics in your life, and you really just need to tell them to go away. You are limitless and amazing, just as you are.

I can recall for many years being judged harshly by my family for being single and not settling down with a man. They used to say things like:

- When are you getting married?
- When are you settling down with a nice man?
- When will you be having a family?
- Why are you still single?
- Why can't you find a good man and settle down?

This used to hurt me as they were always pushing me to be the stereotypical woman who meets a good man, gets married and has a family. They used to make me feel tiny because I wasn't the stereotypical woman. I was single, and they didn't really want or know what was best for me. They wanted to shove a square peg in a round hole and stereotype me.

It used to make me angry and upset me. They couldn't just be happy for me because I was happy with who I was and didn't need or want to be the same as every other woman. I was me, unique and special just the way I was. That was enough for me, but they could not see it. All others could see was what they wanted to see, which was through their own rose-coloured tainted version of the world, and what they wanted me to be like in that version.

It took me many years to get past their critical judgement of me and the way I lived. I had to limit my contact with those people so that their negativity would not bring me down. During my personal development journey, I cared less and less about who others thought I should be and more about what made me happy and who I wanted to be in life. This gave me true self-acceptance and peace of mind. I am much happier now because I now live in my truth and my inner world reflects my outer world. I know that through my life's story, I can and will touch and change the hearts and lives of many people.

You Don't Need To Be Perfect

*"Stop looking to be perfect, as there is no such thing.
To make something perfect means you will always procrastinate
and never complete/deliver it. Near enough is good enough. So
do as they do on agile projects, get the rough/base prototype
delivered and put the improvements in future releases."*

You don't have to have all the answers, you just need to know where to look to get the answers.

I have been in the Information communication and technology industry for twenty-two years now.

When I first started working in ICT, I was twenty-one, and knew nothing about computers, apart from what my partner at the time had shown me. So, I started a diploma in IT at TAFE and got part way through it when I got an IT traineeship with the government. I have been in the ICT industry ever since.

Contrary to what people say, you don't have to be perfect; you don't have to have all the answers to be in the ICT industry as it is an ever growing and ever evolving industry which makes it very challenging at times. I love the challenge of having to keep up with technology, as it has helped me to grow and change personally throughout the years.

During my time in this industry, I have contracted to multiple large private and government organisations in Brisbane and in Melbourne. I have found my way around multiple different systems, processes and so forth to do my job for those companies and have played with the hardware and software components, including multiple different networks, operating systems, and standard operating environments.

I have now been in project management in ICT for twelve years. I have managed multiple different IT, business transformation, communication, network infrastructure and data centre refresh, Adobe cloud, campaign, forms, experience manager and asset management, platform, and web development projects.

Until about two years ago, I used to think that a Project Manager needed to do things perfectly and know everything. With the projects I have managed over the past two years I realised that these expectations I had of myself as a project manager were way too high and because of the size and complexity of the projects that I could not know everything about the project and that I had to lean on the Technical Leads and Lead Business Analysts to get the information I needed for some reports I was doing. These projects were quick paced, with lots of moving parts to them, and not one person on the project could know everything about those projects. This meant that I needed to ask for help and that was hard for me.

I rose to the challenge and engaged with other people in the organisation and on the project more, so that I could learn more about the projects and what the team members did. Eventually, this got easier, and I built up some really strong and healthy working relationships with my team members and the project's stakeholders.

I did this by implementing a strategy of asking for help when I did not know something, and I engaged with my managers when I could see a risk was going to turn into an issue rather than when it became an issue. When people and things challenged me, I would seek advice and guidance from those above me who could help me see things differently and who could show me other options on how to handle different situations.

A manager I had over a year and a half ago told me that the one thing he liked most about me is that I am so easy to give feedback to as I will immediately go implement the feedback as I am flexible in my ways. I love to collaborate with my team and the clients as it not only helps me, but it also helps them.

Perfectionism doesn't exist and does not belong in any industry, let alone one that is constantly changing and evolving all the time. If you don't ask for help or collaborate with people, you will get left behind.

Good open, honest communication with managers, team members and clients is best when you are a project manager. When you use good, open, honest communication with people, you earn their respect, trust and they then want to work with you.

The points I am getting at here are:

- Don't be afraid to not have all the answers.
- Don't be afraid to ask for help
- Don't take all the burden of the issues on yourself if you can escalate up and get the issue resolved quicker
- Don't be afraid to communicate with and ask for guidance from others on the challenges you are facing as they will more than likely have a different view or perspective on it and may be able to help you see and think about things differently.
- Being in a senior role doesn't mean you are perfect, and you have all the answers because you quite simply don't as you learn things as you progress on the project and others can help you with filling the gaps.
- Nothing and no one is perfect so ease up on yourself.

Here is the link to my YouTube video I made about this topic: https://youtu.be/nauRChqD8AM

The Latest SCAM And
The Lesson I Learned From It

"Don't let your guard down too quickly with other people, especially if you don't know them that well. The best way to preserve yourself is to protect yourself."

I have authored this book from a different perspective, as someone who I thought was my best friend in the USA recently scammed me. He scammed me for my manuscript IP of my life's story and most of my life's savings (thousands of dollars).

The scammer pretended to be an author and a motivational public speaker and offered to get me a great publishing deal on my book; he said he had lined up a typist, website developer, and an editor to help me with my book and he also pretended to have amazing contacts with agents for publishing, movie rights, and audio book deals. He promised he would help me put my life's story into a book that would read very well, as I have never authored a book before. I have only written articles and blogs, so the concept of writing in chapters was new to me, and I wanted it to be a success. He pretended he was a wonderful ghost writer that could piece the chapters of my life into a book that would read very well.

He used my dreams of buying and doing up an orphanage to his advantage when getting close to me and getting me to open up to him about my life. We were friends on Facebook for three years prior and had chatted on and off during that time. He would even ring and talk to me from time to time. I was silly in believing that he cared and really wanted to help.

Dario convinced me to courier over to him my manuscript, which I had handwritten asap and once he had it, he would scan it and send me the scanned digital copy back for safekeeping. He promised to ghost write the parts from video interviews, we had done every night for twelve months into my book and turn it into an amazing book. He even had a one-page contract that we both signed, so I really thought he was legit and a genuine friend in what he was offering me regarding his help.

It was only since October 2019 that he started making more regular contact with me. We became close throughout the lockdowns from COVID as we used to do zoom video meetings every night about me, my day, and my life for my book. These zoom sessions would go anywhere between one to four hours in duration.

He made me feel acknowledged, validated, listened to, valued and as though someone actually cared about me, how I felt and what I had to say. I had never experienced a friendship quite like the one I thought we had, as it was deep, respectful, and strong. I thought this friendship would last a very long time, but I was wrong.

I researched him on the internet when things went wrong but because I was searching for his pen\author name, nothing came up in the google search but his website, Facebook, LinkedIn, and good reads reviews. I needed to have searched for his real name, which I did not know until a month before I sent the funds over to him. It wasn't until six months into our friendship that he told me he had some people lined up to help me make my book a success and I fell for his lies as he was a very smooth talker and very good actor, and he came across as genuine.

I thought I could trust him as I had gotten to know him very well over the six-month period. So, when he told me about the professionals, he had lined up to help me with my book and asked for the money to pay them; I sent him the money. I thought I was sending it to him so he could pay the typist, editor, and website developer he had lined up. He told me he had completed the clean-up of the book and added the extra information to my book. He said he was not computer literate and so scanning it and sending it to me would be hard for him to do, but he would get the librarian to help him with it at his local library.

Once he had received the wire transfer, he told me his typist he had on payroll had resigned and he had to find another typist he could trust to type it. I was so annoyed by that. Over the space of four months, he told me about four other typists that either didn't have the time to type it or they cost too much.

I was getting so frustrated with him and so annoyed over it all. He regularly told me he felt humbled and honoured to be helping me with my book and if I ever felt that I could not trust him I could get another ghost writer to help me with my book as it would be a massive success with or without him.

When he finally found a typist, he said she had COVID and needed to recover. A month after she recovered, she had the manuscript on the table at her mother's house and an industrial fan blew the pages all over the place and he apparently did not find out about that until he was out-of-town doing a major motivational speaking gig in America at some of the black rights protests where he ended up getting sick and misdiagnosed with COVID when he had food poisoning. So, he got given a double dose of the COVID medication, had an allergic reaction to it and almost died from it.

He had two of his cousins text me from his mobile while he was in the hospital, giving me updates on his progress every day. Once he was well enough, he had one of his cousins contact the typist and find out where the typing was at and apparently the typist when she found out he was in the hospital went on a holiday with her mother and travelled all around the USA and would not be back for seven weeks to complete the typing.

When the typist finally returned home, she then had problems with her laptop and could not use it to do the typing, which meant that any typing she had done was lost. Dario then tried to recover the data from the laptop but it was too far gone and so he gave her a new laptop to use for the typing. He said she was lazy and kept stalling with the typing and had already been paid $1.5k USD of my money as a down payment for the typing and he gave her another chance, even though I told him to fire her. A week later, he forwarded on to me a very basic query letter for my book. Then he fired her. He told me she never gave him back the manuscript for my book.

Since I had the typist's email address from the forwarded email, I contacted her and told her what he had told me about her and what was going on. I threatened to take legal action if she self-published my book and or didn't send the manuscript back to me. It was odd that she never contacted me back. Dario told me she contacted him and was angry with him, saying she might as well keep the manuscript and the notes for my book since she was going to be sued. I had a massive fight with him on this and he was so mean and horrible, threatening my job and all sorts even though I only had contact with him after work hours and on weekends when I was not working. I rarely do personal things during work hours as I have the work ethic that if I am getting paid to do the work between certain hours, then that is all I will do.

I then looked up the typist on LinkedIn and contacted her again, and that was where the truth came out. He never gave her the notes or the manuscript for my book, and he never paid her to type it up. We compared stories to what he told both of us. I found out that everything he told me, and that we had built our friendship upon was a lie.

I found out that his Facebook profile was his author's pen

name, which was fake and that he did not make any money from his book he had apparently written. He was a broke poor man who lived in the roughest part of his city. He had a son who was in prison and that he was suing his local church for racism, among other things.

When I told him I had the goods on him and wanted my money back and the IP for my book, he refused to return them and started emailing, messaging me on WhatsApp and sending me messages on messenger every hour with nasty horrible things to hurt me. He pretended to be a very religious person, always praying, going to church on Sundays and spurting verses from the bible at me regularly and he was big on preaching forgiveness. Even though he was unwilling to forgive anyone for what they had done to him in the past.

He had me completely fooled, thinking that we were best friends when all he was really doing was scamming me and making sure I could not get my money back.

I found out he wasn't who he made himself out to be and he wasn't doing what he said he was doing in the past number of months, so I had lots of negative emotions to process because of this. I am sure he has done this to other people before.

When I first found out he had scammed me, I was SOOO angry with myself and extremely hurt because this was someone who I let my guard down with and he knew everything about me, things I had told no one in my life. I felt betrayed, as he was a friend of mine for three years prior to us getting close. I felt annoyed with myself for falling for his scam and not listening to my gut instinct when it first told me there was something wrong and for thinking he was a legitimate author as he had the cover of his book as his profile picture on Facebook and LinkedIn.

I was also angry that Facebook and LinkedIn did not and do not prevent people like that from creating fake accounts on their social media platforms. I was very angry at myself as he had played me like a fool for what felt to me like a long time.

However, I don't want you to think of me as a victim, as I have learnt some precious lessons from this. These lessons are below:

- Don't open up too quickly to people on the internet COVID or not.
- Check out if they are legitimate when it comes to what they say they do for a living.
- Never get too involved with people online.
- Always get proof of progress when checking in on a project you are working on with other people particularly if they are online.
- Never wire funds over the internet to anyone use a credit card or a system like stripe or PayPal so you get buyers protection, invoices, and receipts.
- Don't give people too many chances.
- If they are on social media, then they are computer illiterate and don't let them tell you otherwise.
- Always keep a soft copy of whatever you send to people even if it is just a scan of it on your computer with you.
- If it sounds too good to be true, then don't invest in it.
- Always try and find out if people are who they say they are before getting to close to them.
- When my gut says something then trust it as it is always right, so don't give them the benefit of the doubt.
- Don't trust other people to do things for you that you need to make the time to do yourself.
- These scammers are professionals, and they do courses and go through a lot of heavy training to be able to play a person like this so do not blame yourself if this happens to you.

The reason I am telling you this is to make you aware that these scammers are out there, and they will invest a lot of time and effort into getting you to trust them before scamming you, so be careful and learn from my mistakes.

This scammer is releasing another nine books this year, which I am sure are not his work but are from his fraudulent activities online. I have reported him to the authorities (FBI in the USA) and my bank and am unsure whether the authorities will do anything about it. I really hope they do as my bank couldn't get my money back, but they can now protect other customers from sending money to him.

If you think you have been scammed, put a report on SCAM Watch and report it to your local fraud squad. Also report it to your financial institution as they may get your money back if you used a credit card, PayPal, or stripe to send the funds. Be aware that if it is through PayPal, I think they give you protection for six months and credit card companies will give you buyers protection for three to six months within which to get your money back. You must report it to your financial institution as soon as you can. Don't leave it too late.

For internet transfers you may not get your money back unless it is within the first couple of weeks that you report it as it is harder for the bank to get the funds back as the company or person the funds get transferred to has to give permission to send the funds back which is silly and highly unlikely. You may need to take legal action through other means if they can't get it back for you.

How To Process Heavy, Sad, Or Negative Emotions

"Success comes from going deep within the darkest heaviest moments of your past and processing the emotions attached to them. You will become unstoppable as nothing from your past will ever be able to hold you back from your success."

Throughout my life, I have had my ups and my downs. Been through the ringer of life more times than you can count on both hands.

Because of this, I realised that the strength of one's character is not in how you handle the ups but how you handle and get through the downs that lead to learning and growth for you.

When I get really heavy negative emotions, I fall back on a few key things that are in my holistic health support system that I developed throughout the course of my life.

These key things are below:

1. Sit with the emotions in a non-judgemental way and process them.
2. Let your mind, body and spirit experience the sensations and process those emotions in a warm, gentle, and loving way.

3. Do not think, judge, or label those emotions as bad things just stay present with them as you know they will pass.
4. Don't try to avoid them or push them away as they will come back to you but much stronger latter on in life
5. Know that whatever it is that has gotten you down won't stay forever, and you can and will get through it.
6. Don't force yourself before your body tells you it is ready to process the emotions. Just let them come when the time is right.

Once those emotions have left then do the following things:

1. Make a list of things to be grateful for in your life
2. Do something fun that will cheer you up like
3. Read a funny book
4. Watch a funny movie
5. Listen to a funny podcast
6. Exercise
7. Sing
8. Dance
9. Listen to music
10. Meditate
11. Compliment someone on something
12. Thank someone for doing something for you
13. Do something nice for someone else
14. Do personal development courses and learn more about myself?

1. Scream into a pillow or cushion to get some of those emotions out. While screaming visualise all those

negative emotions rising up and out of your body and going into the cushion and being trapped there. Where they can't harm you anymore then throw the cushion far away from you.

2. Make a list of all the good deeds and achievements you have done in your life and how doing these deeds and achieving these achievement/goals have positively impacted your life and the lives of those around you.

3. Call a friend and speak to them about it (vent, scream and cry) if need be.

4. Look at old photos of things that made you happy in your life and reminisce on them and really get into and feel the positive and empowering emotions you got from those experiences.

5. Make a list of the challenging times you have been through in your life and how you got through them to be where you are now. Give yourself a pat on the back and be proud of yourself and how far you have come.

6. Make a list of goals that you want to achieve and break them down into bite sized chunks that you can do daily, weekly, or monthly. Then put them into a plan on paper and challenge yourself to do those things and tick them off every time you do them. Once you have done one of things on your list then celebrating having done it as celebrating the small things you do is just as important as celebrating the achievement of big goals. Sometimes the achievement of the smaller things can be more gratifying than the achievement of the bigger things.

7. Know that you are you for a reason and that you are unique and special in your own way and be proud of who you are. You are an original so "Dare To Be YOU" in every way you can.

I have many other techniques that you can try but for now try the ones above and keep track of how you go. As we are all unique and different, some techniques will work better than others for you. So, find the ones that work best for you and create a ritual that you can do daily with them. As this will embed new positive beliefs within you.

Modern Day Life And Feeling Lost

"When you feel all alone and lost, like the road is dark and there is no way home to that happy place, hold on. Imagine the path to your dreams being right in front of you, take a couple of deep breaths and trust yourself enough to be courageous and go down that path you imagined in front of you one small step in front of the other until you get to your destination. Let your intuition show you the way."

It is so easy to lose ourselves and what we are all about. I mean, there are so many more things to do and see these days. There is the theatre for live plays and musicals, movies to see, there are so many hobby clubs and training organizations you can join and do things in and meet new people. Why wouldn't you feel a little bit lost as you lose yourself in lots of things in the outer world?

There is family life and work life where we are all constantly trying to do things that please others and therefore not doing what is best for ourselves as we deny our own feelings and needs in order to be liked, loved, accepted and to be loved.

How we ever had the time to stop and think about ourselves for a minute is beyond me, as we don't get to think about what we want and need, apart from pleasing others that would give our lives more meaning, self-love, self-respect, and fulfilment?

We know the job won't last forever as we will need to retire one day or move on to something more challenging where there is greater career progression. We know the children will one day grow up and leave home, leaving us all alone. Not all friends are lifers and will leave when time is up. Some friends are there for a short time to teach us the lessons we need to learn in order to grow. Some friends may stay for a while longer because there are lessons, we need to teach them, and others are lifers as we learn and grow with them on the same path. Sometimes it is really hard to tell which is which in this world.

We know that not all romantic relationships survive or are for the long term because of incompatibility, growing apart, falling out of love, insecurities, selfishness, violence whether that is domestic, physical, sexual, emotional, psychological abuse, narcissistic tendencies, manipulation, cheating and not knowing the other person as well as we thought we did, and the list goes on and on...

We know that not all families are close and will stand by each other through the good and the bad times. Not all families love each other in exactly the same way. Not all families do what is best for each other. Whether or not we like it, let's face it: some families use abuse, narcissism, and manipulation to get you to be who they want you to be and to put their needs ahead of your own.

Our modern day lives have become unbalanced and rushed as some of us put family first, or partners first, some of us put our friends first and some of us put our careers and business first. What happened to just being able to take a step back and putting ourselves first for once? Do we even dare to?

The rushing and putting everything and everyone else's needs first before our own is called life! Well, at least that is what everyone I speak to tells me.

SO WELCOME TO LIFE AS WE KNOW IT! ISN'T IT GRAND?

Did you ever think your life would turn out like this when you were a child?

The bright side is that I have been through all of the above scenarios in my life and have helped people exactly like you with my holistic health support system turn their lives around. My program will help you find out who you are, who you want to become, and fill the gap between the two so that you can nurture, care for, and love yourself again. I can help you regain control of your life and to put your needs at the top of the priority list where they belong for you to:

- Know and love yourself.
- Set healthy boundaries that will teach other people to respect you and your needs as well as teaching you how to respect yourself in a healthy and loving way.
- Work towards being outstanding in life by becoming more goals oriented and focused on what you want and your success.
- Work towards being unstoppable with relationships.

In my signature coaching programs, I have put all the knowledge and tools I discovered throughout the years of my life through trial and error, I was never taught or given as a child or adult, by family and educational institutions into these programs. These are programs I developed through life experience that have helped my clients and myself become ourselves, outstanding and unstoppable, in our lives and relationships.

Life Is Like A Book

*"Life is like a book. The blank pages are the parts of your life
that have not happened yet. The chapters are the phases or
experiences of your life. We start our lives with a fully empty book
and as we live our lives, the pages fill up with writing about our
experiences. You can always change the direction of the current
chapter in your life by making a different choice and going down
a different path."*

Life has a beginning and an end, just like a book.

If you think of life in this way, then you will see that what you choose to put in between the front cover and the back cover of your book is your choice.

Your life's book is filled with all your choices and the strategies you run to be who you want to be, do what you want to do, have what you want to have. Each chapter of a book from the beginning to the middle, which is where you are now, has multiple different choices and roads you could have taken, and you enacted the strategies from the decisions you made in the past to reach your goal or destination.

Some people remember the past and how it got them to the present day clearly, and others don't. The reason some people don't remember the roads they have travelled on or the choices they have made in life and the events that followed is that as per a book the pages get old and may fall out of the book or something accidentally gets spilled on some pages and therefore the writing on the pages for those specific chapters becomes unreadable, smudged, blurred or are no longer in the book where they once were.

You can still choose to do things to change like: defining moments, timeline, past life regression therapies.

When we make a choice and run a strategy, we then put an emotional value on them and from that emotional value comes our priorities on what we remember clearly, what becomes a distant and blurred memory and what we don't remember at all.

We are the inventors of our lives and if we choose to in the middle of life/our book we can change, choose a different path or direction to take and make a different decision, become someone new, different, and amazing.

Our past does not make us who we are and does not have to influence our decisions about what we want, who we are or where we are heading in life now. You are who you are in the here and now, so stop blaming the person you are now for your current decisions and strategies you are running from your past.

If you don't like your past then you can choose to change the emotional attachment you have put on the memories for those particular events, turn that story you have told yourself about what happened into something positive that will drive and fuel your passion to be and do better in the here and now and to move you toward the person you want to be in the future.

Don't be afraid to start a new chapter of your life or to simply stop writing in the old book and reinvent yourself by writing a new book. Once you have that, you will feel proud of yourself as you are a new person. Don't let fear hold you back from creating the life you have always wanted and being the most amazing version of yourself that you can be.

Dare to be someone new, brave, confident, and exciting and take responsibility for your life and the choices you have made and move forward with power, grace, and passion.

Dare to be YOU, Yourself, Outstanding and Unstoppable Today!

Here is a YouTube video I have created to tell you about this in more detail: https://youtu.be/-P1vWMnVpIQ

I want you to watch the video and ponder on it and daydream about what the next chapter of your book will turn out like and put a strategy in place to make it happen. There is no time like the present to work toward your future.

Cutting The Umbilical Cord Permanently

*"Empower yourself right now to cut the umbilical cord
to those that have for so long treated you like a doormat.
This will be hard, I know, as you have built up habits to
tolerate this behaviour from others. You are worth so
much more than that. You deserve to be loved and
respected for the wonderful person you are."*

I am going to tell you about something that happened to me where I finally realised that it was time to cut the umbilical cord and move on with my life.

On the night of Sunday February 19th, 2020, some family members who I told eighteen months earlier that I no longer wanted them to contact me because they are very negative and don't treat me the way they should, as they used to use me as their emotional punching bag when things went wrong with my sister, decided that they would get the police on me for not contacting them and not wanting them in my life anymore. They did this by filing a false police report saying that I was suicidal and that they were concerned that I would harm myself.

It was so embarrassing to have the police come to my place at 10pm, just before I was going to bed, and bash on the door, yelling my name for all my neighbours to hear. I live in a unit block and their voices were very loud.

I was in my PJs at the time, and it terrified me, as I was dazed and so exhausted and had had no one do that before. From behind my front door, I debated with myself whether or not to open the door, as I thought maybe it was a crazy person knocking. I opened the door a tiny bit to see who was there and saw these police officers.

I invited them in, and they told me what these horrible family members had reported about me. These family members reported they thought I would self-harm or commit suicide and that someone should stop me. They filed their report in Queensland, and I live in Victoria, so it was certainly odd that a false police report would get actioned from another state away without all the facts being known first. The fact that I had not been in contact with these family members since September the year before when they chose to take my sister on a holiday over fixing the very broken relationship, they had with me on my birthday. I gave the police the background on the relationship I had with these family members and assured them I would never do those sorts of things.

I felt angry, upset, embarrassed and ashamed of being related to these people and because they thought so low and horribly about me as I would never harm myself as that is not the person I am and anyone who knows me knows I am one of the most resilient, stable, and reliable people they know.

I apologized to the police for these people having sent them on a wild goose chase over to my place for no reason just so they could show they still had some control over me. I also explained that I have never had a good relationship with these people and that I had to cut them out of my life quite a while ago because they did not treat me right when they were in my life.

While inside my unit, the police could see the psychology and coaching books I had on my coffee table alongside my work laptop, as I was studying coaching. They also commented on them. They could also see the multivitamins and magnesium powder sitting on my kitchen bench. Nothing in my place looked odd, suspicious, or out of place to them.

I also explained to the police that I have never had these family members even be there for me in my times of need in my forty-three years on this earth and now because they want back into my life they tried to make out as though I am not in my right mind. I told them I found that behaviour concerning, and I also told them I don't want those people back in my life and want nothing to do with them and asked the police to pass my message on to them.

I told the police that maybe had these family members not paid for and taken my sister to America on my forty-second birthday and instead stayed in Australia to work on the very broken and almost non-existent relationship we had, then things may have been different. These family members had always treated me like they did not want me and as though I was a second-rate daughter to them.

The police then apologized for disturbing me and went on their way as they could see that the report that was filed was false. After they left, I tried to go to sleep but could not as it spooked me and annoyed me that these family members could be so heartless and cruel by doing and thinking such things about me. I wondered if anyone else out there has ever experienced this sort of situation before. I wondered why they wanted to show me they still had some form of control over my life after so long of not being in my life. The answers to these questions I will probably never know.

After the police left, I made my last contact with these family members and told them how it made me feel and told them that under no uncertain circumstances would I ever allow them to come back into my life that they were to never contact me again.

Not having them in my life is for the best as my mother is a narcissist and controlling and loves to tell my secrets to the entire world. Like the time I was raped and abducted, she and my father spread that all over their church to people I didn't even know. They should have kept this information private instead it was used by them to get people to feel sorry for them in their church.

I guess I secretly hoped that one day these family members would change and treat me with the same respect as they treat my older sister and that their promises and apologies were not just empty ones with no actions behind them.

For most of my life I have been secretly hoping that my family loved me enough to make the necessary changes that would show me they wanted and loved me, but they never did. Whenever they needed someone to beat up on emotionally, about things not going right for them, they would ring me and tare strips off me, as I was not living the way they wanted me to.

They called me the sinner, the naughty, ungrateful child. I used to hear the words I love you come out of their mouths, but there were no actions to back up their claims. Their actions always contradicted what they said to me. When I was in more contact with them in my twenties and part way through my thirties, their actions would chip away quite a lot at my self-esteem, self-love and confidence levels to the point where I had a very low self-esteem and didn't know that people could treat me differently so I used to attract into my life people exactly like them who would psychologically abuse, emotionally abandon and treat me like a piece of dirt under their shoe.

I tried to break free from them several times and little by little, limiting my contact with them over the years so that I could build up my levels of self-care, self-love, and respect. This was hard as I was so familiar with the comfort zone I was in, whereas I thought that the way they treated me was normal and that was the way every parent treated their children.

It was not until my ten-year de facto relationship where I got to see, experience, and know that this is not the normal way a parent treats their children. I got to see how much love and respect my partners parents gave him and I wished I had that sort of relationship with my parents but no matter how hard I tried to fix things with my family they would treat me with the same amount of disdain and disrespect as they always did as they didn't know any better and didn't want to learn a new way. Their excuse was that when they were raising me and my sister, that there were no books to guide and teach them how they should treat and raise us as children.

I loved how my partners family were always so loving and supportive and there for each other. They never labelled each other or said or did things to hurt or belittle each other. When it counted, they were there for each other. They always had each other's backs.

What I remember most about his family is that when I was going through some rough times after being raped and abducted, they were there for me when my own parents weren't. My mother told me about a day after the attack that it was my fault I was attacked as I had moved out of home at such a young age. Hearing this really cut me up inside, as it was not what I needed to hear after having been through something you would not wish on your worst enemy.

I tried to cut the umbilical cord with her then but was only successful in doing it for six months. Yet I forgave her for it and hoped that she had learnt the errors of her ways, but all she did was make up excuses for what she said and how she treated me and made empty apologies.

I wanted to believe that she had learnt from it, but after a little while, she went back to her old ways. I did not realize just how bad she had gotten with her behaviour until I got the visit from the police that night when she had filed the false report.

It was that night I realized I had not fully broken away from her and her ways properly, because moving interstate had changed me and strengthened me and helped me see I was worthy of love and respect from others because I love and respect myself enough to now put myself first, that I finally told her once and for all that I wanted nothing to do with her anymore and I told her not to contact me under any uncertain circumstances ever again.

I was sad at first, but I know it is for the best and for my well-being that this had to happen, as I don't need people in my life that treat me that way. I am worthy of and deserve love and respect.

I know that since I've had limited contact with my parents in the past, that I will be just fine without them in my life as I have looked after myself and raised myself for twenty-nine years, ever since I moved out of the family home at the age of fifteen. I have done an amazing job of it too.

I am a Digital Scrum Master/Development Manager in my current role and was prior to this role a senior project manager for twelve years in the IT industry, a writer and a coach and my writing about my own experiences and personal growth has inspired many people, so I have been told.

I am a good person with a big heart and someone who is really resilient in life and that makes me successful, as I have a lot of tenacity. Despite all the dramas, I love life and I love being me.

The First Step To Breaking Through Fear Of Public Speaking

"The hardest part is turning the camera on and knowing what to say to your audience. Empower yourself every day to constantly get out there and to push past your fear, because you will reap the rewards in the end. You will have become someone truly amazing from it."

Presenting in front of an audience and speaking publicly has always been a challenge for me, as I have anxiety and terrible nerves. In April 2021 on a Friday morning, I pushed through my fear of speaking, pushed through my anxiety and nervousness to speak in front of forty to fifty people live on WebEx for work as I was invited by someone who had more belief in me than I did in myself.

When I was first asked to do it the Tuesday before, I had lots of fear going through my mind as I am great at speaking when it isn't planned, but this had a set topic and a set timeframe to do it in. When speaking with a set time frame and topic, my mind freezes in fear as I have this strategy in my head telling me I am not great at it and that I should not do it. That strategy then enables the part where my anxiety kicks in and I go into what is known as the fight-or-flight mode. My mind goes blank due to fear of being judged, not being perfect, missing words, umming, too long pauses, and the list goes on and on as my nerves then go into over-drive and I forget what I have to say.

I thought about it for an hour, and you can imagine all the limiting beliefs and fears that came into my head. All the what ifs came flooding in like there was no tomorrow. After that I sat and calmed myself down, took a couple of deep breaths in and sat with those feelings, letting them process for a while.

After processing these emotions, I picked myself back up, remembering who I am, what I am about and where I want to be and who I need to be to get me to the place I want to be in my life. I then positively visualised how I wanted the speech to go and what I could possibly do in the speech to make it run smoother. I then took the plunge and said yes, I would do the speech.

I did some research on the topic and planned what I was going to say. I read it over in my head a few times, still feeling very nervous about it as I am not naturally a person who is great in front of a live audience.

I thought back to a session I had with another coach on this very topic of presenting in front of a large audience and put some techniques I got out of the session to use in the wee hours of the morning before I had to do the speech. They calmed me down and helped me feel at ease and to have more clarity about what I was going to do.

They then introduced me to all the forty to fifty people on WebEx from my work. I paused for a couple of seconds, got myself together and did my speech. I was nervous but remained positive throughout the speech. After the speech, I received some positive feedback which made me feel less tense.

I am now so very glad they asked me to do the speech, and that I took the plunge to do it as I learnt and grew from that experience so much. I now have more belief in myself and know that I can do it. One must do it repeatedly to become good at it. This helps to bring the anxiety level down and the nerves fade away.

I am so glad I did it as it was a challenge and exciting as well as nerve-racking for me. I don't think I would trade that experience for anything now. I am proud I got up and did the speech and pushed through my fears.

In the end, it is like fighting two different parts of yourself. The one that wants to play it safe and not step out of your comfort zone and the other part that is daring, bold and wild and wants to experience new and exciting things outside that comfort zone because that side of you knows you can do it and that you will get so much out of the experience and develop personally from it.

So, I am challenging you right now to take a baby step outside your comfort zone and do something that scares you. Remember, whatever it is, it doesn't have to be perfect, and practice will help you with your nerves and any anxiousness you may have about doing it. All you need to do is take the first small step until you feel comfortable with it, then push yourself to take more steps and practice until, eventually you will be able to completely push past that fear to become outstanding when doing it.

If you want inspiration, then have a look at the "Dare To Be You" YouTube channel and look at just how far I have come with my fear of speaking in front of a camera. Nearly all of these videos I have up there are my Facebook live videos. I have been told by many people that Facebook live videos are harder to do than to do a private recording and to put that up on social media as you have people watching and commenting while you are talking to them on camera.

Facing A Fear Of Presenting

"Many people fake it until they make it when it comes to doing presentations. Research your topic, put your understanding in a slide pack, and rehearse what you want to say before doing the presentation. Be confident and brave because you can do this as you were made for this. It is only a small audience, so face that fear you have and afterwards congratulate yourself for having a go at it."

I have had this fear of doing presentations to a set audience topic and time frame for a very long time now and it only got amplified when I went for an interview with a government department in 2015 where for the second interview; they gave me a night to create and psych myself up to present in the interview the next day on their chosen topic.

This fear had crippled and overwhelmed me for such a long time and not understanding why or how it was doing this concerned me. There has to have been an event from my child-hood that was triggering me when thinking about it. This fear gave me the same symptoms as the public speaking fear I had. The fear has not fully gone away yet, but I am working on it little by little and in different situations.

Anyway, coming back to the story here, I researched the topic and put together a great presentation pack that night and really tried to remember it so that I could present it the next day. I presented it the next day in the interview with the two inter-viewers.

I thought it went okay but could have been improved on here and there anyway. I got some really negative feedback about the presentation that has made me even more fearful of presenting to people ever since.

Statistics say that public speaking and presenting is one of the most common fears in the world and that it is even more feared than death.

When you come to think of it, who really wants to do a presentation in front of people you don't know personally, who will sit there the entire time and judge you on your language, your body posture, what you have prepared and put together and how you presented it.

It's terrifying, right? **Indeed, it is.**

Since that time, I identified that there was a gap and a challenge for me to overcome but I never really did anything about it until the past two years on my coaching journey where I have had to overcome a great deal of that fear, through doing Facebook live videos. And in May this year I did a two-day intensive online public speakers bootcamp where I spoke in front of people live on zoom and presented to them to gain feedback so that I can overcome my fears. I have since started a twelve-month public speaking Protégé program with Speakers Institute to push myself past these fears even more than I do to challenge myself and step outside my comfort zone into the realm of possibility.

I have known many project managers in my industry and in other industries who are exactly the same as me with the fear of public speaking and presenting in front of a live audience and a camera and they say that they have rarely if at all had to do presentations in their roles and have avoided doing them.

Well, now, I am saying I will no longer be a victim to this fear and that I am better than that. I was frightened, YES anxious, and nervous of going in front of lots of people in that bootcamp and presenting to people who watched and judged me when I did the presentation, but I was also excited because this has open up some possibilities and options for me in my current career and also in the coaching industry that I never would have had.

I did it, felt the fear and overcame a portion of that fear, as I know eventually that it will in time make me more confident and capable in many areas of my life.

Here is a YouTube video I did on this topic for you to watch: YouTube: https://youtu.be/TXQU9NjuuL4

Through The Darkness
Into A System That Works

"No matter how tough it gets, no matter how rough and bendy the road is, always know that you have the power inside of you to change things and there will always be a light at the end of the tunnel."

I spent many years as a child and as a young adult in and out of the depths of depression.

The things that put me into depression were:

•The emotional\psychological abuse and emotional abandonment as a child from my parents.

•The restrictive religion I grew up in and being an outcast in that religion because I was not the same age as most the children it that geographical area of that religion.

•Being an outcast because I stood out and was different to all the other children.

•Being kept down in grade one and being bullied for it.

•Being bullied for my entire childhood and adolescent years because the other children judged me and thought I was dumb and below them in intelligence.

•Having people, I thought were my closest friends at school lie to me, back stab me and blab all my secrets all over the school.

•Being bullied by my older sister until I moved out of home at the age of fifteen. I remember the way she used to hold knives to my throat while doing the dishes.

•Having extended family telling me my parents never wanted me and that I was a mistake.

•My father when I was moving my things out of the family home letting me almost fall down the stairs while carrying a large box of my belongings and hearing him yelling at me as I proceeded to take the box down the stairs, that I had a heart of stone, that no one can or will ever love me and that I would never amount to much.

•The men I got involved with as a young adult who could not understand that if you are with someone in a serious relationship that you don't stray into the arms of their best friends even when things get tough.

- The emotional\psychological abuse and emotional abandonment as a child from my parents.
- The restrictive religion I grew up in and being an outcast in that religion because I was not the sent age as most the children it that geographical area of that religion.
- Being an outcast at because I stood out and was different to all the other children.
- Being kept down in grade one and being bullied for it.
- Being bullied for my entire childhood and adolescent years because the other children judged me and thought I was dumb and below them in intelligence.
- Having people, I thought were my closest friends at school lie to me, back stab me and blab all my secrets all over the school.
- Being bullied by my older sister until I moved out of home at the age of 15. I remember the way she used to hold knives to my throat while doing the dishes.

- Having extended family telling me my parents never wanted me and that I was a mistake.
- My father when I was moving my things out of the family home letting me almost fall down the stairs while carrying a large box of my belongings and hearing him yelling at me as I proceeded to take the box down the stairs, that I had a heart of stone, that no one can or will ever love me and that I would never amount to much.
- The men I got involved with as a young adult who could not understand that if you are with someone in a serious relationship that you don't stray into the arms of their best friends even when things get tough.
- The rape and abduction I had happen to me in my early 20s.
- The bullying and sexual harassment in the workplace I experienced at parts in my career.

All these things led me down the rabbit hole of low self-worth, low self-esteem, and no self-respect and at one point I even believed all the bad things that people told me I was and that there was something wrong with me. It led me to being a people pleaser who was easily manipulated by others in her life, so that she could feel some form of belonging, love and as though she was enough.

For years I would get myself out of depression only to have another thing happen that would drag me back into depression but way deeper in the depression than I was before. It was a slippery winding, slide or should I say avalanche of negative emotions I felt every day and I didn't know how to snap myself out of it so I experimented with things one by one that people used to tell me would get me out of depression and keep me out of depression, only to find that some of them didn't work on me at all and that others worked but they were only short-term fixes and after a while they would wear off.

I remember when I had had enough of not feeling anything

because of being on antidepressants as people made me believe they were the best thing for me being burnt out and having a nervous breakdown where I sat on the floor of my apartment in a corner just simply staring into space aimlessly for hours, sometimes days. One time I hit rock bottom and at that point I realised that there was nowhere for me to go but up again and the only way for me to go up was for me to pick myself up and to completely change who I was and my entire lifestyle. My life as I knew it was broken and could no longer be glued back together as they shattered me like tiny shards or fragments of glass all over the ground and I had no one to piece me back together again.

The only thing I could do was to continue on my self-exploration journey and further develop my holistic health support system that supports and serves me today in helping me bounce back from adversity. The system was a mixture of many things within my lifestyle that would pick me up, support me, and help me become resilient in the face of trauma, trials, and tribulations. It helped me change my perspective on life, myself, and the way I dealt with my fear, feelings and limiting beliefs, helped me to heal, become strong and gain a sense of who I was, what I wanted out of life and where I was heading.

My system made me more resilient, gave me self-love, self-respect, boundaries, and things I could cling on to so that I would never have to go back into the depths of depression and despair ever again. My system took me twelve years to perfect and is not for the weak minded or weak at heart as you really need to be dedicated and devoted to the lifestyle that you get from having the system. You really must want and need to help yourself. You really have to have the determination to act and transform yourself.

I took myself cold turkey off antidepressants that made me feel nothing, which were suppressing my emotions I had prior to taking them. Because I went cold turkey off the medication, all the emotions from before taking the antidepressants that were suppressed came flooding back to me almost tenfold.

I went off the medication because I wanted to feel the joy of life that others felt every day as I felt nothing because of the medication. I knew that if I were to take myself off the medication that it would really hurt and it would suck and that I needed to replace the medication with something to support me. So, I did my research and combined everything I tried throughout the years before they put me on the medication into the one lifestyle support system. I knew that once I was off the medication, there was no turning back. I would have to make it work.

My holistic health support system helped me deal with the emotions from the darkest parts of my life, heal and become stronger and more self-sufficient. I have supported myself for many years with this holistic health support system now and I know it works. Be resilient enough to try things out and change them to suit you. This is not for the lazy and is a lot of hard work. You will need to put in lots of time and effort to implement it into your life. It is well worth it, though.

To this very day, I am still experimenting with things to see if they can improve on the effectiveness of my holistic health support system, as some things in the system are short term and wear off in time. With this system, I know that my life is my life and that I can get through just about anything that happens in my life without going back into depression. With this system, I have the power to control my thoughts, actions and to face my fears and still know that I will be fine at the end of the day. Today and every day after today, I win in life because I know I've got this!

I must stress to you, however, that going cold turkey off the medication is not recommended or advised and that one must seek the advice of a physician if they want to come off antidepressants first before doing so.

Dealing With A
Hybrid Vanity Publishing Scam

*"Always do you due diligence and check out the places
you do business with, or you will live to regret it"*

It was at the end of October 2021 when I had completed the final draft of my manuscript for my book "Dare To Be YOU" that I found a good editing and publishing company to edit, design and publish my book.

I felt overwhelmed by the thought of having to get another person or company to help me with my book as I struggled previously for many months by a so-called author by the name of Dario Stevenson who only wasted my time with nightly lengthy zoom meetings to discuss my life and what out of my life should go into my book and my views on things. He scammed me out of $11k, promising me he would ghost write my book, get his contacts in the industry to do the typing, editing, interior book and cover designs, a website for my book and publish my book. He asked me to transfer to him in sums of $800 to $3k in four payments over the space of three months for these services, as he already had people lined up to do the work. They were true professionals, according to him. He pretended to be my best friend for over a year, even pretended to be concerned when I told him about how I

319

was scammed by Tradewell. In the end, he delivered nothing to me as he kept stalling on delivery of services.

I didn't want this to happen to me again as I was new to the book writing arena, so I asked another coach that I knew, respected, and looked up to about who she used for her book she had published. I thought because she had referred me to them, she had used them before, as she gave them such a glowing referral.

So, I contacted this hybrid publishing firm she recommended without doing the checks I would normally do on a company or person to see whether they were legitimate and legal or not before hiring them for the job, as I trusted and respected my friend's opinion.

When I spoke to a representative of this hybrid publishing firm on the phone, they were very positive and upbeat. They told me a little about what they could offer and asked me a few things about my book. I asked the representative a few questions and one of them was are you going to edit and publish the book before Christmas, as I had promised my social media audience that it would be out for Christmas. She said yes, most definitely. I also explained to her I had already gotten a couple of quotes from two freelance editors and that they were too expensive. I also gave her how much they told me they had quoted me to edit my book.

She directed me to a publishing and editing program called a Third Chapter publishing program she said had an editorial assessment, editing, interior and cover design and publishing included in it. The cost was $2.8k. This price was almost half the price of the freelance editor's quote. So, I thought it was a good deal. They even threw in discounts for the next two books I wanted to write and publish in one of their other publishing programs called "First Chapter Publishing" program, where essentially, I would get two books published for the price of one. Which ended up being $1.1k per book, which I thought was a great deal as the editing and designing were included in these publishing programs. At least, that is what they told me.

I signed up and paid all three programs on the spot. I submitted my manuscript, pictures, the original book cover, and their questionnaire about my first book with all the information they needed to edit, design, and publish my book to them within the first two days of signing up.

As soon as they got it, they told me that because it was a memoir and self-help book, that I could not have my name on it as the author because of privacy reasons. I asked them if I can't be associated with my book, how was I supposed to market and sell my book as it is a tool for my business and also had my entire life's history in it. They then sold me one of their Book Sellers return programs for $1.4k. They said that the program would help me sell my book to bookstores as it was like a guarantee that if the bookstores couldn't sell my book, that any books they ordered they could return them and be refunded for the money they had paid. I explained to the hybrid publishing company's representative that they were asking me to completely disown my entire history and everything I had been through and that I would not use a Pen Name for my book. I argued with them until they gave me another way to have my book published as a self-help memoir book and also have my real name as the author.

They told me to:
• Change peoples' genders
• Change peoples' roles
• Change my age
• Change people's names
• Change locations
• When referring to family members to make the reference vaguer and more generic.

Or to write the book as though it was someone else's life.

The original manuscript I had already sent them had made up names, ages, timelines, and some locations were changed in it to begin with.

They put it through an editorial assessment and then told me that my book would need a great deal of editing and that the editing was not included in the program I had paid them for and that it would cost me a further $5k for content editing.

I thought this was odd, as the representative had originally told me the program included the editing when I first bought it from them. I argued with them about this, but because it was mid-November, time was running out for the editing, designing, and publishing to happen and I really wanted my book to be published before Christmas as that was what I had promised my social media audience and I really wanted to make that deadline for the book. So, I bought the program for the editing as there was no way that I could source another editor, book designer and publisher so late in the game and not have it cost me even more money.

That night I was checking my business bank account for tax purposes and found that they had double charged me for the Book stores returns program I signed up for, as I remember only signing for one and not two. I contacted them the next day with pictures of the double charged amount they took from my account and threatened to cancel all the contracts and get a refund for my money. They told me I had signed for two of those programs and not one and I said that the contract for that service was only for one and for half the amount they had taken out of my account, and I asked again for a refund. That was when they told me I had signed for the other one two days after I signed for the first program. That was when it clicked, and I realized that the form they got me to sign for the acknowledgement of the first payment was not for that at all, it was for the second Book Sellers returns program. I read the form I had signed, and it said that it was for the acknowledgement of the first payment, but they used it as a new contract for the extra program I did not sign for. They were very deceptive in doing this.

The editor had completed the editing of my manuscript through track changes in MS Word, but they didn't really change a lot at all, which was odd, apart from a little bit of punctuation and grammar here and there. I did notice, however; the editor had put extra commas and hyphens in and dropped off the end of words some letters, and that parts of the endings of sentences were removed for no reason, which made little sense to me. It was as if the editors' first and even second language was not English or as though a child had edited the manuscript.

I raised it with the hybrid publisher representative as soon as I saw it but remembered reading in the email's body with the edited manuscript attached a sentence saying that the editor would not be touching or editing the manuscript again.

They then told me for my first book that I could no longer have colour pictures in it, only black and white stencil pictures for quotes and chapter setting paragraphs and only fifteen insertions of them but because they felt bad, they said that since there were eighty-one chapters in my book, they would insert forty-one for free so that it didn't look odd and to say sorry for messing me around.

They then got another sales representative to call me and pressure me to buy their marketing campaigns and they kept using the fact that I cared about my book and wanted it done professionally that they wanted to give me some massive discounts on their marketing campaigns, and they wouldn't take NO for an answer. They promised me I would make all my money back that I had paid them for all three books editing, designing, publishing, marketing, and distribution if I bought their marketing campaigns. They claimed other authors who had used their marketing program saw a return of thousands of dollars in the first six months, and more than half of them got movie deals for their books because of the marketing campaigns they ran. I felt pressured by it and desperately needed to make all the money back that I paid them, plus the $11k I paid Dario to help me with my book prior to them getting involved. So, I signed up for their Online Book Ads via Google–Standalone (90 days) Online Booksellers Advertising campaigns, which they told me cost $4k, but they ended up taking $4.8k from my credit card.

I tried to contact their customer service coordinator five times over the next week to see why they weren't doing a good job of the book interior design, and also why I was doing their proof reading and Quality Assurance for them on the interior when I was paying them to do that in their program. Each time, their customer service coordinator was not available for my calls and was not responding to my emails.

Christmas came and went, and they still had not published my book as the quality of their work regarding the book cover and the interior design was very poor and you could tell they did not do any quality assurance checks or proofreading of their own work. They promised me they would publish my book in January instead.

I did the proofreading and quality assurance on five different versions of the book design by them and was getting fed-up with doing the work I was paying them to do as each version was changed in different areas of the text that I did not tell them to change and had made those areas read poorly and so I had to note them down in their interior design changes form and email it through to them to make the changes as the document was not editable as it was a PDF and I could not change the text myself. This process was repeated five times until I questioned them again about why I was doing their job for them.

Their customer service coordinator and their publishing representative were getting harder and harder to contact and that was when I did some checking with a Facebook authors support group and some other writers' groups to see what other authors experiences were with this company and that was when I found out that hybrid publishing company although was attached to a well-known global publishing company was a scam and would never publish my book. They just wanted to get as much money out of me as they possibly could. This was also the time I tried to speak to the person who referred me to them, and she didn't want to hear the truth about what was happening with the publishing company she had referred me to and that she had never used their services but intended to for a co-author book she was writing with six to twelve other coaches.

I then spoke to my bank and put a visa Debit dispute in for all the payment transactions they took from my visa card, had my card cancelled and a new one reissued, and also asked Visa and my bank to do their best to get my money back from this scam of a publishing company.

I then wrote and sent this hybrid publishing company a legal email and letter telling them to cancel the contracts and refund my money as they had deceived and misled me in the way they got me to sign up for their programs to begin with and since they had not really delivered anything to me but a copy of my original cover design for my book, and they had delivered none of the services I had paid them for, that this was illegal.

They never responded to any of my emails in writing. They just tried to ring me every ten minutes to talk me out of cancelling the contract and demanding a refund. I sent them a cease and desist to get them to stop ringing me as I have a day job and am in meetings most days all day and can't pick up phone calls during business hours unless it is something to do with my job or an emergency.

To date, I have sent them four more emails telling them to cancel all contracts and refund all of my money but have gotten no response from them at all.

I told my bank about not getting responses from them about refunding my money and cancelling their contracts so that my bank has more evidence against them when they deal with them and get my money back from them.

I then took my book to another editing company to do the editing at the time I thought they were professional as they communicated to me regularly on the progress of my book. They took my book on as a pro-bono project as they knew that I had been defrauded twice previously with regards to my book. They gave my book an editorial assessment and in that editorial assessment they pushed me to divide my manuscript into two manuscripts for two separate books, one which they would continue to do for free and, the other they would charge me for delivering. They gave me a publishing date of mid-June 2022. When I told them no, that my book was to stay as one book, they did not like it and found all the excuses under the sun to belittle my writing and to delay the publishing date.   They delivered three chapters a week for two weeks under duress and became increasingly difficult to work with.

This editor also read into my manuscript things that were not implied or even written into it. This editor had been triggered by something he had read in my manuscript, from his past that he had not dealt with and so he tried to force his views onto me. This made me feel quite ill as those views were of an incestuous nature. Which I know without a shadow of a doubt never happened to myself or my sister whilst growing up. So, I terminated the editing contract with him.

A week later I found another editor who is in the UK who could teach me a lot more about the book editing, designing, and publishing world which I am now paying on milestone delivery. This arrangement suits me well as there is no upfront costs and I get along well with this editor.   He is the best editor I have had work on my manuscript to date.   I am very grateful to have this editor from the UK working on my book with me.

I believe that my bank and Visa will get my money back from the hybrid publishing company as they have gotten more money back from a crypto currency scam for me a few years prior to now.

What The Holistic Health Support System Is

"How would you like to live your life every day knowing that whatever challenges you face you can and will get through it because you are who you are, and you have a holistic health support system that you can fall back on to keep you strong and positively moving forward spiritually, mentally, emotionally, and physically?"
"Change your lifestyle before your lifestyle changes you!"

In the "Dare To Be YOU" signature coaching programs I have put all the knowledge and tools I discovered throughout the years of my life through trial and error that I was never taught or given as a child, adult by family and educational institutions. These are programs I developed through life experience that have helped my clients and myself become ourselves, outstanding and unstoppable, in our lives and relationships.

This system is a holistic health support system which included personal and professional development, nootropics, exercise, spiritual forgiveness and healing, learning what made me happy and who I really wanted to be by listening to my inner child, gratitude, learning life lessons, Coaching, hypnosis, cognitive behavioural therapy, timeline therapy and acceptance therapy, meditation, grounding myself, Biofeedback sessions, infrared sauna and floatation sessions, frequency healing, eating healthy, and finding out what foods reacted with me so I didn't eat them, removing negative people from my life and surrounding myself with positive, successful people who love and support me, facing my fears head on and also changing what defining moments in my past were that caused the fears and limiting beliefs and replacing the limiting beliefs I had with new positive empowering beliefs, listening to good music (theme songs) that lift you up, watching funny movies.

I will now step you through each of these items one by one with the things that worked best for me in my life. Remember to change the system to suit your own life and situations so that you have in it what will work best for you as we are all different and our spiritual, emotional, and physical bodies will all react differently. This does not mean to say that you should not try any of them. You just need to mix them up and try them all out to see what works best for you. As I have said before, this system is fully modifiable to suit each and every one of us.

Personal development books that will get you thinking differently

Some great and insightful books to get you started on your Personal and professional development journey are listed below:

- Emotional Healing: PSH a new therapy for a new millennium by Frank Wright, Sue Bushell, et al
- Divine Magic: The Seven Sacred Secrets of Manifestation by Doreen Virtue
- Secret: Volume 1 by Rhonda Byrne
- How To Win Friends And Influence People by Dale Carnegie
- Intuition: Keys Unlocking Inner Wisdom by Paul Fenton-Smith
- The 7 Habits Of Highly Effective People by Stephen R. Covey

- 21 Irrefutable Laws of Leadership: Follow Them and People Will Follow You by John C. Maxwell
- Entrepreneurial Leadership by Wilson Luna
- The Abundance Book by John Randolph Price
- Beyond Doorways by Alexis Cartwright
- Australian Bush Flower Remedies by Ian White
- Find Your Courage: 12 acts of becoming fearless at work and in life by Margie Warrell
- Manifesting: The secret behind the law of Attraction by Alexander Janzer
- Feel The Fear And To It Anyway by Susan Jeffers
- The Feeling Good Handbook by David D Burns M.D.
- Eat Pray Love by Elizabeth Gilbert
- The Power of Now – Eckhart Toll
- Personality Plus by Florence Littauer
- The Five Love Languages by Gary Chapman
- Empower Yourself by Clive Murphy
- E2 by Pam Grout
- He's Just Not That Into You by Greg Behrendt and Liz Tuccillo
- It's Just A Date: How to Get 'Em, How to Read 'Em, And How to Rock 'Em by Greg Behrendt and Amiira Ruotola Behrendt
- Find Your Courage: 12 Acts for Becoming Fearless at Work and in Life by Margie Warrell
- 10 Days To Great Self Esteem by David Burns, D Burns, et al.
- Ten Simple Solutions for Building Self-Esteem: How to End Self-Doubt, Gain Confidence & Create a Positive Self-Image by SCHIRALDI G
- Reinventing Your Life: The bestselling breakthrough program to end negative behaviour and feel great by Jeffrey E. Young and Janet S. Klosko

Each and every book on in the above list I have read, and I highly recommend reading as they give you a different perspective on life and how to see and think about the world. Some of these books help you trace your behavioural patterns to childhood events and give you an understanding on why you are the way you are, others will help you replace those unresourceful behaviours, habits, and beliefs you have with new positive empowering behaviours, habits, and beliefs so that the past is no longer holding you back. Some of these books will give you the pick me up you need when you are feeling down, and others will give you an insight into your personality and relationships to help you understand why you are the way you are and why specific things happen within the relationships, you have or have had in the past.

Nootropics.

The benefits of taking magnesium are:

Magnesium is involved in hundreds of biochemical reactions in your body. Every cell in your body has magnesium and needs it to function. One of magnesium's key roles is acting as a cofactor or helper molecule in the biochemical reactions continuously performed by enzymes. Magnesium engages over 600 reactions in your body, including: Converting food into energy, assists in the repair and creation process of RNA and DNA for maintenance, assists send messages throughout your brain and nervous system by regulating neurotransmitters, boosts exercise performance, can be used as an anti-inflammatory, help fight type 2 diabetes, assists with lowering blood pressure, assists in the prevention of migraines, assists in creating new proteins from amino acids, it is part of muscle shortening and relaxation, your insulin resistance is lowered, symptoms of PMS are improved, assists in the fighting depression.

· · ·

The benefits of vitamin C are:

Our body tissues rely on vitamin C for development, growth, and repair, It aids in the formation of collagen, absorption of iron, gets the immune system functioning properly, healing of wounds and the maintenance of bones, teeth, and cartilage, protects against free radicals such as arthritis, cancer, heart disease, toxic chemicals and pollution. It protects against stress, colds, flues, strokes, and skin aging by reducing wrinkles.

The benefits of taking Lavandula Calm are:

Lavandula Calm relieves symptoms of mild anxiety and stress, help support emotional wellbeing, calms and relaxes the nervous system, reduces restlessness and sleepiness, induces sleep, reduces excess nervous energy, decrease flatulence, is an antispasmodic agent, eases digestive discomfort and spasms, settle, and supports the nervous system, encourage energy levels, helps to maintain muscle relaxation.

The benefits of taking Stress Ease are:

Stress Ease helps relieve the symptoms of mild anxiety, beneficial during stress, helps to reduce and relieve nervousness.

The benefits of taking a good probiotic/prebiotic are below:

It supports digestive health and gives immune system support, balances your weight, helps you feel lighter, more energized, and healthier, helps to build your immune system up again after taking antibiotics and antibiotics not only attack the bad antibodies in your body when you are ill but also the good antibodies. Helps keep you protected against cold and flu and common everyday viruses.

· · ·

The benefits of taking a good, activated B complex are below:

Activated B complex helps with the maintenance of general well-being, support energy production, maintain nervous system function and supports a healthy stress response in the body and emotional wellbeing and Aids in the metabolism of carbohydrates, this is also very good for the relief of normal everyday stress and anxiety.

The benefits of taking flower essence formulas are:

Relationship (Australian Bush Flower Essence formula)

This bush flower remedy blend enhances the quality of all relationships, especially intimate ones, releases emotional pain and turmoil, removes resentment and blocked emotions of a turbulent relationship, and also helps you to have a healthier internal relationship with yourself.

Abund (Australian Bush Flower Essence formula)

They specifically created this bush flower blend is to assist with the emotional care and wellbeing of people. It helps in releasing family patterns, negative beliefs, sabotage, and fear of lack and it aids people in achieving goals and having more ambition.

Purify (Australian Bush Flower Essence formula)

This bush flower blend promotes a sense of release and relief, spring cleaning, and it aids in the releasing and clearing of emotional waste and residual by-products, helps to clear built-up emotional baggage.

Confid (Australian Bush Flower Essence formula)

This bush flower blend resolves negative beliefs, helps us feel comfortable around other people, helps us to realise and take

DARE TO BE YOU

responsibility for situations and events that happen in our lives and brings out the positive qualities of self-esteem and confidence in people.

Dynamis (Australian Bush Flower Essence formula)

This bush flower blends harmonises and centres one vital force, renews enthusiasm and passion for life, and is formulated specifically to aid with emotional care and wellbeing.

Rescue Remedy (Bach Flower Essence formula)

Rescue remedy works on emotional imbalances associated with daily stressful situations, relieves feelings of anxiety, nervous tension, stress, or agitation, and provides a sense of focus and calm. It can be used to relieve feelings of terror and panic, irritability and impatience, inattentiveness, shock, promote calmness and mental clarity. Rescue Remedy helps people rediscover the positive side of themselves.

I used Rescue Remedy when I took my practical drivers license test many years ago and it was amazing at keeping me calm and focused on what I was doing. It really settled my nerves and anxiety.

The benefits of using space clearing sprays are below:

Space clearing sprays relax, purify, and soothe you, melt away the stress of the day, cleanses yourself and your space of negative psychic energy from environments, awakens your senses, creates safe harmonious environments.

Infrared sauna and floatation sessions,

I highly recommend once or twice a month going to https://

333

beyondrest.com.au/ and booking in for an infrared sauna and floatation tank session.

Infrared Sauna

The infrared sauna will help you relax and get negative toxins out of your body so that you feel renewed and revitalised. It gives you a deep penetration within your tissue and muscles so that your physical and mental wellbeing improves. This is done through a gentle, soothing a cleansing therapeutic sweat. It uses a dry heat to relax and detoxify your body. This will improve your breathing and will detoxify your body. Health Professionals have widely used it for years.

Floatation Tank

The floatation tank has many health benefits, and they are stress and anxiety relief, pain relief and recovery, and deeper meditation and focus. It promotes calmness & relaxation, healing in people with fibromyalgia, heightened visualisation, deeper meditation and expands your awareness.

It alleviates things such as pain from injuries, arthritis and migraines, mental and physical stress, jetlag, and fatigue.

It reduces: ACTH & adrenaline, which helps reduce stress and relaxes you, the production of cortisol, vulnerability to addictions, habits and phobias, fear, anxiety and depression, pulse, blood pressure, oxygen consumption and heart rate.

It enhances: sleep, recovery, rehabilitation, endorphin production, workplace motivation, distribution of nutrients and oxygen and improves circulation, improves productivity, improves self-hypnosis and hypnotherapy, athletic performance, speeds the healing process and general motivation.

It stimulates: Immune function, vitality, and energy, shifts brainwaves from beta to lower frequency levels, alpha, theta &

even delta wave, problem-solving abilities, creativity and learning functions, expands awareness, visualisation and deepens meditation and synchronises the left/right brain creating alertness and mental clarity.

The floatation tank uses deep meditation music, chakra light therapy and it gets you into a deep state of relaxation, which heals many conditions.

I use the infrared sauna and Floatation tank once to twice a month. And I highly recommend people try them. Using them makes me more focused, calmer, increased my clarity on things and made me feel more holistically healthy. This also helped to flush out of my body the toxins that were left in my body from the COVID vaccine that was reacting to my body and making me feel ill.

Frequency healing,

My naturopath gets me to play these frequencies throughout the day on YouTube. These frequencies are for healing, love, abundance, and prosperity. I highly recommend you look these frequencies up on YouTube and give them a go, as they have really helped me to move forward.

To find the frequencies, go to YouTube and search on: abundance frequency, healing frequency, self-love frequency etc... YouTube has many frequencies that you can listen to for many things.

Eating healthy

In my twenties, I ate lots of junk and processed foods. In my thirties, I stopped eating those types of foods and only eat healthy foods now like salads, chicken, salmon, fresh fruit and vegetables and I can now feel the difference in my emotional state. By doing this, I also dropped two dress sizes and felt better about myself. I noticed my concentration levels picked up and I can focus on things for longer periods of time now.

Junk foods and processed foods will always make you feel low in energy, as they don't have the level of nutrients your body requires, and they lack vitamins and minerals.

I strongly suggest you speak to a naturopath or nutritionist about putting together a good healthy diet for you so that you get the right number of vitamins and minerals in your diet to help you function better throughout the day.

Food intolerance and allergy test

I highly recommend you go to https://www.allergytestaustrali a.com and get a food intolerance and allergy test done as the food we eat and the environment we surround ourselves in massively impacts our physical, mental, and spiritual health. I got mine done in 2019 and there were some foods I was intolerant to that I loved to eat but didn't know I was intolerant to peanuts, hazelnuts, and olives.

I couldn't figure out why I got IBS and a lot of bloating and gas after eating and why my energy levels depleted so quickly after meals. Also, after meals, I wasn't as happy and got emotional. For years I struggled with these symptoms trying different things to change this, but nothing worked until I got the food intolerance and allergy test done and it blew my mind with the foods, I was intolerant to and the things to which I was allergic. After cutting those foods out of my diet I was highly intolerant to, I now have much more energy, No IBS, no bloating after meals and I am much happier.

Removing negative people from your life and surrounding yourself with positive, successful people who love and support you

We all have negative people in our lives weighing us down and making us feel miserable about ourselves and life in general. These people, whether or not we know it, drain us of our positive energy and hold us back from achieving great things.

It is important that once you know who these people are to clean them out of our lives by reducing or cutting all contact. It is difficult, but you will find that once you do this, you will attract more positive and successful people in your life who will inspire and empower you to go beyond your comfort zone into the great unknown and to live life to the fullest to become our truest selves.

For me, the most negative people I had in my life were my parents, and they constantly did things to hurt me and make me feel bad about myself. After many years of being made to feel not loved and not enough through their actions and empty apologies, I cut them out of my life and now I feel freer than I ever have before, as I am now attracting the right people into my life.

Facing fears head on

My philosophy is if you don't face your fears and step outside your comfort zone, then you will never really truly know what you are capable of or if you can have the life, you have always dreamed of.

Sometimes facing your fears means going back to a painful childhood memory and changing the feelings you have attached to that experience to be more empowering.

Other times it is like taking a leap of faith, like I did when I had my fear of heights and went skydiving.

Changing the defining moments in the past that caused fears and limiting beliefs and replacing the limiting beliefs with new positive empowering beliefs

This is done through going deep into our subconsciousness

and figuring out what event from our childhood is impacting our lives and holding us back from achieving the things we want to achieve. Then through hypnosis figuring out what the old beliefs, old actions and old results are from that event and then changing the emotions we have attached to that moment by giving your childhood you the resources, techniques, comfort and support they need to be able to positively move forward by attaching new positive learnings, beliefs and actions to it to get the results you truly want in your life in the here and now and letting go of the past limiting fears and beliefs.

This is a very powerful technique and gets significant results from people. You can also use timeline therapy and anchoring for this.

Listening to good music (theme songs) that lift you up

The theme songs below I had for very specific reasons throughout the years, and they have helped me tremendously through a lot of things in my life. They give me that more hope to continue on and to know that I am on the right path for my life.

You will need to choose theme songs that resonate with you for the theme song to work for you the way they have worked for me.

Theme Song: Battles (1 mic 1 take) – LaPorsha Renae
YouTube Link:
https://www.youtube.com/watch?v=3xTG0Livh8Q&list=RD3x
TG0Livh8Q&start_radio=1
Year: 2021
Significance: This song got me through most of the downs in 2021 especially when I had to cut my parents out of my life and also when I lost my job at the start of the year due to covid.

Theme Song: This is me – The greatest showman
YouTube Link:
https://www.youtube.com/watch?v=5J29YsEfYlo
Year: 2020
Significance: This song reminds me that being unique and different is a good thing and to continually grow and change and never to give my power away to those who will judge me.

Theme Song: Ready to love you - Hedegaard
YouTube Link:
https://www.youtube.com/watch?v=i_ZUBj2xeq8
Year: 2019
Significance: This was my theme song for 2019 as I was ready for love and a long-lasting relationship.

Theme Song: Firework – Katy Perry
YouTube Link:
https://www.youtube.com/watch?v=QGJuMBdaqIw
Year: 2018
Significance: I really related to the lyrics, and it hits a cord for me. It pretty much says that we should be true to ourselves and show people what is on the inside and to let it shine as an original.

Theme Song: Most girls – Hailee Steinfeld
YouTube Link:
https://www.youtube.com/watch?v=qBB_QOZNEdc
Year: 2017
Significance: This one made me feel strong and it helped me

embrace that I am different and don't want to be the same as other people.

Theme Song: Pray - Sam Smith
YouTube Link:
https://www.youtube.com/watch?v=hhREiAarjVY
Year: 2016
Significance: This song helps me to keep the faith in the higher power and in love when I need it.

Theme Song: Beautiful – Christina Aguilera
YouTube Link:
https://www.youtube.com/watch?v=eAfyFTzZDMM
Year: 2015
Significance: When I got sad in 2015, I used to play this song as it empowered me and made me stronger.

Theme Song: I was here – Beyonce
YouTube Link:
https://www.youtube.com/watch?v=i41qWJ6QjPI
Year: 2014
Significance: I wanted something more out of life and so I built harmony with action my old personal training and lifestyle mentoring business.

Theme Song: Happy – Pharrell Wiliams

YouTube Link:
https://www.youtube.com/watch?v=ZbZSe6N_BXs
Year: 2013 **Significance:** This song is a very happy bubbly song that cheers me up when I am feeling sad.

Theme Song: Roar – Katy Perry
YouTube Link:
https://www.youtube.com/watch?v=CevxZvSJLk8
Year: 2013
Significance: This song is one of the songs that made me realise I wasn't being true to myself enough and that I needed to stand up for myself and roar.

Theme Song: Keep Your Head Up - Andy Grammer
YouTube Link:
https://www.youtube.com/watch?v=CmrOB_q3tjo
Year: 2012
Significance: This song really helped me when I felt stuck in life and was questioning what life was really about. This has amazing lyrics.

Theme Song: Haven't met you yet – Michael Buble
YouTube Link:
https://www.youtube.com/watch?v=1AJmKkU5POA
Year: 2011
Significance: This song was for when I was tired of being alone and needed hope that a relationship would happen.

Theme Song: Not that kind – Anastasia
YouTube Link:
https://www.youtube.com/watch?v=tGYvVQKJfaI
Year: 2010
Significance: This song was from when I was attracting all the wrong types of guys in my life, and I played this song to stop myself from lowering my standards for men.

Theme Song: Jet Lag – Simple plan
YouTube Link:
https://www.youtube.com/watch?v=ntSBKPkk4m4
Year: 2008
Significance: This was when I was working for a global company, and I met someone, but he was always travelling for work and so was I, so we didn't last.

Theme Song: It's too late for apologize – OneRepublic
YouTube Link:
https://www.youtube.com/watch?v=VRUWtag5EFk
Year: 2008
Significance: This song was from when I went to the UK and Ireland and when I first found out I had the pre stages of cervical cancer. The words really picked me up.

Theme Song: Unwritten - Natasha Bedingfield
YouTube Link:

https://www.youtube.com/watch?v=b7k0a5hYnSI
Year: 2004
Significance: This was great for helping me push myself out of my comfort zone to do new things.

Theme Song: I don't need a man – Pussy cat dolls
YouTube Link:
https://www.youtube.com/watch?v=qBsEF7Qx09o
Year: 2005
Significance: This was the year I broke up with my ex of 10 years and this song helped me empower myself and be strong as I lost him and my best friend from their indiscretion together and also my house.

Theme Song: Send in the clowns – Barbra Streisand
YouTube Link:
https://www.youtube.com/watch?v=ODqj9Mq39FM
Year: 2002
Significance: This song hits a cord for me given my childhood and how alone I was.

Theme Song: Fever – Peggy Lee
YouTube Link:
https://www.youtube.com/watch?v=JGb5IweiYG8
Year: 1996
Significance: This is what I thought love would be like when I was a teenager, and it helps me believe that there is someone out there for me.

Theme Song: I'm too sexy - right said Fred
YouTube Link:
https://www.youtube.com/watch?v=P5mtclwloEQ
Year: 1992
Significance: This song was great to cheer me up as a teenager when I was constantly rejected at school by the guys I liked. I would turn this song on and dance to it.

Theme Song: Vincent (starry, starry night) – Don McLean
YouTube Link:
https://www.youtube.com/watch?v=oxHnRfhDmrk
Year: 1980
Significance: This song was one of the songs that would give me hope as a child when I had no love in my life. It still makes me cry.

Exercise

Exercise changes the parts of the brain that stress and anxiety are regulated in. Brain sensitivity can also increase for the hormones norepinephrine and serotonin, which relieve feelings of depression and helps to manage anxiety by the production of endorphins that help you feel happy and reduces the perception of pain.

Studies have shown that people who exercise are 10% more productive and a lot more focused in their work.

The top 10 benefits of exercising are:

1. Makes you feel happier
2. You can lose weight

3. It is good for your bones and muscles
4. It increases your energy levels
5. Reduces risk of chronic heart disease
6. Improves the health of your skin
7. Helps your memory and improves your brain health
8. Improve sleep quality and relaxation
9. Has reduced pain
10. Promotes a better sex life

I exercise twice daily during the working week, once in the morning with legs, core, and weights exercises for forty-five minutes and then for an hour walking at lunch time. On weekends I run 6km Saturday and Sunday mornings. I also do virtual boxing and HIT workout sessions twice a week for forty-five minutes to let out frustrations and relieve the effects of stress.

Spiritual forgiveness and healing,

Spiritually forgiving people for what they have done to you is very important, as it helps you process the negative emotions attached to what has been done to you. It also helps you to let go of the event so that the emotions attached to the event do not build up inside of you and turn into physical or mental illness.

You don't have to tell the person you forgive them if you don't want to and write a letter to them and burn it or visualise the event and the people concerned with you telling them how they made you feel and how you want things to turn out afterwards. I did this visualisation when I had to face up to how I was treated as a child, and I told my parents exactly how it made me feel and why and that I no longer needed them in my life. I came out of this meditation happier at peace with my decision to cut them out of my life, as things with them would never change. This is a powerful technique and if done correctly, does work wonders.

· · ·

Watching good movies like the ones below:

In the below list there is one movie for every event that will make you feel better and get a better perspective on life.

- My Girl
- Coyote Ugly
- No Strings Attached
- Eat Pray Love
- Hitch
- Laws Of Attraction
- Gerry Mcguire
- Erin Brockovich
- He's Just Not That Into You
- Someone Like You
- A Walk To Remember
- Ghosts Of Girlfriends' Past
- Miss Congeniality
- Before Sunset/After Sunrise
- Grease
- Pretty Woman
- Match Point
- Braveheart

Hobbies

Join hobby groups and do things you consider fun. For example, I go to Salsa dance classes every Monday night at the Salsa Foundation here in Melbourne because I find it fun, and it is great exercise and the people there are really friendly and nice.

I also go running on Saturday and Sunday mornings for an hour for cardiovascular exercise. If I can't get outside due to bad weather, then I do a 1 hour virtual workout which includes HIT and boxing which really helps to stabilise me and keep me positive.

Burning ritual

For this, write down everything you want to happen or attract in your life and any new positive beliefs you want to embed into your life. Read what is on the pieces of paper out aloud and visualise those things being in your life and then burn the piece of paper. This tells the universe what you want in your life and helps you to attract it into your life. Remember, though, that with things like this, you also have to take action to bring those things into your life by putting an action plan together and implementing it.

Learning what made me happy and who I really wanted to be by listening to my inner child

Dig deep within yourself and remember the things and events that made you really happy in your life. Write those things on a piece of paper, put that piece of paper where you can see and read it every day, maybe somewhere like your fridge. Every time you are feeling down, sad, or flat, read the list out to yourself and feel the emotions attached to those things and events. It also may be time for you to do those things again.

Gratitude

Practice gratitude every day by journaling ten things that you are grateful for each day. Also, say them out aloud to yourself three times a day. This will help you attract more of what you are grateful for into your life. Gratitude is extremely powerful and will bring into your life the following benefits.

- It makes us happier.
- It improves our physical health.

- Helps us find more meaning and purpose in our work and personal lives.
- It reduces stress.
- It improves self-esteem.
- The quality of our sleep improves.
- Makes us better leaders.
- It helps us be more resilient.
- It improves our romantic relationships.
- It improves our friendships.

Learning life's lessons

When you go through bad things in life, think about the things you need to or have learnt from that experience and write them down.

Things happen for a reason.

So that we get the most out of the situation and we don't repeat the same events and do the same things over and over again, it is important to let go of the negatives and focus on the positive learnings from those things and events.

Once you have the positive learnings write them down and turn them into a milestone checklist and as you implement them in your life tick them off and celebrate the implementation of them. This will help you become more resilient and far more capable of bouncing back from future negative experiences and events.

Do not dwell on the negatives of the situation, learn from it, and adapt what and how you are doing it so that the same things do not happen to you again. It is important to remember that these events will strengthen you and you can positively learn and grow from those events. Look at your fears as challenges to be overcome and if you have a negative limiting belief, then replace it with a positive and empowering one that will serve you better in the years to come.

Coaching

If you have a challenge or fear to overcome that is holding you back and you don't know where or how to overcome them then it is a great idea to seek a personal transformation coach that has been through similar things to what you are going through as they will understand you, assist you in moving forwards and guide you to see more options so that you choose the option that best suits you to overcome them. They are also very good at assisting you to form positive daily rituals replacing limiting beliefs you had formed from the past so that you can move forward in a more positive way.

Coaches do not give advice. They provide you with a safe space free of judgement for you to be comfortable to say what you need to say and work through your thought's feelings and emotions. Coaches will never tell you what to do or how to do it; they merely ask you the question you would not have thought to ask yourself to understand things and for you to see new possibilities/options for your life.

Sometimes Neuro linguistic Programming (NLP) or Meta-Dynamics is used to help you work through the past and move positively forward with your life.

Such things as cognitive behavioural, timeline, acceptance, defining moments and many other therapies and techniques may help move you forward.

Dare To Be YOU have three amazing life changing programs that will help you massively in your life. I list them below:

Dare To Be Yourself Program

Before you can be everything you want, you have to be yourself. This program helps you when you are feeling lost and don't know who you are anymore because of feeling un-loveable. This program will help you find yourself and get to know and to love yourself more. This program will also help people like you build a stronger, more loving relationship with yourself.

The program helps people be themselves.

- Have the ability to take the power back to say NO to pleasing others and putting their needs above your own,
- Explore their needs and where you are denying them,
- Have the ability to quickly improve your self-esteem and self-respect,
- Have the ability to bounce back from adversity fast,
- Have the ability to remove your "fear-based obstacles" that are impeding you living your life true to your values,

Dare To Be Outstanding in life Program

Once you know who you are, the world has no limits. It's all possible. This program helps people just like you to go that one step further in their lives to be outstanding in life by collaborating with them to overcome their fears. The major fears people struggle with everyday are fears of not belonging, not being loved, not being enough. This program helps peoples overcome these fears so that they can live an outstanding life.

This program gives people the courage to:

- Take the power back by saying NO to pleasing others and to put their needs above others,
- Explore which of their needs are being denied and rebalance them,

- Explore what areas are lacking in their lives, whether that is family, career, self/love/care (health) and wealth and rebalance them,
- Quickly improve self-esteem and self-respect,
- Be resilient and tenacious when facing adversity so that they can bounce back fast,
- Understand their 3 primary fears of not belonging, not being loved and not being enough and put a strategy in place to help overcome them so that they can live their lives being truly outstanding,

Dare To Be Unstoppable with relationships Program

Once you know you can do anything, you still may find you need to change your internal dialogue and work on your relationship with yourself. Unlocking your personal power and opening the door to exciting new relationships with people. This program helps people just like you to build unstoppable relationships by collaborating with them to replace those thoughts in their heads that are limiting them and holding them back from attracting the people that will respect their boundaries and love them for who they are.

This program gives people a way to:

1. Find out who they are (Dare to be you)

- What they like and what they don't like,
- Working on a strategy to change the things they don't like about themselves,
- A strategy to love & respect themselves,
- Say no to people (the no accelerator,

2. Be able to build healthier relationships with themselves and others (relationship builder)

- Exploration of your past and the events that are holding you back,
- Start to overcome the internal fears,
- Clean up their internal dialogue,
- Personal development/moves them along further (creation of rituals & habits,

3. Attract the right people (attraction magnet)

- Who the right people are,
- Where those people hang out,
- Putting themselves out there,
- Learning the tools to simply and effectively communicate how you feel and what you want in a conversation with others.

4. Bonus: Have mutual respectful relationships (happiness)

Meditation

Meditate for at least thirty minutes morning and night. You will experience a reduction in your stress levels, you will feel more emotionally balanced, you will experience a reduction in pain and anxiety, your creativity, focus, compassion, memory, and productivity will increase.

I have found that meditating for 30mins morning and night has certainly changed the quality of my life and how I feel about and see things.

Grounding myself

I ground myself once a day by going to a waterfall, listening to the water trickle down the rocks and into the stream and imagining that I am a tree and out of my feet and toes are roots that go deep into the ground and wrapping around the earth's core and sucking up the nutrients with in the core and then carrying that nutrients up and into the different parts of my body and imagining that my arms are like branches of a tree stable, sturdy and constantly having new growth for younger branches coming out of them. This is about a ten minute grounding technique and works really well for clearing the mind and de stressing me.

Scientific Consciousness Interface Operating (SCIO) therapy application sessions

My naturopath uses the SCIO therapy applications which works with over 85 biofeedback therapies, all of which are safe and self–monitoring and used based on the client condition. The SCIO system is the state-of-the-art biofeedback device for the application of Quantum Biofeedback that addresses the stressors and the resulting stress of today's lifestyle and environment. It works by scanning the client. The device resonates with thousands of energetic signatures for a hundredth of a second each and records the degree to which the body reacts. It measures voltage and current potential and skin resistance.

Once your imbalances and stresses have been identified through testing, you can work with unique biofeedback therapies and frequencies tailored to your current condition–cell response on SCIO–to bring you balance, relief and relaxation. These therapies are well known, safe, widely accepted, and used daily by thousands of therapists / clients worldwide.

The accuracy and reliability of the system is based on decades of research conducted in bio-energetic and bio-response. Science has shown that the body is electric, therefore, electrical reactivity in the body can be measured. The things that it measures and helps me with are electro auto-meridian, chakra balancing, spinal, colour auto frequency, spiritual healing, iridology, brain wave, allergy response, relaxation training, TMJ, detoxification, aging, dental, degeneration, injury, pain, metabolic repair, hormonal balancing, digestion, oxygenation, immune stimulation, anti-inflammation, blood sugar balancing.

Anybody and everybody, from an infant to seniors, and even animals.

It has scientifically proven the Biofeedback system to help reduce stress and dis-ease that may be related to illness, injury, or emotional trauma. The biofeedback produced by the device can cause an overall improved sense of well-being, greater mental clarity, pain reduction, and improved physical performance.

My Naturopath Gabriele looks at the following areas:

- Gum and teeth problems
- Detox and cellular rejuvenation
- Allergies
- Hormone imbalances, menopause
- Nutritional deficiencies, skin problems
- Candida and other fungal infections
- Toxicities such as parasites and worms
- Stress reduction, insomnia
- Pain
- Emotional blockages and anxieties that stop you from moving forward
- Mental stressors
- Chakra and energy balancing

Emotional Frequency tapping

Whenever I feel I need to release negative emotions that are holding me back, I do emotional frequency tapping (EFT). EFT is tapping on different parts of the body (psychological acupressure points) to balance energy and reduce physical and emotional pain.

These points are primarily on the face and the head, in a particular sequence.

When you are tapping on these points, you focus on the issue that you want to fix, for example anxiety, stress, depression, lack mentality, etc. It is relatively easy to do, and you can find on YouTube EFT for most things. You can see an EFT practitioner for treatment or treat themselves using this technique.

EFT works with the body's energy meridian points, which are a Chinese medicine concept. It is believed that they are areas of the body through which energy flows.

So, in theory, blocks, or imbalances in the flow of energy cause ill health. According to research, tapping with the fingertips on the meridian points balances and rebuilds the energy flow to resolve emotional and physical issues.

It is very similar to mindfulness, as it can draw a person's attention to their breathing and body. It is also known to serve as an emotional distraction from the issues that are creating anxiety or stress in people's lives.

There are many YouTube videos on how to do this for particular issues that you can look at.

I know this works as I did it for the first time many years ago when I was out of work, and I had a stranger contact me and give me $1000 for nothing. He merely said it was a gift, as he could see how hard I had worked to get ahead of others in my field and to become employable and he just wanted to help me. He never, to this day, asked me for anything in return.

What This System Did For Me And My Life

"There will always be peaks and valleys, swings, and roundabouts. What matters the most is how you handle the ow lows and what you have learnt from those dark times. For that is what will bring you out of the darkness and back into the light."

This system taught me that true love and acceptance comes from within and once you have it you will feel you are loved and enough, and you will attract the right people into your life and belong.

I met my neighbour once when I first moved into the place I had moved into after my ten-year relationship had ended and did not speak to her until five years later. She said she had seen me around the place many times, but she could tell I was in a dark place and so she avoided me. Until five years later, when she sensed I had changed. We then became the best of friends. In one of our conversations, she told me how much she thought I had grown and changed and was more open to people and things and was no longer in that dark place.

It was an exceptionally long and hard journey getting myself out of depression and off medication to live what some would say is a normal life. But to get to that point, I had to completely change my lifestyle and develop my holistic health support system that supports me and moves me forward in my life when things go bad.

My system took several years, and many terrible things had happened to me along the way before I perfected the system.

The system got me out of depression, which I had been in and out of for many years and helped me manage the severe anxiety I had. I have now been out of depression and managing my anxiety extremely well for over sixteen years and have never slipped back into depression. My system also helps me face many of my fears head on and replaces many of my limiting beliefs I had from childhood.

Reflecting back now, I have come an awful long way in my life as I now look at and handle things much differently than what I did many years ago when I was in that very dark place full of depression, anxiety, and fear. I can now reframe my thoughts and emotions, sit with them and work through them if necessary and face my fears head on, which moves me forward from things quickly and makes me very resilient in times of adversity and challenge. I am also now able to see that there are many options/possibilities for me out there and not just one which has given me hope and belief that things can change for the better.

People now call me resilient, and my closest friends have told me at times that they hardly recognise me now as the way I was and who I was back when they first met me are completely different and they like the new, me so strong, so resilient, and always daring to be myself and facing fears and tough times head on.

Many of the things I have written about in this book I had to go through alone, without support from family and friends. I have, because of this system, personally grown and changed a lot to be the person I am now, and I very much love the person I am now.

I hope this book gives you the tools and techniques to be inspired, resilient in the face of adversity, bounce back fast and to see life in a completely different light.

Here is a YouTube video I did for you on personal growth: https://youtu.be/Ojl0If7SV40

Character Testimonial

Here is a character testimonial for the work I have been doing on social media with Facebook live videos, articles, quotes, and posts on my life.

In 2019, I started authoring my book and articles and I have been getting some really positive interaction from my articles about my life and what I have been through. Many people have told me publicly on social media that my life's stories inspire and give them hope that life will get better and that they can make it through the traumas they are going through, as I did. My Articles\Quotes\Facebook Live Videos give people the desire to continue living and moving forward with their lives in the darkest of times. I now also have a recommendation on my writing and my social media videos saying that they helped pull someone out of the depths of despair and depression (darkness) and motivated them to move positively forward with their life, which is a massive complement to me and who I am and the meaning I now have for my life.

One of my clients gave me this feedback from our coaching sessions:

You have been invaluable in my search to find the right answers and to gain a different perspective on my challenges. You are part strategist, part thought provoker, and you provide a gentle nudge so that I take the required actions. You have a masterful knack for knowing when to invoke these different beliefs and habits in order to remove any obstacles or blockages, and it is amazing. The way you repackage my sometimes-confusing thoughts in a way that adds meaningful direction is brilliant, especially when you share related stories from your life.

The testimonial is below.

To whom it may concern.

My name is Darren. I'm writing this testimonial regarding an extraordinary woman with an extraordinary skill set. Her name is Lynette Diehm.

Lynette is the owner and founder of "Dare to Be You' which is a Transformational Coaching Practice.

In this practice, Lynette draws on her own life experiences and Skillset to help others in times of need.

Lynette came into my life at the right time and moment, be it was a sheer fluke when my life had just been turned upside down.

In brief, my situation came about because of a relationship accompanied by betrayal"

Needless to say, I was emotionally compromised and fell into a deep & dark black hole.

I came across Lynette by sheer chance, whilst feeling board & down one night as I was flicking through Facebook, hitting "add friend, add friend. I didn't know who I was adding, and it was just something to do. Nine out of ten times, I wouldn't even open the requests that had been accepted, but this night I did open Lynette's.

Upon opening Lynette's page, four words stood out "Dare To Be You."

This sparked my curiosity. It led me to her articles, blogs, vids, YouTube clips, etc.

Now apart from commenting on one of her articles, we had no contact in person or by phone, however Lynette's words, stories, articles, and clips alone were enough to inspire."

Not all of Lynette's blogs or articles etc.... pertained just to my situation however I read other articles from Lynette on a variety of subjects and pulled out pieces of them as well to create in my mind the tools needed to join the dots so to speak and get back on track.

In summing up, Lynette Diehm literally saved me from a world of darkness and basically saved my life.

All this with words and video clips only and as mentioned we hadn't even met.

Lynette is brilliant, inspiring, a genius with what she can do.

I hold Lynette with the highest regard and respect.

So, drop her a line, find out what she can do and "Dare To be You"

daretobeyou.net.au

Yours Truly
Darren Gough

HOW TO CONTACT ME

Please reach out to me via the following methods if you would like to enquire about anything you have read that may help you in your life's journey or to find out about how my coaching can help you.

https://www.instagram.com/daretobeyoucoaching/ https://www.facebook.com/daretobeyou.net.au
https://www.linkedin.com/company/dare-to-b-you/ https://www.linkedin.com/showcase/daretobyou/
https://daretobeyou.net.au/contact-get-in-touch/
https://youtube.com/channel/UCfGAQevm6z1FhgSBrygbNg/videos/
https://twitter.com/DiehmLynette

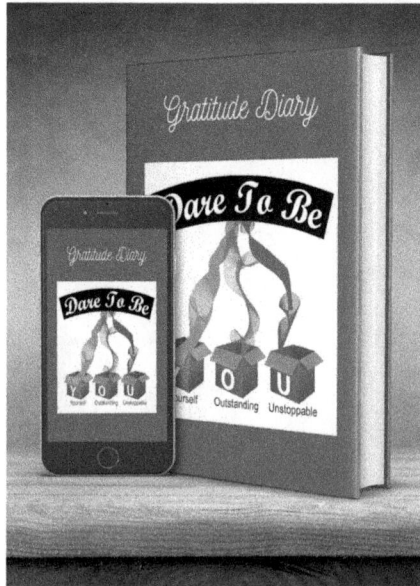

SIGN UP FOR YOUR FREE GRATITUDE DIARY
Click the link below to be redirected to my website where you can download your FREE copy of your gratitude diary.

Take that first step to helping YOU!

Click here to download for free!
Or go to https://daretobeyou.net.au

Enjoy this book? You can make a big difference

Reviews are the most powerful tools in my arsenal when it comes to getting attention for my books. Much as I'd like to, I don't have the financial muscle of a New York publisher. I can't take out full page ads in the newspaper or put posters on the subway.

(not yet anyway).

But I do have something much more powerful and effective than that, and it's something those publishers would kill to get their hands on.

A committed and loyal bunch of readers.

Honest reviews of my books help bring them to the attention of other readers. If you've enjoyed this book I would be very grateful if you could spend just five minutes leaving a review (it can be as short as you like) on the book's sales page. I'd be extremely grateful.

Thank you.

AUTHOR'S NOTE

I'd like to thank you for reading this book and I trust you have gained some valuable insight in to how you can develop your own holistic health support system. This book was written to inspire and give you the tools you need to move you positively forwards past the roadblocks that may come up in your life.

Lynette Diehm

x

Ebook ISBN: 978-0-6454447-1-1
Paperback ISBN: 978-0-6454447-3-5
Hardback(case bound) ISBN: 978-0-6454447-2-8
Hardback (dust jacket) ISBN: 978-0-6454447-0-4

Published By Dare To Be You Media

www.ingramcontent.com/pod-product-compliance
Lightning Source LLC
Chambersburg PA
CBHW051848090426

42811CB00034B/2259/J